We Kept Britain Flying

We Kept Britain Flying
Diary of an RAF Mechanic in World War II

LEONARD F. GUTTRIDGE

Edited by Vivien J. Olsen
and Jan K. Herman

McFarland & Company, Inc., Publishers
Jefferson, North Carolina

ALSO OF INTEREST
AND FROM MCFARLAND

Navy Medicine in Vietnam: Oral Histories from Dien Bien Phu to the Fall of Saigon (Jan K. Herman, 2009; paperback 2018)

Frontispiece: Badge of the Royal Air Force.

All photographs are from the collection of Leonard F. Guttridge.

LIBRARY OF CONGRESS CATALOGUING-IN-PUBLICATION DATA

Names: Guttridge, Leonard F., 1918–2009, author. | Olsen, Vivien J., editor. | Herman, Jan K., editor.
Title: We kept Britain flying : diary of an RAF mechanic in World War II / Leonard F. Guttridge ; edited by Vivien J. Olsen and Jan K. Herman.
Other titles: Diary of an RAF mechanic in World War II
Description: Jefferson, North Carolina : McFarland & Company, Inc., 2023. | Includes index.
Identifiers: LCCN 2023041663 | ISBN 9781476693361 (paperback : acid free paper) ∞ ISBN 9781476650814 (ebook)
Subjects: LCSH: Guttridge, Leonard F., 1918-2009—Diaries. | World War, 1939–1945—Aerial operations, British. | Aviation mechanics (Persons)—Great Britain—Biography. | Great Britain. Royal Air Force—Non-commissioned officers—Biography. | Great Britain. Royal Air Force—Military life. | World War, 1939–1945—Great Britain. | World War, 1939-1945—North Africa. | World War, 1939–1945—Personal narratives, British.
Classification: LCC D786 .G88 2023 | DDC 940.53/41092 [B]—dc23/eng/20230906
LC record available at https://lccn.loc.gov/2023041663

BRITISH LIBRARY CATALOGUING DATA ARE AVAILABLE
ISBN (print) 978-1-4766-9336-1
ISBN (ebook) 978-1-4766-5081-4

© 2023 Vivien Olsen. All rights reserved

No part of this book may be reproduced or transmitted in any form or by any means, electronic or mechanical, including photocopying or recording, or by any information storage and retrieval system, without permission in writing from the publisher.

Front cover image: The author with Hawker Harts at RAF station South Cerney, Gloucestershire. These vintage twin-seat biplanes, designed during the 1920s as light bombers, were indicative of what was still in the RAF's inventory on the eve of World War II. Guttridge would spend many hours patching up these "relics" which were put to good use training pilots; *background*: Leonard Guttridge's entry from the original diary dated June 6, 1944, says it all in just five words: "Second front? Christ, at last!"

Printed in the United States of America

McFarland & Company, Inc., Publishers
  Box 611, Jefferson, North Carolina 28640
    www.mcfarlandpub.com

To Dad,
For your inspiration, for your passion for life,
and for the privilege of knowing you better through your diary.
And to your mates of the RAF
who worked tirelessly to "keep them flying."
—Vivien K. Olsen

Contents

Preface	1
About the Author	3
A Note to the Reader	7
Abbreviations	11
The RAF versus the Luftwaffe: September 1939	13
The Diary: 1937–1945	15
Afterthought	216
Glossary of Aircraft Mentioned	217
RAF Bases Where Posted (1937–1945)	220
Index	221

Preface

I never knew that my father, Leonard Guttridge, had kept a war diary. Frankly, I had never heard him talk about his wartime experiences. A few times he had mentioned the name of his closest friend, Arthur Wilson, who had been killed in the war, but not much more about the war itself.

After my father died in 2009, many of his belongings, including his writings and research materials, were moved to my home halfway across the country. At that time, I was engaged full-time with parenting, working, and various other commitments. Years passed before I was able to fully peruse the many boxes of Dad's papers, research notes, and collections.

My father authored eight books and kept boxes of source materials and related documents and information. I eventually examined their contents and came upon the diary in an aging plastic three-ring binder with "Diary 1937" written in ink on the front cover. The binder was full of pages of typed and handwritten diary entries in chronological order. Some pages consisted of pieces of paper that had been taped to what appeared as original parts of his journal. Once I scanned the contents, I knew I needed to put the diary in electronic format for preservation and safekeeping. And perhaps, more importantly, I wanted my dad's insightful words to be read by family and friends. Few people besides me have been able to read my father's handwriting, so I set out to read his diary while transcribing it.

Dad copied his original diary, initially typing portions of it and then writing the rest in longhand. He must have made a new copy for the purpose of preserving it in its entirety. Then he reproduced passages from notebooks and pieces of paper kept throughout the years. But those segments had become loosened or detached without regard to whether anyone else would read it. He did include a notation in red ink on the last entry of 1942 that says: "March 1992 on completing this copy." Mentioning the omission of the rest of 1942 and all of 1943 from

1

his diary, he commented: "I probably continued to keep a diary of sorts but if so, it has long been lost."

I am grateful to have found and transcribed Dad's diary. With repeated readings, his entries have allowed me to know my father better, and they have also prompted an interest in World War II history. Each reading of this "service diary," as Dad often referred to it, brings me close to him. I have learned about life with his mates in the barracks, his excursions to and through the British and Moroccan countryside, and the pubs, cinemas, dances, and concert halls he frequented. The diary entries reveal his developing personal philosophy, questioning Allied strategy, condemning the evils of fascism, and growing weariness with wartime bureaucracy. Dad's eyewitness accounts of the Battle of Britain and the Blitz are realistic and grim, yet riveting and breathtakingly detailed.

I completed the electronic transcription in December 2020 and sent it to Jan Herman, a dear friend of my father's and a professional historian. Dad had mentioned the existence of his diary on several occasions to Jan but had never shown it to him. After Jan read the electronic transcript, he suggested that I try to get the diary published, emphasizing that it was a rare, primary historical document. Jan added that Dad's diary was unusual in that most surviving wartime records are written by members of the elite officer corps, not by enlisted men whose experiences are typically from a vastly different perspective.

Jan and I agreed to share the editorial tasks required to publish the diary. We provided footnotes to help the reader understand the historical events and identified abbreviations that Dad used. In order to maintain its integrity and present my father's thoughts as he wrote them, we did not rewrite or make any changes in the diary. To help illustrate the text, we have provided photos from my father's service in the war.

My dad's diary vividly recounts—on a very intimate level—a cataclysmic time in the last century when democracy's fate truly hung in the balance. I hope the reader will enjoy the diary, perhaps feeling transported back in time to share Corporal Leonard Guttridge's observations from his distinct vantage point as a young enlisted man in the RAF. His diary will relate his eyewitness accounts, his experiences, and his thoughts and questions about the war, a worldwide conflict that shaped his life all those years ago.

Vivien J. Olsen
St. Marys, Kansas

About the Author

Leonard Francis Guttridge was born in Cardiff, Wales, on August 27, 1918. He was informally adopted and brought up by George and Clara Thompson in a working-class area of Cardiff. George, his first adoptive father, a quiet man, was a veteran of World War I who served on the Western Front and suffered the effects of poison gas attacks. As a result of those devastating gases, he died at an early age. Leonard later wrote, "But with affection I remember the photo of my father erect in British army uniform and the Bicycle Thief handclasp."*

Leonard developed a very loving relationship with Clara, who often took him to silent films where he quietly whispered the subtitles to her because she was illiterate. The couple also adopted a daughter named Edna, a few years older than Leonard, who tragically died of tuberculosis at twenty-six, leaving behind a husband and two young children.

Leonard attended church with his adoptive family and, when not playing football on the streets of Cardiff, he and the neighborhood kids scoured the local dump in search of batteries to power their crystal radio sets. On his crystal radio and later on the "wireless," Leonard listened to American jazz, all varieties of musical concerts, and news reporting from around the world. In 1932, at the age of fourteen, he completed his formal education and worked until he was eighteen. At that age, he enlisted in the Royal Air Force (RAF), identifying his occupation as "Garage Hand."

It was not until that point in his late teens that Leonard found out that his surname was Guttridge, not Thompson, and that George and Clara were not his biological parents. In 1947, more than a decade later, he was further surprised to learn that his biological mother was not only living but that he had brothers and sisters somewhere in England.

---

*This unusual phrase is a reference to the poignant final scene in the 1948 Italian film *Bicycle Thieves*, in which the dispirited protagonist, Antonio, tightly grips his young son's hand. Leonard Guttridge likened that scene to his father George holding his own young son's hand with the same firm "I'll never let you go" handclasp.

About the Author

In World War II, Leonard served as a flight mechanic in the RAF, being promoted to corporal in 1942. He served in Britain and North Africa, was "mentioned in despatches," as he recalled, and was awarded the Africa Star. In his comprehensive "service diary," kept from 1937 through 1945, he chronicles, philosophizes, and comments on political and wartime events, people he met, books he read, musical shows he attended, movies he watched, and records he bought, played, and replayed for many years.

After separation from the RAF in November 1945, Leonard remained in the RAF Reserves until his final discharge in the spring of 1947. Always a supporter of Britain's Labour Party, he stated that he was a loyal "trade union man." He was also a member of the National Society of Metal Mechanics, working for Birmingham Small Arms Company Limited, "testing the hardness of steel bars," he recorded. That large company, known as BSA, was a major British industrial combine—a group of businesses manufacturing military and sporting firearms, bicycles, motorcycles, cars, buses, and steel.

In May 1947, Leonard finally took the trip to America he had been planning for years. Nevertheless, "the sudden imminence of departure to a new land, to an uncertain future, to strange people," as he wrote, elicited a variety of thoughts and emotions. With only $80 in his pocket, he made the transatlantic crossing on the Polish liner MS *Batory*, recently repainted after having her "war-paint" as an Allied troopship scraped clean. He settled in Washington, D.C., with a new job as a librarian at the Embassy

Leading Aircraftman Leonard Guttridge strikes a jaunty pose, 1941.

of India. Leonard began his new duties within weeks of India's independence in August 1947.

From the late 1940s through the 1950s, Leonard wrote jazz articles for *Melody Maker*, a British weekly music magazine, as well as other jazz publications. He also penned short stories for *Fantasy and Science Fiction* plus hundreds of articles for magazines of the now defunct "pulp" genre: *Saga, Male Stag, Man's Magazine*, and *True Action*, to name but a few.

Early on, Leonard enjoyed sharing his love of jazz. During the war, he sent a notice to *Melody Maker* asking jazz aficionados to contact him. He received many responses, so many he soon realized he couldn't keep up with the correspondence. In Washington, a cultural center, he soon became acquainted with jazz fans and musicians he had befriended and written about.

While working at the Indian Embassy, Leonard met Canadian Jean Freeland Stoddart, who had emigrated from Toronto, Ontario, after the war to find secretarial employment. Jean was an executive secretary for the Indonesian and Indian embassies. Leonard and Jean married in 1956, and their daughter, Vivien, was born in 1958. They moved to Alexandria, Virginia, in 1961 when their son Bruce was born. It was then that Leonard would begin full-time self-employment as a writer.

Although they eventually divorced, Jean and Leonard remained lifelong friends, sharing a passion for classical and jazz music, enjoying conversations with mutual friends, driving to local parks, and delighting in musical and historical events in the Washington, D.C., region. Jean frequently assisted Leonard with research and editing tasks.

Leonard Guttridge died in June 2009 in St. Marys, Kansas, but up to the week prior to his death, he was actively writing. He never ceased to be a brilliant conversationalist on many subjects, particularly jazz, American and British history, and politics. Throughout his lifetime, his friends could always rely on him as a source for accurate and factual recollections.

He left behind several widely acclaimed books:

Jack Teagarden: Jazz Maverick, with Jay D. Smith (1965)
The Commodores: The U.S. Navy in the Age of Sail, with Jay D. Smith (1969)
The Great Coalfield War, with George S. McGovern (1972)
Icebound: The Jeannette Expedition's Quest for the North Pole (1986)
Mutiny: A History of Naval Insurrection (2002)
The Ghosts of Cape Sabine: The Harrowing True Story of the Greeley Expedition (2003)

Dark Union: The Secret Web of Profiteers, Politicians, and Booth Conspirators That Led to Lincoln's Death, with Ray A. Neff (2003)

Our Country: Right or Wrong: The Life of Stephen Decatur, the U.S. Navy's Most Illustrious Commander (2006)

A Note to the Reader

"Never in the field of human conflict was so much owed by so many to so few." Winston Churchill's immortal words of August 20, 1940, paid tribute to the brave young pilots who manned the Hurricanes, Spitfires, and other aircraft. These men of the hour turned back the Luftwaffe and thus won the Battle of Britain. Churchill may well have included the Royal Air Force personnel on the ground. They were the unsung mechanics, armorers, and other ground crew who patched bullet holes, repaired engines, refueled nearly empty tanks, and replaced spent ammunition. They enabled nearly exhausted and outnumbered RAF pilots to return to the skies for another crack at the enemy.

This diary reflects that time of war through the eyes of one important member of the ground crew, an enlisted RAF mechanic who chronicled the war from his own perspective. For seven years, Aircraftman Leonard Guttridge gathered his words in tiny notebooks, occasionally with a few phrases, sometimes in long, descriptive paragraphs. With a borrowed pen or pencil, he often dashed off observations after long hours of duty hunched over a battered aircraft to repair and dope the fabric of a bullet-riddled wing or to replace the throttle linkage on a disabled Lysander scout plane.

More than once, Leonard Guttridge came under enemy fire. Following one such episode, he recorded his close encounter with death after German planes bombed and strafed his barracks. "I awoke to an awful bang followed by a heavy clatter—a bomb burst and cannon-fire. I was aware too that my bed frame was no protection against bombs and 20-millimetre cannon-shells. I braced for steel thudding into my back then crawled ... from under useless shelter and groped for the door, outside of which I eventually stood under a cold moonlit sky, my only attire, boots, a shirt and shorts—and a tin hat."

Chroniclers of war have traditionally been the educated and the powerful—politicians, journalists, professional historians, and the officer class. Too frequently, those writers, blinded by limited perspective and access to the facts, offer only two-dimensional results. Less frequently do we witness war through the eyes of the enlisted man.

The aircraftman's diary is unique in several respects. It is the product of a young man possessing the innate gifts of language and writing skills, an insatiable inquisitiveness, knowledge of current events, and an extraordinary sense of history. Going through almost day-by-day diary entries, the reader can easily be duped into thinking that these accounts came from a man with a Cambridge education and years as a seasoned war correspondent. Instead, the diary is a product of someone barely out of his teens who lacked a high school education.

Leonard Guttridge was born in 1918, the year the Great War ended. He was raised as an adopted son by a lower middle-class family in Cardiff, Wales. His stepfather, a veteran of the trenches and a victim of poison gas, was unable to work, and he died young when his damaged lungs gave out. Leonard joined the Royal Air Force in 1936 at age 18 after working briefly as an auto mechanic in a local garage. The RAF offered him room, board, a skill, and a ticket out of a dead-end life.

He was largely self-educated with a voracious appetite for books, magazines, and newspapers, and his eclectic reading list included works of the sixteenth-century philosopher Michel de Montaigne, Charles Dickens, Fyodor Dostoevsky, Winston Churchill, D.H. Lawrence, Noël Coward, and Damon Runyon. He somehow always managed to obtain current newspapers. Between those daily and weekly publications and news broadcasts, Leonard kept well informed about local news, world events, and especially war news on all fronts. With his self-developed writing skills, he even generated short stories, one of which he submitted to *Lilliput*, a British monthly literary magazine. That exercise, unfortunately, ended in his first rejection.

The young airman also devoured American jazz and Hollywood films. He inevitably fell hard for Ginger Rogers. "How I remember those Depression years, when a bright spot in my otherwise fairly drab life was dear Ginger. I used to pray that one day I would go to the USA and meet her." His diary is filled with references to attending jazz performances in London and other cities, as well as catching Louis Armstrong, Count Basie, Duke Ellington, Benny Goodman, Fats Waller, Glenn Miller, and other musicians over his shortwave radio. Most of these "extracurricular activities" were punctuated by the nightly wailing of air raid sirens, anti-aircraft fire, and bomb blasts.

During many postings at RAF bases throughout England and later in Morocco, the young jazz lover rounded up amateur musicians and organized base concerts. After he learned that Rabat's Radio Maroc was available for RAF personnel who wished to air their talents, Leonard arranged for those musicians to broadcast to British and American personnel stationed in the vicinity.

As with his mates, also in their 20s, Leonard delighted in "pub crawls." He frequently enjoyed a pint or two, sometimes to excess, while socializing with young women who congregated at those ever-crowded public drinking houses. Scattered throughout his diary are references to dating local young women. Leonard became easily susceptible to a comely smile or to females who could hold up their end of a thoughtful conversation.

Leonard Guttridge's diary reveals an extraordinary perception of his comrades and humanity in general. His closest human studies were the enlisted men he lived with, worked with, and drank with. He selectively became friends to only a few, one of whom he considered his dearest mate. Arthur Wilson later died during a bombing mission over Germany. The loss cut deep. "The grievous news outweighed in emotional impact the description of my other letters contained of V-E celebrations at home, the flags, the bonfires, speeches, floodlit buildings, and street-dancing. Wilson was a friend whom I shall never forget."

As American soldiers and airmen poured into Britain in preparation for the invasion of France, they became objects of derision and jealousy. More than once, Leonard found himself defending the Americans whom his mates claimed were stealing their women. British personnel at that point were already grumbling that the Yanks were "overpaid, oversexed, and over here." His comrades also expressed their lack of confidence in the American soldier's prowess on the battlefield. Leonard frequently reminded them that without their American allies, victory was anything but certain. After George Patton's tanks eventually began slicing through enemy lines deep into Germany, his mates were forced to agree with him.

During much of the time that Leonard kept his war diary, Britain stood alone, certainly until the United States entered the war in late 1941. Most of Europe had already been conquered by the German Wehrmacht. Under incessant bombardment by the Luftwaffe night after night, and later attacks by V-1 "buzz bombs" and V-2 ballistic missiles, the citizens of Britain endured.

Leonard heard the same air raid sirens and shared the same crowded underground shelters with them. But he learned that the will and fighting spirit of the British people could not be broken—even amid the rubble of their homes and even with the deaths of thousands of their countrymen. The Germans were also coming to that realization. Leonard Guttridge's ability to describe it all in such stunning and personal detail is what this historic and highly insightful diary is all about.

Abbreviations

AA	Anti-aircraft
AACU	Anti-aircraft Cooperation Unit
AC1	Aircraftman First Class
APO	Acting Pilot Officer
ARP	Air Raid Precautions
ARS	Air Refueling Squadron
ATS	Air Training School
ATS	Auxiliary Territorial Service (women)
BBC	British Broadcasting Corporation
BEF	British Expeditionary Force
CC	Confined to Camp
CLS	Central Landing School
CTO	Chief Technical Officer
DFC	Distinguished Flying Cross
DRO	Daily Routine Orders
FAP	First Aid Post
GPO	General Post Office
GWR	Great Western Railway
ITS	Initial Training School
LAC	Leading Aircraftman
LTTB	Local Trade Test Board
MO	Medical Officer
MP	Military Police
MSFU	Merchant Ship Fighter Unit

Abbreviations

NAAFI	Navy, Army and Air Force Institutes
NCO	Non-commissioned Officer
NDF	National Defence Corps
OO	Ordnance Officer
PT	Physical Training
RAFVR	RAF Volunteer Reserve
SDO	Special Duty Officer
SHQ	Sector Headquarters
SP	Service Police
WAAF	Women's Auxiliary Air Force
WO	Warrant Officer

The RAF versus the Luftwaffe: September 1939

On September 1, 1939, the day German forces invaded Poland igniting World War II, the RAF's first-line aircraft numbered about 1,150 planes. Other operational aircraft were reserved for reconnaissance and training. Many were obsolescent. British aircraft factories produced one modern fighter in 1939, the Hurricane. The relatively new, high-performance Spitfire was just coming into production and did not enter the air war in large numbers until early 1940.

Germany was far ahead of Britain in combat aircraft, having steadily increased its production since it began serious rearmament in 1935. The numbers rose progressively until the outbreak of war when Germany had an operational force of 1,000 fighters and 1,050 bombers. Its planes were superior to nearly all British classes. And unlike many of the planes in the British inventory, few, if any, of these German aircraft were outdated.

The gravity of the emergency was not universally acknowledged in Britain until German tanks rolled across the Polish border, introducing the concept of "blitzkrieg" into modern warfare. The relentless destruction of Polish cities by German bombs presaged what would shortly befall London, Birmingham, Liverpool, Sheffield, Coventry, Cardiff, and countless other cities and towns across the British Isles. Nevertheless, aircraft plants continued to operate on a pre-war schedule, hindered by a pre-war bureaucracy. Shortages of parts and materials affected production of essential fighter aircraft. In fact, the aircraft production pipeline was so dangerously clogged that nearly completed planes sat on factory floors because they lacked engines and instruments. Shortages of parts, which were destined for new aircraft and those planes requiring routine maintenance, would shortly reach unacceptable levels.

The RAF's ability to defend the homeland against an aggressive Luftwaffe, bent on wiping out Britain's air defenses, depended entirely on the nation's capacity to produce and repair fighter aircraft. And the odds seemed to be with the enemy, especially after the fall of France in June 1940.

That precious resources were limited was a fact not lost on the men charged with keeping aircraft airworthy and ready to fight. One of those mechanics, 21-year-old Leading Aircraftman (LAC) Leonard Guttridge, found himself posted at several RAF training bases where both novice and veteran pilots honed their skills. Leonard's job was repairing and maintaining both training aircraft and an assortment of second echelon planes, such as the Airspeed Oxford trainer, the Fairey Battle, the Westland Lysander scout, the Bristol Beaufighter, and, occasionally, a de Havilland Puss Moth. In the modern age of aluminum and all-metal construction, some of these aircraft still had fabric-covered wings and control surfaces.

Hamstrung by these circumstances, Leonard Guttridge and his mates needed to work with what they had, often improvising to keep their "kites" in the air. In July 1940, when the Battle of Britain had just begun, the motto "keep them flying" would be a tough order to fill.

The Diary: 1937–1945*

1937

Henlow, Herts.†

Wednesday, December 8. Icily cold. Glad I'm no longer on Salisbury Plain,‡ though, where seven-foot drifts reported. I hope to be home in a fortnight. Lots of foreign war news, Japs at the gates of Nanking,§ Barcelona bombed in that other conflict [Spanish Civil War].

Saturday, December 11. Railway disaster in Scotland, the Glasgow-Edinburgh express crashed into a stationary train in a blizzard.¶ At least 35 dead. Here we had heavy snow and sleet yesterday.

Monday, December 13. Light sprinkle of snow. Freezing all day. Stayed in over the weekend. Tales of heroism in the Scottish rail crash. Daily Express emphasizes the danger of wooden coaches, calls for steel ones. Mussolini announced last night that Italy will withdraw from the League of Nations. This was expected.

Thursday, December 16. On a strange parade today. Monday night on the Henlow-Shefford road a local girl was attacked and raped by three

---

* Several months of 1941 are missing as is the entire year 1943. Notebooks from those dates did not survive.
 † Located in Bedfordshire, RAF Henlow, a Royal Air Force station, began as a military aircraft repair depot in 1917. Henlow continued as an aircraft repair base during World War II. "Herts" refers to the county of Hertfordshire, which borders Bedfordshire.
 ‡ Salisbury Plain, located in the county of Wiltshire, is a plateau covering about 300 square miles and was used as a military training ground since the 1890s.
 § The Nanjing (Nanking) Massacre or the Rape of Nanjing was the murder and rape committed on a massive scale by Japanese troops against the residents of Nanjing during the Second Sino-Japanese War. The massacre, which took an estimated 40,000 to 300,000 lives, occurred over a period of six weeks beginning on December 13, 1937.
 ¶ A London and North Eastern Railway Edinburgh-Glasgow commuter express, traveling 70 mph in white-out conditions, passed a danger signal and rear-ended a local train standing in the station; 35 were killed and 179 seriously injured. This is known as the "Castlecary rail accident."

men. Victim finally got to Shefford police station after tramping miles. Well, heard last night there was to be an identity parade on this camp, that her assailants were airmen though they had been wearing civvies. So everyone owning civvies out on parade 8 am. Hundreds of us in our civilian garb, standing in raw wind and sleet. Our clothes, needed next week for Christmas leave, got soaked. We stood there, stamping feet, over two hours. Girl slowly walked past, along each rank, accompanied by her mother, two detectives, plain clothed, and cluster of RAF officers including CO [commanding officer]. As she passed me (my heart foolishly skipping a beat as she appeared to hesitate). I saw she was pale-faced beneath veil. Before our dismissal, word had spread among ranks that she had pointed out a man, who was marched away.

Sunday, December 19. Little item in News of the World,* which specializes in this sort of "news," that at an RAF identification parade, two men had been picked out by victim. Charged, both pleaded guilty.

Next Thursday not coming quick enough. Feeling a bit browned off tonight. I hear roads are icebound all over the country. Hope our coach will make the 200-mile journey into Wales safely. I'm all set. Expecting a picket Tuesday night. Won't get much sleep Wednesday but that doesn't bother me. So long as I get home.

In Hitchin last night to pay the 30 shillings balance on a new brown coat from Foster Brothers. Hitchin packed with shopping crowds. Windows sparkling. Paddy tried to get me into a dance, one shilling and sixpence. I resisted, must go easy on cash. Returned to camp alone, handed my pass into the guardroom. Hands in pockets, walked across the crisp grass between the [Nissen] huts.† Stopped in a clearing, looked around. From the hut came sound of choral singing, on radio. "O Come, All Ye Faithful." Bright full moon, frost thick on hut roofs. Christmassy.

War crisis between Japan and USA. Seems Japs held up and boarded US gunboat Panay and four hours after the boarders departed, Jap planes bombed the gunboat and sank it.‡ Roosevelt has protested to Tokyo. British too have been harassed by the Japs.

And war in Spain goes on. What a cheery world for Christmas. Still, according to statistics, there is more money flying around Britain than ever before.

---

* *The News of the World* was a weekly national tabloid newspaper published in the United Kingdom from 1843 to 2011.

† A prefabricated structure for military use, especially as barracks, made from a half-cylindrical skin of corrugated steel.

‡ On December 12, 1937, Japanese warplanes sank the U.S. Navy gunboat *Panay* on the Yangtze River, killing three Americans and wounding 30. In the daylight attack, many of the escaping survivors were repeatedly machine-gunned.

Friday, December 24. Christmas Eve. In town Tom and I met Renee, a girl whose acquaintance I made at a party last August. She asked us to meet her and Doreen, a friend, at Victoria Park Christmas night, 6 pm. We agreed, a decision not met with approval at home. It had been assumed we would all be together.

Selfish, really, of me. Foolish too, we'd have to walk way out there, no transport.

Saturday, December 25. Christmas Day. News full of war threats. Spain, Panay incident, etc. But Ambrose band* on the radio. And the King. Took afternoon walk returned home and found Doris Green there. Have disliked her ever since the fiasco of last August and her presence, more than anything else, decided me. After a glass of wine, I set out with Tom. Three miles in drizzling rain on Christmas evening. We waited half an hour. No one showed up. Cursing myself and everything else, I turned back with Tom.

All's well when we return. Doris and her friends have gone. Hot tea and cakes, and Don's brother and sister have arrived. I talk affectionately with Edna. Don, old man,† Fred, myself off to the Moira Hotel for drinks. Return, we play record after record, jazz and rumbas mostly, laughing it up, Don and I dancing weirdly. So everyone reasonably jolly. Later after all had retired, I was still up, listening to an American station on the shortwave.

Next day, Edna very ill, cannot be left alone. That night I went over to Jim Parry's home. Jim's on leave, too, five days. He and Tom and I seek two girls for Jim's party Monday, celebrated this year as Boxing Day, December 26 being a Sunday.

It was some party. Wine, women, dancing. Met all the old crowd, Hutch, George Parry, Stockholm, their girls. Also, newcomers, including a nice pair of girls Tom and I claimed for the inevitable game of Hyde Park (darkness, someone who is "it" wanders around with a flashlight, and whoever he/she catches kissing, thereupon becomes "it"). Got home 3 am, let myself in quietly. Light burns all night in Edna's room. And she is still awake, calls my name as I'm halfway along the passage. I go in, she says she can't sleep—Don slumbers beside her. I chide her gently. "Go to sleep now, that's an order."

With each new day, she appears to be brightening, only at night does she become depressed. Don returns each evening to a thin and wasted wife, and two unthinkingly mischievous boys.

---

* Benjamin Baruch Ambrose was an English bandleader and violinist. Ambrose became the leader of the British dance band, Bert Ambrose & His Orchestra, in the 1930s.

† Edna was LFG's sister and Don, her husband. The "old man" refers to LFG's foster stepfather.

At the cinema, saw Cary Grant and Constance Bennett in "Topper." Delightful.

Friday, December 31. New Year's Eve. Edna slipped into a coma. I met Mam in the passage, she was quietly sobbing, "My poor girl," and in the front room Edna and Don were in each other's arms both crying, and I stopped the kids from dashing into the room. Mam fears Edna will die with the old year. The doctor was sent for, Doctor Llewellyn. He gave Edna a tablet told Don at the door, "There is nothing else we can do." I wondered whether I should stay at home but there seemed no reason. Tom and I went to St. Margarets where we had understood a New Year's Eve dance was to be held. We found the place in darkness. We walked aimlessly through the mild damp last night of 1937. Looking for parties to gatecrash.

1938

Friday, January 7. A week since I returned to camp from home. Tonight, the hut is half empty. My leave was saddened. My sister is dying.

The Welsh contingent had boarded two coaches at dawn December 23. As the day brightened, the bus rolling through Bedfordshire and into Buckinghamshire, we sang old songs, new songs, "Cwm Rhondda"* and Hoagy Carmichael. Sunlight on wet highways. Oxfordshire, over the Chilterns, Gloucester first stop. Taff Williams, who organized the trip, passed the hat around for the driver. I dropped three pennies into it. Fellows living in this region left the bus. Choruses of "Merry Christmas." Chepstow, Newport. Cardiff.

West Luton Place. Mam met me at the door, we embraced. She took me into Edna's room. I kissed her, feeling how terribly thin she had become. She broke off the kiss, turned her head and began to weep. Mam rushed to her with words of comfort and over Edna's shoulder, her own eyes glistening, said soundlessly, "She's dying."

That was my welcome, this Christmas homecoming.

When I re-entered the room, Edna apologised for crying and then was bright and apparently happy. I gave her the colorful cushion-cover I'd bought. Welcomed the kids home from school. Went out with Tom Parry that night. Bought a George Formby record for Edna and the

---

* This Welsh hymn, taken from the Welsh name for the Rhondda Valley in Wales, is a popular hymn tune also known as "Guide Me O Thou Great Jehovah." Composed by John Hughes with lyrics by Welsh minister William Williams, "Rhondda" was one of LFG's favorite hymns.

Lecuona Cuban Boys for myself. That night welcomed Don. Kids were in bed asleep. I heard the truth, that Edna was desperately ill, that recently she was so low she sobbed for a pastor to visit her and pray with her. She had then recovered slightly.

Throughout Edna's illness, mam and the old man have slaved daily at the housework. Kids naturally a distraction. Don out at work all day.

Sunday January 23. Full pack, rifle drill, CO's inspection, left me with an aching back and limbs. But last night to Biggleswade with Cox. Cinema and pub. Returned to camp drunk. Today from 7:30 am to 6 pm with few breaks, entire hut on duty in cookhouse. Greasy work, dishing out food. And I've got toothache or neuralgia. Bloody awful day.

Week culminated in sensational Braddock–Farr fight at Madison Square Garden Friday night. We listened to transatlantic relay. Fight awarded to Braddock, he crossed ring to shake hands with Tommy Farr who, furious at what he considered wrong decision, turned his back and deliberately kicked his bucket over. "I'll go back to the mines," he told reporters bitterly. "I can get a living there."

Gladys writes, says it's her birthday Tuesday.

Tuesday, January 25. 10 pm. Remarkable phenomenon. The Northern Lights. According to the radio they are visible tonight all over Britain.

Thursday, January 27. Most of Europe saw the aurora borealis. Peasants panicked in Portugal. Princess Juliana, pregnant, considered the spectacle a good omen. North Sea fishermen couldn't catch any fish. Scotsmen fear the phenomenon augurs ill. Compasses swung two degrees off, and shortwave radio from America blacked out.

Cox and I watched the sky show after seeing Charles Laughton in "Rembrandt," in the camp cinema. Some at first thought the glow a fitful reflection from a fire. But as Dean said, "It can't be a fire, it's all over the sky." My impression was of great sheets of crimson with a pale bluish tinge about them, stretching across the heavens. Stars in the vicinity were lost in the greater glory. Jock said it's often seen in Scotland. At ten, the BBC announced reports from all over, John O'Groats, to Land's End.* Occurs rarely this far south and is apparently caused by a super sunspot one million miles wide.

January 30. Sunday afternoon. Showery and cold. Wish I was in the Cambridge Theatre, London, where Stephan Grappelli, Django Reinhardt and the Hot Club of France, are giving a concert. In Bedford last

---

* John O'Groats is the extreme northern point of mainland Scotland. Land's End is located eight miles west of Penzance, and is the most westward point in mainland Britain.

night saw "The Good Earth," Louise Rainer says no more than fifty words in the long film but is magnificent. So is Paul Muni. Another tiptop show I saw recently was Spencer Tracy, wonderful as Manuel in "Captains Courageous."

War in Spain goes on, bitter fighting around Teruel. Japs continue to insult the Stars and Stripes. And hundreds dead in an Italian weapons factory explosion.*

Yesterday morning we had 2½ hours of gas drill, and in a lecture following it, we were told by Sgt. Hope, "Your respirator is your best friend."† Proceeded to amplify, describing different gases—chlorine, phosgene, mustard, etc—and their effects on humans, like choking, burning, destroying sanity. And their different smells, musty hay, garlic, sweet flowers, peardrops.

This morning I read the Sermon on the Mount to myself.

Tuesday, February 1. Gales. Heavy air raids on Barcelona 85 bodies of children recovered. And one of Franco's submarines sank a British freighter, eleven seamen drowned.

Tail plane strut fell on my middle fingernail with a terrific whack, blood spurted out. Trying to splice today with a bandaged finger.

Will be home soon. Letter from old man tells me they didn't see the Northern Lights. And Edna weaker.

Thursday, February 3. Going home tomorrow. Haven't written home though, I'll surprise them. Last night Paddy and I set off for a dance, took short cut, wallowed for half a mile in mud and water and darkness. Joined another group of airmen, also lost but armed with flashlights. Finally reached Arlesley, only to find no dance. So, a pub crawl, got drunk. Long walk back but this time kept to the road. Woke up in the night feeling sick. Okay now.

Heard Lew Stone's band yesterday, first broadcast in months.

Battleships in the Mediterranean are hunting a pirate submarine.

Sunday February 13. 9 pm. Feel lonely tonight. Thoughts repeatedly return to Cardiff. And sometimes think the past seven days all part of a dream. Almost immediately after arriving home Friday 4th, I went into the front room. Edna was sitting up in bed propped by a chair behind her. She said "Hello" in such a weak whisper. Someone sits with her all

---

* On January 30, 1938, two violent munitions explosions in a factory near Segni, a small town 30 miles from Rome, killed at least 15 men, and injured about 200.

† In 1938, a year before World War II began in Europe, the British government issued 35 million "General Civilian Respirators." It had been 20 years since the end of World War I, when chlorine gas—and, later, mustard gas—had first been used.

through each night. She became worse Saturday night and when Tom called for me to go out with him, I said no.

My brief weekend was quiet, a record I had bought left unplayed. Before leaving I went in to see her. Her cheeks were white and swollen, her eyes dulled. Lips cracked. I made some humorously chiding remark about the GWR* allowing only one train for me to leave on, a too early one at 5 o'clock. I kissed her and said goodbye. She barely managed the same word and in the passage at the front door Mam told me tearfully she would send a telegram if—

I crossed the road accompanied by Tom. Turned and waved. Between the curtains, in the glimmer of the front room, Edna raised a hand and feebly responded.

That was the last time I saw her alive.

In the train I prayed that God would save her.

Jenks was on the same train. It was only 9 pm when we reached London. We left Paddington Station and walked up to and along the Edgeware Road. It was thronged by mixed crowds, returning church-goers, the usual prostitutes, right up to Hyde Park Corner. In the bright glow of the Regal we entered Hyde Park, passed orators and their hecklers, and came upon a large contingent of London's Welsh, who were, of course, singing. Old Welsh hymns. We joined them, listened to the swell of voices above the clatter of traffic.

I fell asleep in the train from King's Cross. Finally, at Henlow about 1:30 am, awoke to drizzling rain and the darkness of Camp. Handed in my pass, and the NCO [non-commissioned officer] who received it told me I was wanted in the main guardroom. I got there, reported to a group of NCO orderlies, and an SP [service police] corporal took me into a back room and said, "This arrived for you a few hours ago." I took the telegram out of the envelope and read: Guttridge, Henlow RAF Camp. Return Home. Sister Died.

The corporal advised me what to do next morning, there being nothing I could do immediately. I slept five hours and when I got up, sewed a button on my greatcoat. I would have to wear uniform at home, of course. My civvies are brown not black. I passed up breakfast and parade, and at the squadron office applied for seven days leave. Sergeant Humphries, sympathetic, sent me over to 2 Wing Orderly Room. And that was the beginning.

I filled out the application Flight Sergeant Roberts handed me and returned to Sergeant Humphries who got Flight Lieutenant Metcalf to

---

* The Great Western Railway (GWR) was a British railway company that linked London with the southwest and west of England, the West Midlands, and most of Wales.

recommend it with his signature. Back to Roberts who said he'd see to it, and meanwhile I should report to my workshop. Over in 188 Hangar workmates and instructors were sympathetic. After a while, Sgt. Roberts sent for me and said the Chief Technical Officer [CTO] wouldn't grant my application, would permit only a day's leave for the funeral. There was nothing (the CTO said) I could do at home, and I would be missing valuable instruction. I stammered something about being unable to concentrate on work, and I must have been close to tears. Roberts agreed it was rotten for me, but said all I could do was wire for the date of the funeral and he'd see I got away early after duty the day before.

A cursing rage against the entire Royal Air Force gave way to a cooler determination. Slamming the lid of the tool chest on my overalls, I stalked off and saw Flight Sergeant Turner, then Flt. Sgt. Daniels, who took me before a technical officer named Wicklesea, who promised to talk with the CTO. I went back to the hangar. It was still forenoon.

Forty-five minutes passed then Flt. Sgt. Daniels and Wicklesea came by to tell me the CTO had reconsidered. I could get away today and be back by Sunday. All that remained was for the CO to sign my application. In the afternoon I was told he wouldn't sign it, wanted me back the day after the funeral.

I didn't know the date of it yet, and more time would be lost if I wired to find out. I guessed it would be Thursday, and was advised to mark the application accordingly, which I did. All okay then but for a week's pay. I had practically to beg for it. I finally left camp at 4:20 pm.

A lonely journey, by bus to London then train to Wales. Half past ten found me plodding the wet pavement of Adam Street and Windsor Road and into West Luton Place to the silent house where the curtains were drawn and a dim light glowed in the front room. The padding placed on the doorknocker to deaden its sound had been removed. Don opened the door. Mam embraced me and said, "You're all I've got now." Edna had died at 8:40 pm. When she felt her life going, said the old man, "She struggled a little, then went."

(Note later added by LFG)

(Of Edna's death and funeral, some pages of description lost. I have a few scribbled references to the motor cortege, the watchers in the street—they included some of Edna's schoolfriends, even an ex-beau or two. A fine day but gusty, wind whipping two wreaths off the hearse as the procession wheeled over Crwys Road Bridge, and it paused for an undertaker to alight and retrieve them. At the cemetery church we sung "Abide with Me." Don looked awfully lonely at the graveside. A prayer was said for the

motherless children, sorrowing relatives, grief-stricken husband. At home afterwards, it was the traditional veneer of strained and subdued conviviality concealing mingled emotions of grief and relief. Beer and sandwiches and cigarettes. Even a joke or two. It's the custom. Or was then. And we all shared the belief that Edna was no longer suffering. No one asking why, aged only twenty-six, she had to be destroyed by tuberculosis.)*

April 1938.

Graduating (if that's the word) at Henlow. Examined by a "sarcastic swine of a Flight/Sgt.," and then by a friendlier W.O. [warrant officer] to explain "the theory of flight." Etc.

Thursday, April 28. An "easy" day but for the tension of awaiting results. "Rumour floating about that there are six failures. Hope to goodness I'm not one of them." I wasn't, but neither did I score enough to become Aircraftman First Class. "Flight Sgt. Spearpoint gave us a fine lecture, bade us all do our jobs properly when on our squadrons, and wished us good luck. All over. I'm no longer a trainee but a tradesman. Next Friday will be posted."

Duke Ellington on the radio tonight. Half an hour ago heard Hore Belisha† on ARP,‡ appealing for recruits, saying "There is no need for panic. There is need for reparation."

Wednesday, May 11. No. 3 Flying Training School, South Cerney, Gloucester. Arrived here last Friday following a hot dusty journey carrying kitbag, equipment, two suitcases, gasmask, etc. from Henlow to Cirencester via London. Cirencester is small and old with a lovely church but no food sold after ten. A new aerodrome, plenty of construction going on. Three modern hangars in use. This is No. 3 Flying Training School, with Hawker Harts§ soon to be replaced by Oxfords.¶ I'm in ARS [air refueling squadron], dealing with repairs only. About 450 airmen, fifty or more APOs (Acting Pilot Officers), very young. Posted here with me is Ron Allaway, also from Cardiff. Plenty of other Cardiff chaps here. Weather's fine, and I have a weekend pass coming.

---

   * Social conditions in Wales during the Depression, particularly poor housing and diet, most likely contributed to the higher rates of tuberculosis than in England, where by 1939, disease rates had fallen by 70 percent; in Wales they had only fallen by about 40 percent.
   † Leslie Hore-Belisha was Secretary of State for War from 1937 to 1940.
   ‡ Air Raid Precautions was an organization dedicated to the protection of civilians from the danger of air raids.
   § A Hawker Hart was a British two-seater light bomber biplane.
   ¶ An Oxford was a two-engine monoplane.

The author with Hawker Harts at RAF station South Cerney, Gloucestershire, 1938. These vintage twin-seat biplanes, designed during the 1920s as light bombers, were indicative of what was still in the RAF's inventory on the eve of World War II. Guttridge would spend many hours patching up these "relics" which were put to good use training pilots.

Tuesday, May 17. Had a nice weekend. Friday afternoon walked two miles into Cirencester, took a 3.50 train to Kemble, changed for Gloucester where I caught the express for Cardiff. The old man has enlisted in the city's ARP. Surprise visit by Billy Allen, who has just got married, having got the girl pregnant. They obviously think a lot of each other—although I was taken aback somewhat when, she having left the room, he whispered to me, "When she comes back, take a look at her legs. She has bloody fine legs." The baby is due in July.

Early August 1938.

(Note later added by LFG)

(A Sunday—reviewing a furlough which had coincided in Cardiff, with the Eisteddfod* held there that year.)

Monday, August 1 or 8. Tom Parry and I to Barry. Weather hot, with thunderstorms. Barry railway station crammed with soaked holiday

---

* National Eisteddfod of Wales is an annual Welsh cultural competition in the fields of dance, music, drama, and literature.

makers who, caught by a sudden downpour, flocked from the beach to the station for shelter. Cooler later and we had a good time there.

Had a few nights out with Don. He, Olwyn, Fred, and myself in Fred's car, a pub crawl around the city's outskirts. (Another somewhat memorable night with Tom in the home of one Dr. Myerson, whose daughter and housemaid entertained us mightily until 1 am.) Tom and I also made the acquaintance of two Canton girls, the one I was with was named Eileen. Nineteen and sweet, pleasant moments alongside the Weir at Llandaff, in the shadow of the cathedral.

Saw "Hurricane," "Dead End," "Private Life of Henry VIII," all good films, and I bought a Count Basie record. Basie's band is one of the few modern outfits with real guts. Lester Young terrific on sax.

Cup of tea in bed each morning.

Had a rather drunken Saturday with Jim Parry, also home on leave. Started in the Carlton and finished at the Railwaymen's Institute. In civvies all this time, forgot I was in the service until my leave all too quickly ended.

Disastrous return to camp. Arrived 2 am instead of midnight (my 10:55 train from Cardiff had reached Kemble 1:15 am where I disembarked, got a lift on a mail van to Cirencester, and walked up the lonely road to camp). Put on a charge, up before S/Ldr. [squadron leader] Rowlands who silenced my attempts to explain by saying I'd had twenty-six days to make sure I caught the train in time. He awarded me seven days CC [confined to camp] and a further seven without privileges. A bad time, for I've also learned that Tuesday I am on LTTB [Local Trade Test Board] for my AC1 [aircraftman], which, if I pass, will increase my 24 shillings weekly to thirty. And on Wednesday a CO's inspection, full pack parade. Never rains but it pours. (Precisely. It stormed day after day while I went through the ordeal known as "jankers,"* slaving in the cookhouse, periodically reporting in full pack, etc., and causing me to think, for a mad moment, of deserting.)

During my leave, I read that Benny Goodman came over here to escape the jitterbugs.† Stayed in London day or two, hid in France three days.

Sunday, August 14. Ominous news of German troop movements on Czech frontier. Doesn't worry me. Have decided to go home Friday week, plan to buy six swing records, of Ellington, Spike Hughes, Chick Webb, etc. Also expect to have heard of my promotion to AC1.

---

* In the British military, "jankers" or "restrictions of privileges" (ROP) is an official punishment for a minor breach of discipline, as opposed to the more severe punishment of "detention" which would be given for committing a more serious or criminal offense.

† A jitterbug was an aficionado of swing music or style of dance known as the jitterbug and who followed the styles and fads of other jitterbug devotees.

Tuesday, August 16. Quite busy today, fitting center section struts on an Audax.* There's a big battle brewing along the Ebro in Spain. Lots of flying here last night, noise kept up till 2 AM.

Sunday, August 21. In bed till noon reading papers. Bombs wrecked Barcelona Zoo. Another British ship sunk. Stayed in last night and over in the canteen heard Eric Fearn, a hopeful musical comedy writer in civvie life, played "Smoke Rings" (Casa Loma band's theme) very prettily. The other night saw Cary Grant and Irene Dunne in "The Awful Truth." Delightful. Last night on the radio heard, from USA, Benny Goodman. Played "Alexander's Ragtime Band and" and "A Tisket a Tasket," then the battery faded.

Monday, August 22. AC1 at last. So I succeeded that Tuesday when, homesick, miserable and on jankers, I went through the Test. Corporal Smith looked up at me as I hung halfway out of the cockpit, leaning on the center section of the Audax, and he said, "Have you seen the notice board? You're an AC1." What's more, out of the eight riggers and mechanics who sat for that board, I had the highest percentage—66. Extra five bob [shillings]† a week. Nice birthday gift. Will celebrate at home next week. Will now have a pint of water, go to bed. Plenty of work tomorrow. Putting up a set of mainplanes,‡ make the Audax look a bit more like an aeroplane.

Thursday, September 1. Nip in the air. Blackberries out, fields yellow with corn. Autumn upon us. And Europe dangerously near war. I've had a weekend at home. Drank a lot of port wine and bought five great records: Ellington, "Saturday Night Function," "Willie the Lion Smith," "Old Stamping Ground;" Lang-Venuti, "Beale St. Blues," "Chicago Rhythm Kings," "Who Stole the Lock from the Henhouse Door?", and Spike Hughes, "Air in D Flat." With Tom Parry most of the time. Weekend overshadowed by Czech crisis. Next week Hitler will address Nuremburg Rally. I can't believe he'll start a war. Anyway, I'm going by car up to London Saturday afternoon to see Fats Waller.

Monday, September 5. Beginning a week's fire picket guard. (Sleep in firehut, occasional fire drill, daily parades at 6 and 10.) Nice time in London over the weekend. Saw and heard Waller. Took a boat ride from Westminster Bridge, down the Thames to Greenwich and back. Waller—he ambled onstage at the Holborn, grinned expansively at the audience, sat at the piano and captivated all, non-jazz fans included.

---

* An aircraft used by the British Army, based on the Hawker Hart light bomber.

† A bob was the popular slang for a shilling in British currency prior to 1971 (12 old pennies, 1/20th of a pound).

‡ The wing of an airplane that provides most of the lift.

"Margie," "Flat Foot Floogie," "St. Louis Blues," "Sweet Sue," etc. And an appealing "Loch Lomond" for an encore. Waller always seems in a happy-go-lucky mood, has been called the Peter Pan of jazz.

Saturday night I stayed at the Union Jack Club. After breakfast Sunday, I crossed Waterloo Bridge, turned east to Tower Bridge, Tower Hill, the Tower itself. Wandered on into the evil-smelling slums and dives off and in Cable Street ... savouring the smells and flavors of this dockside neighborhood ... into Limehouse. Then turned back. Had tea after the Thames boat trip. Caught the Tube at Piccadilly and reached Uxbridge half an hour after the appointed time, eight, when Mac (who had driven me to London in his Austin) was to collect me. He turned up late—on a motorcycle. He'd had an accident with the car. So I rode pillion* across Middlesex and Oxfordshire and the Cotswolds at a 50 or 60 mph clip. Eventually Cirencester, and I tumbled into bed at half past midnight.

Wednesday, September 7. Week of fire picket drags on. News yesterday that all frontier leave for army troops cancelled in France. World still awaiting that speech from Hitler, he's keeping everyone on tenterhooks. But the general opinion is there'll be no war. A scare yesterday morning when WO "Monty" Kemp rounded up 25 airmen, told them to rush into full pack and marching order, with gasmask, utensils, etc. and get down to the guardroom. They did, stayed there some hours. Some say it was a test to see how quickly a local mobilization could be carried out. Another theory is that the 25 are on standby for duty at some unknown location where a "shadow factory" might be affected by the threatened nationwide strike. They would presumably protect blacklegs,† if any.

RAF plane crashed on a house in North London, killing ten and the pilot.‡

Thursday, September 15. Sensational news. [Prime Minister Neville] Chamberlain has decided to fly to Germany and talk directly with Hitler. Fear still exists, crowds in Whitehall, demonstrators in Trafalgar Square with "Stand by Czechoslovakia" banners. Sudeten vs. Czech skirmishes in Czechoslovakia. ARP tests in Paris, Runciman§ dithers

---

* Seat for a passenger behind a motorcyclist.

† A term used by laborers to denounce their peers, also called "scabs," who were unwilling to join a strike.

‡ The Hawker Audax was being flown by a 19-year-old pilot. Twelve people on the ground were killed, including four children.

§ Sir Walter Runciman was a prominent Liberal politician and former member of Parliament. Neville Chamberlain sent him on a diplomatic mission to Czechoslovakia to negotiate an accord between the Czech government and Germany. The mission was unsuccessful but it eventually led to the Munich agreement and the policy of appeasement on the eve of the war.

in Prague. Hence this desperate gamble of Chamberlain's. After flying to Germany (his first air trip, they say), he will talk to Hitler in Munich. Most Czechs are bitter, feel that whatever comes out of this will be to their disadvantage. US warships at Gravesend, waiting to evacuate US citizens if war breaks out.

Hope the folks at home aren't worrying too much about all this. And unless we go to war, I'll apply next week for a weekend pass.

Civilian workers here are getting measured for gas masks.

Westminster Abbey open all day and night so people can enter and pray for peace.

Last night, going out with King and Tuck, passed motor hearse entering camp with casket containing remains of APO Winters, killed six miles away in a crash. Funeral tomorrow, expect I'll be on the funeral party.

Sunday, September 18. Chamberlain back from Munich. <u>Daily Express</u> assumes he's been confronted with a demand for a plebiscite.* He said at Croydon that he was going to confer with the cabinet and soon return to Hitler "who has intimated that he will meet me halfway." Cheers from the airport crowd. Tonight, Chamberlain is at Buckingham Palace conferring with the King. Chamberlain is 69. On arrival at Berchtesgaden† he was greeted with a double handclasp from the Fuehrer.

Fighting meanwhile in Palestine, Spain, China. Weather here is fine and frosty, and I sent a "don't panic" letter home.

Monday, September 19. Henlein‡ is in hiding in Czechoslovakia, near the border, a price on his head. Thousands of his party fleeing into Germany. His followers have formed a Free Corps [paramilitary shock troops] and are attacking Czech border posts. All this in defiance of the Prague government. Something definite should happen when Chamberlain meets Hitler again tomorrow or Wednesday. Crowds pray in Westminster Abbey while, nearby, demonstrators with "Down With Hitler" and "Stand By Czechs" banners clash with police. <u>Daily Express</u> says Britain will not be involved in a European war.

I hope to go home Friday on what might be the last weekend pass before war begins. To my limited sight, war seems inevitable.

Thursday, September 22. So much has happened. And still is hap-

---

* The direct vote of the electorate on an important public question.
† Location in Germany of chalets of Hitler and other Nazi leaders.
‡ Konrad Ernst Eduard Henlein, a leading Sudeten German politician in Czechoslovakia.

pening. Following Sunday's Chamberlain-Daladier-Bonnet* talks, plan proposed and sent to Prague. Details made public, reaction includes much anger and charges of treachery. What it amounts to is France, Britain, saying they won't protect Czechoslovakia against a German invasion unless she gives in to Hitler over the Sudetenland. British leftists, and New York papers scornful of Chamberlain's "surrender." Czechoslovakia stunned, a weary [Edvard] Benes [President of Czechoslovakia] asks for time to think the proposal over. And Poland now demands return of Polish minority area, Hungary behaving likewise. This morning Chamberlain flew once more to Hitler, in an American aeroplane, got to Godesburg. Czech govt has fallen, Benes forming a new cabinet.

My weekend washed out. I am on this "special party" business, which still puzzles me. Twenty-five picked each week, must have full marching order ready, and if alarm goes off, report at Hut 8A. My guess is, this must be sort of mobilization.

Saturday, September 24. Headlines full of grave news. Yesterday the Chamberlain-Hitler talks broke down. Czechoslovakia reported mobilizing. Polish-Czech frontier skirmishing, Czech-Hungary border closed. Russia threatens war on Poland if she invades Czechoslovakia. Aircraft and tanks in Germany swarm to the Czech frontier.

While everyone excitedly jabbering over breakfast, the orderly sergeant came into the dining hall, demanded silence and ordered all of the third "special party" confined to camp. So tonight, as the rain pours, I'm in the billet. I hear the station radio is open all night, wireless runners standing by. Flares are out on the airfield, God knows why. From American radio on shortwave tonight came ominous broadcast that British press not told Royal Navy ships moving into positions in the North Sea where they can intercept German submarines.

Sunday, September 25. Possibly last Sunday of peace. Am writing this in bed. The memorandum, or ultimatum as some call it, has been delivered from Hitler to President Benes via Chamberlain. The contents not published but presumed to be a demand that Czechoslovakia withdraw troops from the Sudeten zone and that region be ceded to Germany.

Tuesday, September 27. At 6:30 am yesterday (hours after Benes announced that Hitler's demands are neither feasible nor acceptable) I was the only one awake in the room. Then everyone was aroused by a

---

* Édouard Daladier was a politician and the Prime Minister of France at the beginning of World War II. He was among the signers of the Munich Agreement on September 30, 1938. Georges Bonnet was a leader in the French-Radical Socialist Party and Minister of Foreign Affairs at the beginning of World War II. He was also a signer of the Munich Agreement.

siren wailing, an alarm bell ringing. Wondering and cursing, buttoning tunics over pyjamas, men rushed out into a misty dawn. Above the chatter a bawling voice—"Panic party outside!"

McGeehan, Croft, Jock Hawkins, myself, slung on musketry order, full packs, dragged our laden kitbags, and groped through the grey light. Everyone but the "panic party" was eventually dismissed. Monty Kemp, minus false teeth, danced around. OO [ordnance officer] and SDO [special duty officer] took charge. Fifteen men drew rifles, cooks brought hot tea, boxes of rations.

RAF transport trundled up. Obviously not mobilization, I thought, for the decree would have been read out to the whole camp. But something was up. We clambered aboard, were trucked through sleeping Cirencester. Finally reached Camp Kemble. Fell out where we now are, our beds consisting of two trestles and three boards per man, with "biscuits," blankets, and sheets. In newly-built civilians' canteen (only civvies on this camp).

First ten men drawn out, taken away to guard four camouflaged hangars containing incendiary bombs. I was on duty from 4 pm yesterday to 4 pm today—two hours on, two off. Base is a tiny guardroom.

Following a vivid sunset, torrential rain all night, pitch blackness except for occasional lightning flashes, and the beam of my flashlight. I felt doubly burdened by kit, rifle, bayonet. Surrounded by bushes alive with rats and rabbits and noisy frogs. A stagnant swamp with me in the middle of it. No spies or saboteurs, though. Climbed to the top of hangar, a grassy sod and soil-covered low curving roof. It's quite invisible from the air, I should say. Although while on guard today, I was somewhat concerned by a plane looping and spinning directly overhead.

Today's newspapers carry Hitler's "patience is exhausted" speech, in which he delivers final warning to the "madman Benes." And in London, trenches are being dug in the parks. I feel somewhat resigned to a likelihood of war now. Perhaps I'll never go home again.

Wednesday, September 28. In an hour, tender will take night guard, including me, from here, the civvies canteen, half a mile or more away to the C Site bomb dump, the guardroom of which will be our base until 4 pm tomorrow. Padre from South Cerney came over yesterday with cheering words and a promise of periodicals, which arrived today. I hear reports of naval mobilization, of Hitler's reply to Roosevelt's peace appeal. Evidently, it's a new ultimatum to the Czechs. Chamberlain has broadcast to the country: "Keep calm and hope."

Friday, September 30. War averted, for the time being at least. The averter, so to speak is Chamberlain who, in Parliament yesterday, announced smilingly that Hitler had agreed to four-power talks and he Chamberlain, would make a third trip to the German dictator. Many MPs cheered. A proud Mrs. Chamberlain sat in the visitor's gallery with Queen Mary and the Duchess of Kent. Today's news photos show more smiles, of Daladier, Mussolini, also Hitler and Goering.* Czech territory will be surrendered, Czech borders guaranteed.

I finished a 24-hour guard yesterday at 4. Was peaceful and sunny and fresh around the bomb dumps in the afternoon, but fifty men had worked feverishly all through the previous night digging soil, dropping grass seeds as the effort to finish camouflaging the dumps reached near panic.

Raining today, it will be a quagmire up there. I go on at 4 again today. Last night, crossed fields to an inn called the Trouble House. Reputedly haunted. I got rather drunk to celebrate the peace. Still have no shaving tackle here. No sign of a relief party but at least the sense of danger has slackened. The good news yesterday coincided with a burst of brilliant weather, but today more rain. Exodus from London of thousands, ranging from crippled children to American celebrities.

Crisis jokes banned on the BBC.

On guard throughout Wednesday night, alone and cheerless, wandering to and fro over the turf-covered bomb dump, beneath the ghostly searchlight beams that fingered the sky.

Saturday, October 1. Crisis over. Chamberlain is back, proud and smiling. Country relieved, gives him warm welcome. On the balcony at Buckingham Palace with his wife, and the King and Queen, he yelled to the rain-soaked crowds, "Here is the paper.... It bears his name on it as well as mine." Holding aloft the agreement that "Never again shall the German people go to war against the British." The papers reported that an elated Chamberlain had even forgotten his umbrella.

We left the Kemble bomb dumps, I'm now back at South Cerney. Approved of Legs King's choices on my behalf for the Littlewoods Football Pools. Had a good dinner. Washed my aching and mud-encrusted feet while the radio played dance hits. Tomorrow being hailed as "Peace Sunday." Last week it was "Gas Mask Sunday."

Sunday, October. 2. Hitler told Chamberlain: "This is the last territorial ambition I have in Europe." Well, he's made promises before. I

---

* Hermann Goering was a political and military leader and the highest-ranking member of Hitler's inner circle. He held the title of Reich Marshal of the Greater German Reich, a rank Hitler bestowed on him, making Goering senior to all field marshals in the military, including the Luftwaffe. As a result of this promotion, he was the highest-ranking soldier in Germany until the end of the war.

said to Jack Hawkins last night, "History will show whether Chamberlain was right." Hardly a resounding observation compared with Johnny King, who said of the pats on the back accorded Chamberlain, Daladier, Mussolini and even Hitler himself. "Bilge, bilge and more bilge." "We should have stopped him even if it meant war." And as the radio began its coverage of the National Thanksgiving Service conducted by the Archbishop of Canterbury, he spat.

The Czechs, being left alone, accepted Poland's ultimatum and Polish troops have crossed the border. Hungary today presses for her share. Germans occupying parts of the country, Czech soldiers reluctantly retreating to make way for them. By Thursday, all Sudeten areas will be part of Germany. And Britain is getting back to normal, ARP, trench-digging, gasmask-fitting continue. But the Navy is demobilizing. The six-mile radius limit and 11:30 pm curfew on this camp will shortly be lifted.

I celebrated by going to the Regal, saw Emlyn Williams in "Dead Men Tell No Tales," and a crisis newsreel. Afterwards, two pints in the Bishop Blaize Inn with young Britton, storesman [quartermaster], just back from Halton where forty storesmen had assembled to hurry 5000 full kits into readiness for RAF reserves expected to be called up. The nightmare of guarding the Kemble bomb dumps is leaving my thoughts. Hope to be home for weekend.

So tonight truckloads of German troops rumble through Czech towns and hamlets. The rest of Europe sleeps on what just might have been the first Sunday of the Second Great War.

A stormy night here, wind howling mournfully.

Monday, October 3. Fierce wind, rain lashing the windows like steel rods. Huge pools flood the camp roads, the blackness of an early winter's night envelopes everything. I wouldn't go ten yards on a night like this. Am in a large room, brightly lit, thumbing through last week's "Echo" sent from home reading how South Wales passed through the crisis. Trench digging in Cardiff—200,000 gasmasks distributed. When the four-power conference eased tension, Lord Mayor Purnell [of Cardiff] flew the German swastika flag from the top of City Hall with British, French, and Italian flags. Protests followed, aldermen took the offending flag down, Purnell replaced it.

Last night, final demands on Czechoslovakia accepted. Chamberlain back in London for Commons debate. Duff Cooper's resignation* not likely to be the last.

According to the papers, at least four suicides in Britain due to the

---

* Alfred Duff Cooper, Conservative politician and First Lord of the Admiralty.

war scare. One man, whose sons are in the forces, threw himself under a Tube train.

Storm continues tonight, windows rattling, doors banging.

Tuesday, October 4. Commons opposition lined up against Chamberlain. "I have nothing to be ashamed of," he declared. Duff Cooper, resigning his cabinet post, said, "The Munich demands stuck in my throat... I have ruined perhaps a political career, but I can hold my head high." [Clement] Attlee called Chamberlain "the man who saved the peace but brought us to the brink of war."

I spent all morning out on the 'drome where a gang of us pushed in a half-wrecked Oxford, blown over by last night's gale. Storesman Billy ?, back from a weekend in Manchester, told me a man there digging trench for an air raid shelter struck coal. Kept on digging and got up five tons of it. He's still digging. Bradshaw told me he has built an air raid shelter at home and when his wife nags him, he retreats to it with pipe and newspaper.

Wednesday, October 5. Hip, Hip, and several loud Hurrahs! The general ban on leave lifted. So I go home tomorrow for the weekend.

Churchill attacked Chamberlain's government yesterday, said we were allowing Hitler to grow into a stronger menace.

Wednesday, October 12. First chance of writing about an interesting weekend, the first leave since the war scare. In front of huge fire, the folks and I exchanged our stories (mine dealing mainly with how I staggered over hillocks and through waterlogged ditches, carrying my rifle with bayonet fixed, guarding a bomb dump set deep in a forest). The folks were issued gasmasks, fitted for them at local schools. I walked into Cathays Park [Cardiff], where the gales had blown down trees and where, quite close to the War Memorial, the newly dug trenches for another war were half-filled with muddy water.

Had a few drinks with Don, who told me of the anti-aircraft guns installed near the Dowlais Steel Works. On Sunday night, Tom Parry and I took 20 swing records up to Ron Allaway's house in Lisvane Street and I met 18-year-old Eileen Allaway, a very attractive blonde, who said I reminded her of a film star but wouldn't say whether she had in mind Robert Taylor or Popeye.

Sunday, October 16. A boring Sunday. Papers dominated by question: Was Britain ready during the war crisis? Majority say no. A week ago tonight, I was at Ron Allaway's house and fell for his sister but have no chance unless she breaks off with the Territorial* she is going with.

---

*Member of the Territorial Army, a volunteer force locally organized to provide a reserve of trained and disciplined manpower for use in an emergency.

Allaway is in the next bed as I write this. And he is singing, "This is my first affair…. So please be kind…."

According to Cavalcade,* many think the reason war didn't erupt was because God answered prayers for peace. An equal number prefers to believe that mobilizing the Navy did the trick.

Talking of tricks. A poster I saw in Cardiff says that on November 11, the Reverend Dick Sheppard will speak on peace. It's a spiritualist meeting, but still quite an event, Sheppard having been dead a year or more.

Wednesday, October 19. Monday night was a lively time at the Bishop Blaize Inn, Cirencester, the whole town celebrating the Mop [local fairs], mostly in the town square. Then into the Bull Inn, where a radiogram played Dorothy Lamour and Fred Astaire. Fell in with an overpainted, non-adventurous blonde called "Peach." Later met Jean Smith, whose glove I had retrieved during a near-fight at the Cirencester Carnival last June. Came back to camp slightly tipsy in pouring rain.

Yesterday we were all out on the 'drome trying repeatedly to jack up an Oxford bellied down in the muck. It was difficult to see the kite† for the crowd swarming over it, and King and I, inconspicuous in the mob, enjoyed lots of laughs. After a carpenter had sawed planks for packing, a dozen of us heaved under one wing. "Watch that Peto [pitot] tube,‡ you big stiff," yelled Flt/Sgt. Black. I was the big stiff. Dusk was falling, but as fast as we got the Oxford up on jacks, the jacks sank into mud. Out came a mobile searchlight to illuminate the brisk and futile activity. NCOs yelled. Rain started to pour. Finally, the undercart [landing gear] was lowered securely and twenty men trundled the Oxford across to the hangars.

Thursday, October 20. Aided by the RAF, British army went into action in Palestine against Arab rebels, recaptured the old city of Jerusalem. This land is caught between two promises one by Balfour§ to the Jews, the other back during the war by Lawrence of Arabia to the Arabs.

Monday, October 24. Japanese have captured Canton [China]. Hankow their next objective. In the Spanish Civil War, Madrid shelled. Letter

---

* *Cavalcade* was a British weekly news magazine from 1936 and 1950 and modeled after America's *Time* magazine.

† RAF slang for airplane.

‡ A pitot tube is affixed to the fuselage of an aircraft that measures fluid flow velocity to determine the plane's airspeed.

§ The Balfour Declaration, named for Foreign Secretary Arthur Balfour, was a public statement issued by the British government in 1917 announcing support for the establishment of a "national home for the Jewish people" in Palestine.

from home tells of a mock air raid on Cardiff, part of ARP drill, was followed by a dance at City Hall.

At New York World's Fair they just buried a time capsule, to be unlocked and read 5000 years from now. Its contents include a newsreel film and a recording of "Flat Foot Floogie." The <u>Daily Express</u> asked its readers what they would choose to typify our age for the folk of 6938. Replies ranged from zip fasteners and football coupons to beer bottles, the Bible, a Mae West movie, and Hitler's "Mein Kampf."

Marijuana said to be on the increase in America. It's often referred to in jazz tunes as "tea," "reefer," "weed," and has found its way to London. Its effect is said to make one "high." I fear the growing publicity linking drugs with jazz might ruin the music. If the excesses of jitterbugs don't do it first.

Sunday, October 30. A win on the Pools is always welcome. We work a three-draw system, "we" being King, Tuck, Sgt. Pile and myself, at a 3/6 outlay, and it came up yesterday. We got the news in Cirencester while awaiting the train to Swindon. Tuck bought a paper—its front page told of a Marseille fire, heavy loss of life, of a cabinet dispute on Chamberlain's handling of national defence, and the latest in the Canterbury asylum murder. Tuck ignored all this, turned to the sports page and sure enough, four of our seven draws had clicked.

King, Tuck, Sam Britton, and I into Swindon, but over drinks at the Rifleman's Arms, we argued over what we should do—dance, movies, or a pub crawl. Argument lasted until it was too damn late to go anywhere and our pool win momentarily forgotten, we headed, sulkily back to camp. But drank Horlicks [malted milk hot drink] at the railway station and were our old selves when we reached Cirencester.

Monday, October 31. Morning papers say dividends on three draws 30 shillings. Boils down to 11/4 each, nothing to rave about but welcome.

Tuesday, November 1. An amazing incident in America. Big panic caused by a radio broadcast of H.G. Wells' "War of the Worlds." Octopus-like creatures were described as crossing the New Jersey marshes.... "We warn the people.... The Martians are approaching. Evacuate New York. Our army has been wiped out." The radio sponsors have apologized, say they announced several times throughout the play that it was a play.

Thursday, November 3. Startling news of a naval battle off the Norfolk coast, the Spanish rebel battleship <u>Nadir</u> shelling the Spanish government steamer <u>Cantabria</u>. The town of Cromer trembled to the roar of gunfire, crowds lined the coast with binoculars. After three hours, Cantabria sinking, British vessels rescuing crew.

Saw "Snow White and the Seven Dwarfs" last night. Beautiful, but a bit scary for kids, I'd say.

Big parade in town tomorrow. Civilian rigger Geordie Middleton asked why he wasn't going on the RAF Comrades Association march, said he didn't believe in it. "The Girl Guides, Boy Scouts, and so forth, being brought up on war. Why don't they forget it? My brother came back from France in 1918. Know what it's done for him? Every month he goes into the backyard and bangs his head on the door. It was so awful to watch him. My mother dies broken-hearted a few years later. Armistice Day, shit."

Sunday, November 6. The big parade this morning had soldiers, naval cadets, RAF. Church service followed by another march, augmented by the British Legion. Lots of us fell out of step in the narrow Cirencester streets and had to endure much sidewalk ribaldry.

Wednesday, November 9. 9:30 pm. My roommate and pal Ron Allaway posted to Iraq and he is badly shaken, being affianced to a girl in Bedfordshire. He sails December 23, after a week's leave at home. I've decided to go home myself instead of to London.

Thursday, November 10. Armistice Day tomorrow. Widespread persecution of Jews in Germany. Synagogues ablaze. Jews arrested and beaten.* Today Mussolini passed a decree forbidding Italians to marry Jews. And in Palestine, on goes the Arab-Jewish war, which we are trying unsuccessfully to halt. War in Spain, China … and our government announces that gasmasks for civilians will cost the Treasury 5 million pounds.

Friday, November 11. Here it is, the Day of Remembrance. <u>Daily Express</u> front page: "Anti-Jewish Mob in Control of Berlin Streets." Local celebration a hapless affair. Three clergy presiding as we paraded on the square. High wind blew away their hymnbooks. We started "Onward Christian Soldiers" too late. Halfway through the third verse a gun rocket sounded, signaling 11 am. After the Silence (broken by the noise of a passing car), the Padre prayed, then we sang "O God Our Help in Ages Past," followed by "God Save the King." And our CO crossed the square, presuming the ceremony at an end, just as the Padre began the Benediction. Well as they say, "At the going down of the Sun…

And in the Morning

We shall remember them."

---

* Kristallnacht (Night of Broken Glass) was a pogrom against Jewish communities throughout Germany on November 9–10, 1938. More than 90 Jews were killed, and more than 30,000 Jews were arrested and sent to concentration camps. Thousands of Jewish homes, businesses, and shops, were sacked or destroyed, and more than 200 synagogues were ransacked and burned.

(Note later added by LFG)
That was the last national Two Minutes of Silence to commemorate the dead of what was then called "The Great War" and is now in the history books as "World War One."

Saturday, November 12. World horrified by the Pogrom continuing in Germany. Jews ostracized, forbidden to attend cinemas or theatres, forced to pay for the damage done to their homes and shops by Nazi hooligans. Says Goebbels:* "We must make them suffer."

Sunday, November 27. Bitter wind blowing. In these well-lit blocks though, the rooms are large and warm.

Wednesday, November 30. King and I posted to the flights—me to ATS [Air Training School], Legs King to ITS [Initial Training School]. A nasty shock. King and I gave our tools in. Nothing appeared in orders yesterday, but we had been kicked out of ARS. We weren't certain where we belonged. So Legs and I set forth on a long walk in the sunshine that steadily dried the pools from last night's storm. Crossed the 'drome, climbed a low wall, and headed down the South Cerney Road, singing softly, quieter than the birds. Felt wonderfully free. Breaking rules and regulations, but nothing else surely by drinking in this glorious English countryside morn. Found an inn in South Cerney village, had half a pint each and two games of darts. Got back into camp safely, went straight to our billets, made our beds. After dinner studied DROs [daily routine orders] which said King and I both posted to ITS. Too bad we can't repeat our escapade tomorrow.

Thursday, December 1. Another "freedom" day. We hunted up two mechanics who, like us were posted to ITS. They said they weren't going up until break, 11 o'clock, because they had to wind things up at ERS [Engine Repair Service]. King and I said fine, suits us, and we were off again this time via the Officers' Quarters and down into Cirencester where we toured the Abbey. Back in camp after break—closer to two, in fact, but no work in progress, rain had arrived and the wind rose again, so Legs and I kept to our billet reading the newspapers until teatime.

Sunday, December 4. In Room 3 of ITS Block, King in the next bed. We service Harts at ITS. The room's radio is one of the new pushbutton types.

Thursday, December 8. An uneasy "crisis" feeling in the air again. All aircraft are to be camouflaged. Camouflaging training planes is

---

* Joseph Goebbels was Reich Minister of Propaganda from 1933 to 1945.

unusual. Painting to be completed by the end of the year. Green and brown dope,* sickly smelling stuff, and it gave me a headache yesterday. Everyone at the task, working into the night, hoping all is finished by Christmas.

Sunday, December 11. In Swindon with Legs King last night. Town thronged with Christmas shoppers. The hangars as well as the planes are to be camouflaged.

Thursday, December 15. When I don't go out, which means six nights out of seven, I get to bed remarkably early, 8:30 or thereabouts.

1939

Wednesday, March 29. Spanish Civil War ended yesterday. Madrid surrendered to Franco's troops. Nine IRA† terrorists sent to jail in London. Here at South Cerney we have a double hangar guard against possible IRA outrages. Plenty of flying today. But Easter is coming.

Monday, April 3. 7:30 pm. In M Flight office, warm and cozy. I'm on hangar guard, which means simply that I sleep here in the hangar office instead of my billet. So quiet, can read in peace. Far as I'm concerned, this is one blessing the IRA has conferred. But big news is Chamberlain's statement that Britain will declare war on Germany the moment Poland is threatened, or rather, invaded. Poland has what Czechoslovakia never had, a firm assurance of help.

Tuesday, April 4. Some day! Big ARP‡ test this morning. Bugles sounded alarm. We all donned gasmasks, dispersed to posts or air raid trenches, but right in the middle of the panic, an Avro Tutor landed. "Dingle" Bell and I, like gargoyles in our masks, raced across the drome, splashing through mud and sweating like cobs, to greet pilot and push the biplane towards the hangars. "All clear" sounded at 11:25. Forty-five minutes later a number of men emerged from an air raid trench complaining they hadn't heard it.

Friday, April 7. Good Friday. Italy invaded Albania. That night, Don, Stan, and I with girls, in the Unicorn where everyone seemed to be at

---

* Aircraft dope is plasticized lacquer applied to fabric-covered planes to make them waterproof and airtight.

† The Irish Republican Army or the Provisional Irish Republican Army, was an paramilitary organization that fought to end British rule in Northern Ireland.

‡ In December 1937, the British government passed the Air Raid Precautions or ARP Act, requiring local authorities to ready themselves in case of air attack.

least tipsy, but occasionally "Albania" could be heard amid the general chatter and mirth.

Bought Easter eggs for Don's kids. Met Al and Doreen and another girl. Took them home to Ely, quite a bit of kissing.

Sunday, April 9. Very warm. Queenie Titselis, a very pretty Greek girl of sixteen, called at our home bringing a seventeen-year-old friend Betty Barrel. Lots of beer and swing records. I rather fell for Betty, also she for me.

Easter Monday, April 10. Watched Cardiff City beat Southend, 1-0.

Tuesday, April 11. Left on same train as Stan, who detrained at Gloucester.

Wednesday, April 12. 9 pm. On bed knees raised, pillow at my back. Taste of chips in my mouth and recollections of Easter leave in my thoughts. Train got me into Cardiff two hours late. Greeted by Don, who told me Stan was on the same train. So he was, tanned after global traveling. All three brothers were there. Fred as well.

Friday, April 14. While I was at home, Stan amused me by confessing that he'd arrived back in Britain not remotely knowing what ARP stood for and too embarrassed to ask. When I told him and of the general preparations for war, he said, "Oh, there'll be a bloody bust-up shortly."

War scares or no, Duke Ellington and orchestra touring France and Scandinavia.

Monday, April 24. Had three days confined to camp last week. 72 hours of completely undeserved punishment.

Saw "You Can't Take It with You" in Swindon the other night. Marvelous.

Passing through the village of Shrivenham, 5 miles the other side of Swindon, saw a brass plate on the wall of a house. It said "Mr. Tooth, Esquire. Dentist." And a blacksmith's shop whose door was adorned with the dried heads of dogs, fish, otters, etc.

Thursday, April 27. On hangar guard tonight. No sound but the overhead drone of night-flying ATS machines.

Historic announcement in Commons yesterday: Conscription. All fit men of 20-21 will be called up. Attlee attacked the government, challenged Chamberlain on his promise never to introduce compulsory military service in peacetime. Chamberlain retorted that the present state of affairs was hardly peacetime. I think the majority of the country is with Chamberlain on this.

Monday, May 1. Interesting weekend at home. On Friday I was changing from uniform into civvies at 1:45 pm. Half-dressed, I switched on the radio. Hamburg. Heard the thick tones of the Fuehrer, his manner of speech not as hysterically strident as usual. But though subdued, deliberate, to the point (whatever the point was since I don't know the language). Had difficulty separating Hamburg from a BBC regional, so heard Hitler's voice against the sentimental background of Sandy MacPherson on the theatre organ.

In the train going down to Wales, conscription chief topic. At home on Saturday, I inspected the back-garden air raid shelter. Four feet deep, looks sturdier than I had imagined. Gladiolas planted in the soil covering its corrugated iron roof.

Bought a Bob Crosby record. Cinema in the afternoon. Lots of flags flying on Queen Street buildings, wave of patriotism sweeping the country.

Coming out of the Capitol [theater] at 6:45 pm into crowds gazing upwards. Rumble of anti-aircraft gunfire and nine aircraft roared overhead. Said a youth near me, "Aren't those Spitfires?" Actually, they were Hawker Harts. Puffs of gunfire. Air raid drill, nothing more. News agent's placard saying "Wolves Will Be Tamed" showed war hadn't broken out. Long live soccer.

Girls hanging on to uniformed fellows in town made me half regret my decision to wear civvies.

Wednesday, May 17. Now I'm a Leading Aircraftman. LAC. I get a nice lump of back pay and six bob a week raise.

Glad it's over. I wasn't much prepared when the word came to leave for West Drayton. Three of us—Croft, King and me. Civvies in suitcases. West Drayton was cold, damp, NCOs surly, and food sloppy and unappetising. Into London on the Saturday afternoon. "National Service" posters at the base of Nelson's Column [monument in Trafalgar Square]. Usual buskers alongside theatre queues. One, a strong man, asked me to try bending a 6 [penny] nail to show he wasn't cheating. I couldn't. Another somersaulted, turned cartwheels. He must have been fifty if a day.

Friday, May 26. Excessive overtime. (Isn't all overtime excessive??) Very warm weather. Mutinous spirit, we all passed the sports-subscription table without dropping the usual tanner into the box, the contribution mandatory, towards subsidizing the sports. What chance do we get for sports, working 7:15 till noon, 1:15 to 3, 4 till 7? Then, often, on again at 9 pm for night flying. Work all day tomorrow, Whit Saturday,* also Sun-

---

* The day before Whit Sunday. In Britain and Ireland this holiday celebrated on the seventh Sunday after Easter by Catholics, Anglicans, and Methodists, as the Christian festival of Pentecost.

day, Monday, while civvy street and the rest of the RAF enjoy holiday. Oh, for a war. Or something. Anyway, I'm LAC. That Monday after the ordeal before the board, splicing, tested on rigging, etc., we celebrated in London.

Empire Air Day [air show] last Saturday. Worked from 7.30 am till 8 pm. Among things I noticed—the special enclosure for officers' ladies and families, set apart from the NCOs' and airmen's wives and kids. The strawberries and cream laid out for the former while the airmen's canteen sold cups of tea and cold meat pies at double the normal prices.

And—oh, yes, mock aeroplane out on the drome, wired to explode as Fairey Battles [light bomber] roared overhead in simulated bomb runs. The Battles came in on schedule to some feeble ratatat from ground gunners. They circled, came in again. Stubbornly the sitting duck refused to cooperate by blowing up. We pushed the darn thing into the hangar afterwards.

Tuesday, June 13. Last fortnight overshadowed by tragedy of the Thetis.* I was home on brief leave when first news on the radio told of a missing submarine. Then the hours of agony, the sub's stern actually rising above the surface of the water, yet each attempt failed to save the vessel. The final plunge. Over one hundred men inside. At 11.30 pm—I'd just come in slightly drunk. I turned off a Gene Krupa swing record program to pick up a news bulletin. "The Admiralty regrets to announce it has no reason to continue to believe there is any hope." The sub was in only 130 feet of water. The feeling of loss following the last announcement was acute. Somehow, we had all been part of the fight for life. The foreign messages of sympathy next day included one from Adolf Hitler.

I had flown home for that leave. With Sgt. Pile and at the controls, P/O Skene. Took off 2 pm Thursday, crossed the Severn and down to Cardiff, landing about 2:40. My first flight. Weather warm up to 86. Following week, home again, with Legs King as guest, and we even took a day a trip to Barry.

Thursday, June 22. Off home again tomorrow so can't complain. No upsetting news these days, all seems calm. King and Queen a big hit in America, especially at the New York World Fair. King munched a hot dog.

Another sub disaster. First the USS Squalus,† 26 drowned. Then

---

* The submarine HMS *Thetis* sank during sea trials in Liverpool Bay on June 1, 1939. Nearly 100 crew members drowned. The submarine was salvaged and renamed HMS *Thunderbolt*, which sank in the Mediterranean in March 1943.

† USS *Squalus* sank during a test dive off the coast of New Hampshire on May 23, 1939. The submarine was salvaged and renamed USS *Sailfish*.

our Thetis, 99 lost. Now French Phoenix,* 77 gone. I sent for "Cook's Tours Abroad." King and I have decided on a trip to Paris late this summer. Eight days, 5 pounds, seventeen and sixpence.

Monday, July 3. Jittery weekend. Germans invaded Danzig.† Looks as if the Nazis plan to scare the Poles into such a state of nerves they'll be only too glad to surrender Danzig. But the Poles are asserting their resistance. So there's a crisis period ahead, likely to wreck my August leave. I saw Chamberlain in Cardiff the weekend before last, at the National Government Display. Popular songs piercing the gloom include "Little Sir Echo," "Hold Tight," and "Beer Barrel Polka."

I'm not in favor of concessions to blackmail, but it's fantastic that Britain and France should contemplate going to war over some distant, not very large, seaport. Total camouflage of hangars and preparation of "blackout" blinds. I'm corresponding with a 24-year-old Chelsea girl who has a ready wit and is an excellent conversationalist.

Monday, July 31. An unlucky month ending. After receiving 2 pounds twelve shillings pay and credits, I placed most of it in my tunic pocket, foolishly left the tunic hanging up in the hangar annex all afternoon. Found all the money gone. Notified service police, SWO etc. but no results. Damn bad show when you can't trust your own workmates. I suspect Humphreys, a shifty-eyed character who recently failed his LAC exam. He is often short of cash and bets on the horses. He was working in the vicinity of the annex. Well, it makes a big hole in my savings for the Paris trip.

Most fellows sympathize with me, and there is some anger at the thought of a thief in our midst. Few weeks back Reggie Metcalfe had five quid [5 pounds] stolen. Anyway, my bad luck.

Am writing these days to an Evelyn Gomm, a good-looking young lady of charming conversation that I met on the Cardiff-Gloucester train. She lives in Sloane Square, London. Recently she sent me a copy of "Gone with the Wind."

After well over a hundred days, an Anglo-French-Soviet pact seems

---

* French submarine *Phenix* sank during diving exercises on June 15, 1939, off southeast coast of Indochina (Vietnam).

† Germany didn't actually invade Danzig on July 3. That would happen on September 1. As one of the provisions of the Treaty of Versailles, Danzig, largely an ethnically German city, became a "free city" under the protection of the League of Nations but with special administrative ties to Poland. This territory, known as the "Polish Corridor, was Poland's access to Danzig and the sea. Hitler, however, was determined to thwart provisions of the Versailles treaty and include ethnic Germans in the Reich. In the spring of 1939, he demanded the annexation of the Free City of Danzig and rail access for Germany across the "Polish Corridor."

in the making. But no Nazi move yet except military preparation in Danzig. Security tightened at RAF camps, including this one, following new outbreaks of IRA terrorism. Bombs exploded at King's Cross and Victoria stations recently. Don and Queenie are getting married in three weeks, are now in Jersey.

Tuesday, August 8. Tuesday. Wheadon, Sandy, Will (at the wheel) and myself, drove into camp about 1 pm after what was for me a memorable weekend. Pete. That's the name she told me to call her when I sat by her side on the sands at Barry. Tom and I had been sitting behind these two girls in a relatively uncrowded patch of beach. Struck up a conversation with them and I fell for the one who rather resembled Sonja Henje. (Her father is Scandinavian, her uncle the South Wales Echo cartoonist J.C. Walker.) On the warm sands we drank lemonade and talked happily and Tom seemed quite content with the other girl, Kathleen. But a special warmth developed between Pete and me. She is anxious for us to meet again. So am I. Her full name is Dorothy Peterson, and when I left her yesterday, she was close to tears.

Wednesday, August 9. At midnight tonight we have a blackout and gas attack drill and I'm on guard at the water tower.

Tuesday, August 22. War—scary day. A non-aggression pact signed between Germany and Russia, right in the middle of negotiations between Russia, France and Britain aimed at a pact resisting German aggression.* Hitler is now expected to invade Poland any minute. He speaks at Tannenberg on Sunday—my 21st birthday.

This past weekend at home, saw Pete again. Hated to leave her and after a hurried kiss, I dashed off in a thunderstorm to rendezvous with Will Price, for a drive back to camp through rain and lightning.

Thursday, August 24. Dim blue lights, almost impossible to write by, emergency conditions. War seems inevitable. All museums, galleries, etc. in London closed. Parliament recalled.

Sunday, August 27. Sunday. My birthday. Twenty-one. And all Europe faces war. Secret messages flying between chancellories, presumably in a last-minute endeavour to avert it. Evacuation of schoolchildren. Ration cards. Advice to owners of pets. ARP. All the familiar news features of last September's crisis once more fill the columns. Friday's Evening News headline: "A Little Nearer the Brink of War."

Thundery weather.

---

* German Foreign Minister Joachim von Ribbentrop and Soviet Foreign Minister Molotov signed the German-Soviet Nonaggression Pact on August 23, 1939,

Last night I sat through the film "The Sisters" (Bette Davis,) nursing an aching tooth. Pete writes that she still loves me and says, "In our shop, customers constantly ask 'Will there be war?' Until I feel like throwing the inkstand at them."

Evelyn writes, "Most of us feel grateful to you (RAF) in your curtailed freedom." This reference being to the general stoppage of all furloughs.

Camouflaging here mostly completed. Thousands of square yards of rope netting coloured by worn and green drape hangars, roofs, and sides, and entering through the side door, one has to stoop through them. It's like creeping into Ali Baba's cave.

When night falls now, reading and writing cease. These dull blue lights are quite useless. Here it is my birthday, and nothing to do but sit amid newspapers with the black headlines unable to read the smaller print and forbidden to go out.

I was born in a time of war. And I reach man's estate, whatever that entails with another one imminent. Looking back, I can remember being four or six years old, living on Eisteddfod Street (now obliterated to make space for a huge new bus center) and seeing horse-drawn GPO [General Post Office] vans and at nine writing my name in the snow on the only white Christmas Day of my childhood. Great blizzard in 1928, February, and the death of my foster father, lungs destroyed by wartime gas. Other memories, equally sad. But lots of pleasant ones too, laughs with friends like Tom Parry and (no relation) Jim Parry while working at Sid Jones's garage. Loves with Pete and Doris and briefer flirtations. Mourning for King George V in 1936 and his son's [Edward VIII] abdication before that year ended. Countless movies and much much music. Religion at the Foursquare Gospel, harvest festivals at the Salvation Army. Edna. Don. The RAF and an altogether new life.

Wednesday, August 30. Peace still in the balance. I've just helped put up the blackout screens. Doing that each night will enable us, thank God, to enjoy normal illumination. But these great black rectangles all around the room produce a feeling of claustrophobia. Birthday cards and letters from home so pedestrians won't stumble in the blackout ("they are painting the kerbs [curbs] white"). Pete sent me, as a birthday gift (an ornamental dog) which beheaded with a flick of the thumb to become a cigarette lighter.

To the dentist with my aching tooth the other morning. After freezing the gum, he sang, "Hands, knees, and boomsadaisy..." and on the boom, yanked out the tooth.

Thursday, August 31. General evacuation of schoolchildren from the big cities. "Children must carry attache-cases containing underclothes, toothbrush... Gas masks must be taken, slung over the shoulder, not packed away...."

Walking about the camp are men in their fifties and sixties, boys of the old brigade, members of the newly formed National Defence Corps [NDC]. Pete writes that there is a barrage balloon in Roath Park and an air raid shelter in her garden. Tonight's Evening News headline: "We are on the Brink."

Friday, September 1. War began today between Germany and Poland. I am half-drunk as I write this and my mind is confused.

Saturday, September 2. 4.45 pm. In a couple of hours will go over to the hangar. We are working 12-hour shifts, I'm on 7 pm–7 am. Yesterday's news from Poland shook us all up. Warsaw bombed, etc. The canteen was crowded with airmen, reservists, khaki-clad NDC men, singing, laughing, cheering, and cursing, all drinking. I've never seen so many bottles. Blackout screens kept light from escaping, but also ended ventilation. Tobacco smoke thick. Someone at the piano thumped away at "Tipperary." The deafening din subsided abruptly, and rather creepily, for a radio bulletin to be heard. War is as good as started. A thunderstorm is banging away just now. I packed my civilian clothes, will send them home. God knows when I'll need those again. I never thought, though had often feared, that Hitler would take such a step, plunging us into war. But he has.

Sunday, September 3. 2:20 pm. Since 11 this morning, Great Britain has been at war with Germany. As I write, only the faint stirrings of a newspaper page turning over, and somebody whistling "South of the Border," and the sigh of the wind outside. Nothing else disturbs the stillness. Even from the direction of the drome, no sound of aircraft, though it is a twelve-hour working day. We, the night shift, came off at 7 am. Some of us now reading the Sunday papers, others writing home.

An electrician awoke me at 11:50 am and said without emotion, "It's started. We declared war at 11 o'clock."

The King will broadcast tonight at 6 pm. Chamberlain has already been on the air. Our CO Group Captain Iron gave everyone available (which didn't include the night shift) a lecture, saying that our Flying Training School work is of major importance, also that Right was on our side, our consciences clear, and "in the end, the British Empire will prevail," at which point the lads all cheered.

Warsaw was bombed 6 times yesterday.

Last night I and two others were on guard outside ATS hangar.

Rain fell continuously, with vivid flashes of lightning. I watched the leak and wild dawn creep over the soaked earth and thought of home, of Pete, of so many things.

Around noon, the BBC announcer said, "This is the Home Service Station broadcasting on two wavelengths. Since 11 am the British Empire has been in a state of war...." A heavy mirror propped on a window sill near my bed slid off and smashed to bits.

Because of the war, I won't be able to take my library book back into Cirencester yet. It's "The Struggle for Peace" by the Right Honourable Neville Chamberlain.

Well, he worked hard to preserve it. And who can disagree with this passage from the foreword he wrote? "To me, war is not only the cruelest, but the most senseless method of settling disputes. But man of peace as I am, there is one claim which if it were made, must, as it seems to me, be resisted even, if necessary, by force. That would be a claim by any one State to dominate others by force, since, if such a claim were admitted, I see no possibility of peace of mind or body for anyone."

Tuesday, September 5. 1:30 pm. Third day of the war. Widespread disgust over sinking of the Athenia.* German radio blames the British, alleges we did it to bring America into the war. (The ship's 1400 passengers included 300 Americans.) French troops in action. The RAF flew over north and west Germany dropping leaflets. Six million of them. But the RAF bombers that flew over Kiel† last night dropped bombs.

I was again on guard at the ATS hangar. A brilliant night, moonlight defying the blackout. Night before last, was on scatter patrol—on the far side of the drome, alongside the South Cerney road, where Harts and Oxfords are parked in scattered fashion, picketed [tied] down. That night, thunderstorms alternated with bursts of moonlight. Sunday night before going to work—this was the day war began—I rode into Cheltenham in Will's car. Quiet in the town. No signs of jingo hysteria, and the only flags I saw were two Union Jacks in a village on the Birdlip.‡

We are allowed out daily from three till seven.

Monday, September 18. After almost a fortnight of monotonous communiques from the Western Front ... inconsequential French advances, RAF leaflet raids, U-boat attacks on Atlantic shipping, and the futile if brave struggle in Poland against the invader, two big shocks: The Soviet

---

* SS *Athenia*, a transatlantic passenger liner, was en route from Scotland to Montreal, when it was torpedoed by U-30, killing 117 civilian passengers and crew. The ship was the first British vessel sunk by Germany in World War II.

† German port city on the Baltic Sea.

‡ A village in Gloucestershire.

Red Army has crossed into Poland on the pretext of defending White Russia and the Polish Ukrainians. And the aircraft carrier Courageous* has been sunk in home waters.

I was in Swindon Saturday night. Town packed with evacuees and the military. After a meal in a cafe, spoiled by an elderly reservist who persisted in loudly reciting the merits of the Bren gun ("fires a distance of 40,000 feet ... twenty-seven shells a minute"). I escaped into the blackout, sought a movie. "Love Affair" with Charles Boyer and Irene Dunne, and it helped me to forget the war. A newsreel showing Athenia survivors shoved me back to reality.

Taking some while to get used to the blackout. People barging into one another. Gasmasks entangling. Wrong buses boarded. My bus took ninety minutes to travel fifteen miles back to Cirencester.

Don was married to Queenie yesterday. I sent a gift.

The BBC is doing rather well, considering it is now confined to only two wavelengths. There is just one program, but swing music often featured. The news is on now. The Red Army and German troops have met at Brest-Litovsk [Poland] and will discuss the carve-up of Poland.

Courageous death toll feared above 600.

Thursday, September 21. Just been listening to the radio, Roosevelt speaking in favor of repealing the Neutrality Act.† He wants to lift the embargo on arms, which will be to our benefit. Still working 12-hour shifts. Am on days, prefer nights. New training term begins Monday. Hope to squeeze in a weekend home.

Sunday, October 8. Managed to get home for a day. Cardiff appears so strange, blacked out. St. Mary Street half empty by ten at night, Citizens picking their way about with shaded torches [flashlights]. Searchlights constantly probing the sky. Saw the newly-weds Don and Queenie. Ma is on good terms with Queenie, they go to the Capitol Theatre every Monday.

U-boats rumored in the Bristol Channel.

Walking back from the Horse and Groom last night with Beverley and Sid Mills when a car came up from behind and knocked Sid ten yards or more. The car, going fast, raced on, to be swallowed up in the blackness. We got Sid to the camp hospital. He is bruised by the gasmask over his shoulder [which] may have saved his spine from injury.

---

* HMS *Courageous* was torpedoed and sunk off the coast of Ireland on September 17, 1939.

† The Neutrality Act of 1935 imposed a general embargo on trading in arms and war matériel with belligerent nations. The subsequent Neutrality Act of 1937 allowed European belligerents to buy materials and supplies as long as the recipients arranged for the transport and paid immediately with cash. However, the arms embargo was maintained.

Much singing in the Horse and Groom of "We'll Hang Out the Washing on the Siegfried Line."

Friday, October 27. Couple of weeks ago began seven days leave. The second day of it—a Saturday—I bought a war map which now covers a quarter of one wall in the living room. That night, met Pete and after a spot of lovemaking I dashed back into town met Don at the Royal Hotel and got drunk. Saw Pete again Sunday night, we went up on Penylan Hill and looked across the blacked-out city to the Bristol Channel beyond. The sky shimmered with stars, an occasional searchlight beam fanning across it. Spent most of the morning in various suburban pubs, drinking and dart-playing. Wonderful weather, every day a bright blue sky flecked by drifting clouds and stationary barrage balloons. Grim news that weekend though, of the Royal Oak* sinking. Tom Parry knows a sailor who was among the 800 drowned. Some nights our radio brought in the silky English tones of this anti–British propaganda-broadcaster we've been hearing about lately.

Tuesday night Don being at work, Queenie came down. I danced all night with her, bought the kids chocolates and lemonade. Queenie and I got on very well indeed, and I feel rather odd about this. I took her home, quite innocently, but was there when Don arrived at 10:15. Wednesday night she took me to see her mother, who is very deaf. It's necessary to shout at her, something the kids enjoy hugely.

Friday night I saw Pete, apologised for my three-nights-in-a-row neglect of her and she told me she loves me intensely.

Eight days leave was it? Went quick.

The U.S. has voted to repeal the Neutrality Act.†

One of our Harts crashed today. This is the third crash of a kite from this station since the war started. Several friends of mine posted—Elms, Taff Jones, and Lofty Horner (all of whom I converted into swing fans) posted to France.

Sunday, October 29. Two close friends posted: Will Price and Sandy Powell. Bound for France. Frankie Keene and Johnny "Legs" King are my remaining friends. Did I say I converted Lofty Horner to swing? Actually, he knows more about jazz than I do. Sandy and Will and I all live within twelve miles of each other in Wales, and we used to ride home in Will's car. Fed up with the monotony of this twelve-hour day work,

---

* On October 14, 1939, a German U-boat torpedoed and sank HMS *Royal Oak* while the battleship was anchored at Scapa Flow, Scotland.

† The Neutrality Act of 1939 lifted the arms embargo and put all trade with belligerent nations under the terms of "cash-and-carry." American ships were still barred from transporting goods to belligerent nations.

The Diary: 1939 49

I wish I was going to France, too. Will turn in now, read "War Weekly, Part One." A war map, enclosed with it is now on the wall above my pillow.

Thursday, November 2. Butter and bacon rationing due next month. Four ounces of butter weekly. Tommy Handley on the air the other night—"Hitler has to be a teetotaler—he can't even get a port on the Baltic." Frankie Keene, one of my best friends, posted to the Fleet Air Arm, leaves Thursday for Scotland. Just listened to Hamburg's "Lord Haw Haw"* talking of the "alarming rationing of butter and bacon in England." Is this chap actually English? "Is this the freedom," he asks us, "for which you are fighting?" And after gloating over the torpedoing of the Royal Oak, this fairy-tale teller asks in a slimy voice, "Which way is the wind blowing now, England?"

Saturday, November 11. Day off. At 11 this morning, no silence. The radio broadcast dance music to the BEF [British Expeditionary Force] in France. Beer-cellar bomb mystery. Who planted the bomb in the Munich beer cellar that killed eight old-guard Nazis while Hitler escaped, having left ten minutes before detonation? Radio Hamburg, as I myself heard, claims "Providence guards the Fuehrer," says Chamberlain and his "murderous" secret service are behind it.†

A British mystery, the "accidental" explosion that wrecked the submarine Oxley,‡ killing 53 men.

Am going into Swindon today. My application for a weekend pass washed out.

Monday, November 13. Service in the hangar yesterday. Sang "O Valiant Heart" and a bugler sounded "The Last Post." We had leaflets, printed originally for pre-war (this war) Remembrance services for the British Legion. In a corner of the leaflet it says "Revised, 9-10-39" and

---

* Lord Haw-Haw was the nickname of Brooklyn-born William Joyce, who renounced his British citizenship in 1940. His broadcasts of Nazi propaganda began with "Germany calling. Germany calling." Joyce was captured by British forces in northern Germany when the war ended. He was tried and hanged for treason in 1946.

† On November 8, a time bomb concealed inside a pillar in the Bürgerbräukeller was set to go off during Hitler's Beer Hall Putsch address commemorating the so-called Putsch in 1923 in which Hitler and the Nazi Party attempted to overthrow the Weimar Republic. The bomb exploded, killing eight people and injuring 57. Hitler had cut short his speech and had already left. A critic of Hitler and the Nazi Party, who planted the bomb, Georg Elser, was arrested, imprisoned for 5½ years, and executed shortly before the end of the war.

‡ On September 10, 1939, HMS *Oxley* became the first British submarine sunk in World War II. *Oxley* was torpedoed off the coast of southern Norway by HMS *Triton*, another British submarine that mistook it for an enemy submarine. Wartime security hid the details of this "friendly fire" tragedy until the 1950s.

it contains a new prayer for "Victory over all the powers of evil," with a new hymn that begins, "Lord, while for all mankind we pray, O hear for us the land we love the most." I thought of peacetime remembrances at the War Memorial in Cardiff. Mam always wept at 11 o'clock. She lost two brothers, indirectly her husband, and a third brother came back with one leg. A letter from home tells of Cardiff's first air raid warning. And from Pete a letter which doesn't mention the air raid warning but she longs "to have your arms about me."

Tuesday, November 21. Home Friday night and much of Saturday. Had a few beers with Don. The two kids seem well and happy. Saw Pete Friday night and we are still fond of each other, but I had some pleasant moments on the train coming back with a 17-year-old girl named Helen Hawkins. Too bad she had to detrain at Newport. At the NAAFI* concert last night, third-rate singers doing that horrible thing about "hanging out the washing on the Siegfried Line."† A violinist played Lizt's "Liebestraum" and "The Lost Chord," both out of tune and a soprano sang "Trees."

One wartime benefit: magnificent night-sky views during the blackout. Returning from the NAAFI, I contemplated the moon as it peeped between scudding black clouds. Someone in the dark said, "Nice night for an air raid," ruining the moment. There have been scattered raids, in the North, Scotland, east Yorks, also Thames Estuary, where parachute mines [German naval mines] were dropped. In Swindon Friday saw well-rated if somewhat harrowing "Dark Victory" with Bette Davis.

Sunday, December 3. Finns fighting off the Russians, their gunners picking off the parachuting invaders before they hit the snow. Petsamo, up near the Arctic Circle, was one of the first towns to fall, but the Finns, fighting like tigers, have recaptured it. In Swindon Friday night saw superb "Wuthering Heights," and afterwards spent pleasant hour or two in moonlit blackout with a blonde named Theobold (that's her second name) to whom I shall write. If I have the time. Already corresponding with Evelyn Gomm of Raglan, Helen Hawkins of Newport, and the intensely loving Dorothy "Pete" Peterson of Cardiff. Christmas near. Must buy gifts for folks, nephews, and a girl friend or two. And for myself, a Damon Runyon collection and some records.

---

* The Navy, Army and Air Force Institutes (NAAFI), a company created by the British government in 1920 to run recreational establishments for the British Armed Forces. NAAFI also sold goods to servicemen and their families.

† "We're Going to Hang Out the Washing on the Siegfried Line," first published in 1939, was written by Ulster songwriter Jimmy Kennedy while he was a Captain in the British Expeditionary Force.

Monday, December 18. Sensational climax to the Graf Spee saga.* Loss of life heavy on the Exeter and Achilles, but the scuttling of Hitler's crack battleship is worth the price.†

Last night, for the first time in weeks, the sky throbbed to the drone of Cheetah engines‡ as three Oxfords kept on monotonous circuits over the flare-path which winked steadily in the blackness. On tables in the crew room the young pilots, mostly APOs [Acting Pilot Officers], dozed, awaiting their turn to fly, and still wearing their sidcots [flying suits]. I forget how many solos were done. We packed in about midnight. What with refueling, pushing in, and DIs, it was 1:30 am before I got down to about four hours sleep. Parachutes make fine pillows. Tonight, Harts would be flying but probably won't. It's raining.

Thursday, December 21. Thursday, 10:30 pm. I go on night-flying duty in half an hour and am somewhat drunk following some wild boozing and even dancing (all males) in the canteen. Found myself jitterbugging with Champion, who has a harelip, while the station band, a corny outfit if ever there was one, played "Roll out the Barrel." Proceedings marred by (a) near fight which Sq. Leader Mathieson, whom we all genuinely love, managed to subdue, and (b) LAC Borden playing "Smiling Through" on a saw. Even the unpopular Warrant Officer "Monty" Kemp got up on stage and told filthy jokes, winding up with an appeal for cooperation from the men in his herculean task tomorrow of supervising the departure of some 700 of us off on Christmas furlough. It's a moonlit night, so the Oxfords will be flying. Just when I need the sleep....

Monday, December 25. Christmas day in Fred's (Don's brother) car we rode to the cemetery and placed a wreath on Edna's grave. That night, though, a party at Don's with over twenty guests, including his new wife Queenie. Lots of drinking and dancing to records, mostly to my latest hot ones, and too many requests for a record I had reluctantly bought, under extreme pressure from non-jazz addicted parents: a medley

---

* *Admiral Graf Spee* was an (armored ship), nicknamed a "pocket battleship" by the British. On December 13, 1939, HMS *Exeter* and light cruisers HMS *Ajax* and HMS *Achilles* engaged *Graf Spee* off the Rio de la Plata. After a brief but intense battle, the outnumbered German warship took refuge in the neutral port of Montevideo, Uruguay. Trapped there by the three British warships, four days later, *Graf Spee*'s commanding officer, Hans Langsdorff, ordered his ship scuttled. Churchill heralded the naval victory, declaring, "This brilliant sea fight takes its place in our naval annals and in a long, cold, dark winter it warmed the cockles of the British hearts."

† During the battle, *Exeter* was hit by a total of seven 283mm shells that killed 61 of her crew and wounded another 23. *Achilles* had 4 killed and 47 wounded.

‡ The Armstrong Siddeley Cheetah, a seven-cylinder aircraft radial engine, powered many wartime British aircraft. The Oxford was equipped with a pair of Cheetah engines.

including "Hang Out the Washing on the Siegfried Line" and the nauseating "There'll Always Be an England." A great deal of kissing games in almost total darkness into the final hours before dawn. I staggered home through frost-coated streets under a brilliant moon.

Friday, December 29. A strange leave, a Christmas of goodwill and gasmasks. What a year 1939 has been. I remember how it began for me—standing at midnight outside a Swindon phone-box with Legs King, while Basil Smart phoned for a taxi. An Easter night in some Tiger Bay dive with Al and two girls. Pat Lewis's fantastic kisses at Olwen's 21st birthday party. A slightly pleasant affair with a girl named Betty Barrel. And all that political high-tension summer. I had begun poring over Cook's Tours' travel folders, decided on Paris for four days in September. The war nipped that plan in the bud. Meanwhile, I'd met Pete. And there was that harrowing night of foredoomed effort to save 99 men on the Thetis off Liverpool.

Well, what a Christmas. Bought brooches for girls, cigars for old Man, a purse for Ma, and numerous cards. Shops and streets thronged despite the blackout. Bought four new swing records for myself. Friday night before Christmas, I had a date with Pete but before I could keep it, Doris Green and Phyllis Evans showed up. Doris looked very attractive. They and Tom persuaded me to join them and off we went. I made love to Doris in an air raid shelter and caught one hell of a cold. All these shelters seem so infernally damp. I also felt bad about the broken date with Pete, never saw her at all Christmas week. She sent me a gift of a Rolls razor and a note saying, "This must be goodbye."

Sunday, December 31. Back in camp for New Year's Eve. Half a dozen of us brought beer, smuggled in port and sherry out of the sergeants' mess and threw a party in the sub-depot canteen. Among the highlights—a soldier from a Gloucester regiment who gave such a remarkable impersonation of Hitler we all goose-stepped around the canteen bawling "Deutscheland Uber Alles." Reg Metcalf, performing "The Chestnut Tree," too vigorously with a stomach full of ale, had to make frequent trips outside into the snow. Legs King, generally scornful of "The Lambeth Walk," danced it. At midnight, about a hundred of us swarmed across the ice and snow to the main square where we joined hands and sang "Auld Lang Syne." Someone struck forth with "God Save the King," then we all dispersed to our quarters. I was up again at seven, did little work, on guard that night, first of the year.

1940

Sunday, January 7, Night. Feeling lousy. In bed, though it's only a quarter to eight. Fever or something. Eleven hours in a damp cold hangar working amid black and yellow grease, clutching cold metal tools on a fog-clammy Sabbath with the same in store for tomorrow. "Freedom is in Peril. Defend It with all your Might." How fed up I am with that hypocritical phrase.

Friday, January 12. In bed with a sore throat. Enemy bombers were reported over the East Coast and Scotland today. No bombs dropped. Also, a big Finnish victory.*

All night flying last night left two kites unserviceable. One's oleo leg† busted, the other cracked up in the middle of the drome was brought in this afternoon, a sorry looking sight, and I took part in its dismantling. ATS flying tonight, Oxfords [communications aircraft] ceaselessly overhead. One of our Oxfords, taking advantage the other day of clear weather, flew across to Grantham then crashed, killing ITS pupil. And this morning another Oxford, ATS this time, piled up near Swindon, killing both pupil and instructor. Someone passed the hat around, collecting for a wreath.

Tuesday, January 16. Day off! A gang of us are heading into Cheltenham for a movie, a good meal, winding up with a dance at the Town Hall. Yesterday little excitement broke the freezing monotony of 30 and 60-hour inspections. An air raid warning, the first we've had around here. Men filed into trenches. Machines [aircraft] running up cut engines. Nothing in the blue sky however, not even a cloud. I ran down to the Decontamination Centre where I'm on duty in the event of a gas attack. All leave has been stopped for the BEF and RAF in France, so something is in the wind.

Saturday, January 20. Last Tuesday, Legs King and I hitch-hiked 14 miles through a blizzard to attend a dance at Cheltenham Town Hall. It was a "dry" dance, so we smuggled in a bottle of port. The following night at the Pantomime Ball. This wasn't dry. Whiskies, ports, beers, chased each other down my throat. Some interesting acquaintances

---

* From December 7, 1939 to January 8, 1940, at the Battle of Suomussalmi in northern Finland, the Finns' smaller forces fended off the larger attacking Soviet forces.

† An oleo strut is a pneumatic air-oil hydraulic shock absorber used on the landing gear.

made. A flashily dressed man discharged from military service (he said) on health grounds and now an office manager. Full of sickening patter such as: "Though I'm in civvies, my heart's with you lads," so we let him buy our drinks as we ogled the brunette he introduced as his secretary. She raised a glass in toast of "Victory," a ritual I rather spoiled by tipsily asking, "Whose?" Met another brunette with whom, unfortunately (a common failing when I overdrink), I talked too much and smooched too little. The quiet chap, who occasionally materialized at her bare elbow, proved to be her husband, but she said to me, "Don't mind him. He's partial to blonds, really."

We took a taxi back to camp and, it being 2:30 am, had to break through a frozen hedge and run at a crouch across the snowclad airfield to reach our hut without the guards spotting us.

Tuesday, January 23. Half past two pm. Day off. Reclining on bed. Winter sunshine steaming through the window. Cold though. Tonight, Legs and I will go into Cirencester, see a film, followed by eggs and chips, then back to camp on the 9:40 pm bus.

Odd view outside. Camouflaged square patchworked with snow. Barracks blocks also camouflaged, bleak and gloomy in shadow. Beyond the sergeant's mess, the 90-foot-high water tower with a Lewis gun [light machine gun] atop of it and a gunner bobbing up and down trying to keep warm. Two Whitleys [medium bombers] far above in the blue, their heavy engine roar drowning the drone of our own Harts [light bombers] aloft and gleaming in the sun.

We've lost a destroyer, the Grenville,* with 80 men. The Russians have launched a fierce attack against the Finnish lines. Some of the neutral countries are sore at Churchill for his blunt criticism. Americans annoyed over this mail-opening business. Understandable. Most Americans sympathize with the Allies, I think, but they want to keep out of the war. Also understandable. Can't they see, though, that if Britain and France lose this war (not impossible), they, too, will go under?

Another destroyer sunk. The Exmouth. No survivors.†

Sunday, January 28. 8 pm. Everything covered by ice this morning. Trees, grass, roads, sheathed as if tightly in glass. Icicles hanging from bushes and rooftops. No flying, of course. Acres of camouflaged netting covering the hangar walls stiff with ice. The camp is isolated, all phone wires down. No traffic into town. The flag couldn't be hauled up, the

---

* HMS *Grenville* hit a mine on January 19, 1940, off the southeast coast of England.
† HMS *Exmouth* was sunk by a German sub on January 21 1940, north of Scotland.

ropes like steel rods. Still raining, and freezing as it falls. This the Nazi's secret weapon we've been hearing of lately?

Sunday, February 11. 6:30 pm. In B flight office on hangar guard duty.

That freeze-up last week was so paralyzing we were permitted four days leave. I got away at six Friday night, but ice and sleet so bad my train didn't reach Swindon until eleven and it was four next morning when I got into Cardiff, where streets were icebound. A pleasant leave, though, and a pleasant acquaintance struck up with the barmaid at the Tredegar pub. Tom and I together much of the time, including a rather wild night in and out of pubs and cafes down Tiger Bay.* In one establishment, a good-looking half-caste girl I talked with said suddenly, "We have some of Louis's here," and forthwith produced an [Louis] Armstrong record "Jeepers Creepers." Followed, on the gramophone, by some Maxine Sullivan and Fats Waller, so in no time we were dancing.

Yesterday the King and Queen paid our camp a visit. During the usual tiresome preparations various unpatriotic remarks made. But the Queen smiled brightly at we overalled jerks† as her car sped all too swiftly past us. I only got a glimpse of the King in a corner of the car, but those who saw him more distinctly say he looked bored stiff.

Wednesday, February 14. Saw damn good film last night, "Bachelor Mother," with Ginger Rogers and David Niven. Felt rather an urge, not for the first time, to abandon this darkened war-wracked country of ration cards, gasmasks, and casualty lists, and get to the United States. Land of light by night. I don't think I have too many false illusions about the USA. But I hope to visit there someday.

Big battle raging in the Karelian Isthmus.‡ Some say equal to the Somme, 1916 [high-cost French-British victory over Germans].

That half-caste girl I danced with in Butetown, when I was home last week, refused at first to play the other side of Maxine Sullivan's "Loch Lomond" because some nights previous, some Finn sailors were in the café and when they recognized "Dark Eyes,"§ they threatened to wreck the place.

---

* Tiger Bay was the local name for an area of Cardiff which covered Butetown and Cardiff Docks.

† RAF slang for a low-ranking member of the ground crew (aircraftman).

‡ The "Winter War" between the Finland and the Soviet Union took place from November 30, 1939 to March 13, 1940. In December and February 1940, the Battles of Summa were fought between the Gulf of Finland and Lake Ladoga in northwestern Russia. Finnish forces held off the Soviets in the first battle. The Soviets triumphed in the second.

§ "Dark Eyes" is a well-known Russian folk song.

Sunday, February 18. Listening to [Anton] Rubenstein's "Melody in F." Feel rather weak and red spots have broken out on my legs. I'll report sick tomorrow. Yesterday a great "battle" here at South Cerney. Maintenance men headed by F/Sgt. Henderson trooped on to the snow-blanketed drome. We spread out in a long line, armed ourselves with snowballs, and advanced through the whirling flakes. The "enemy" was Operations Flight. For an hour or more, the air was dense with hurtling snowballs as well as flakes. This way and that, surged the titanic white struggle. Which we won.

Too bad the warring nations couldn't settle their conflicts so beautifully and bloodlessly.

Good news, though, that of the Altmark* boarding by Navy men. 300 prisoners liberated from the Nazi prison ship.

Sgt. "Tiddler" Pile got back from leave in Plymouth where he saw the battle-scarred Exeter. He said the cruiser dodged a lurking U-boat to get into port and that the Ajax put in a few weeks ago only after an RAF bomber had sunk a submarine.

Wednesday, February 21. I want to go abroad—soon. We had gas drill this morning, a messy affair, and the drome is a sea of mud and slush. With gasmask fitted, I dreamed up the following potty poetry:

> In the event of a raid
> I'm afraid
> I'll have to ask
> For my gasmask
> And go down to the trenches
> And sit on benches
> Mid an assortment of stenches

Also:

> Most of Hitler's threats generally get scorned.
> 'Tis when we hear the siren
> We feel we've been warned.

Friday, February 23. Men of the Ajax and Exeter got a right royal welcome in London. With free seats at West End cinemas. The Battle of the

---

* The Altmark incident took place on February 16–17, 1940 when several British destroyers intercepted the German tanker *Altmark* in then neutral Norwegian waters. On board the vessel were 300 British prisoners, whose ships had been sunk by the *Graf Spee* in the Southern Atlantic Ocean. The destroyer *Cossack* attacked the German ship, freeing all the prisoners, killing eight German seamen, and wounding 10 others. Germany claimed the attack was a violation of international law and Norwegian neutrality.

River Plate* has really fired the imagination, now that we are hearing eye-witness stories. In honoring those who have returned though, we shouldn't forget those who lost their lives.

Carrying on the war in our own unsensational, often boring, and never-publicized fashion, we on this camp envy those men of the Navy, not only their living it up in London but the opportunity they had for getting to grips with the enemy.

Churchill on the radio now at Guildhall† where the River Plate warriors are being honoured. As usual, he's tough and terrific and often amusing.

I am on 48 hours excused duty while I get rid of these mysterious spots.

Tuesday, February 27. Day off. Weather mild. Will hitch-hike to Swindon this afternoon, see Errol Flynn in "Dodge City." Read in the paper that a Jesuit minister, deploring the decline in religion, says "Christ is less of a reality than Mickey Mouse or Donald Duck." Not surprising, in my opinion. Bombs and blackouts and casualty lists. Nothing very Christlike in evidence whereas Micky M. and Donald D. offer some brief escape from it all.

Wednesday, February 28. Dull day. [Legs] King and I in the fabric workshop most of the time, rebuilding and redoping, carrying out a 180-hour inspection. We hope to have the Hawker Hart ready for flying in a week or so, give it to F/Sgt. Morrad, our dreamy-eyed, easy-going boss, and ask him for a 48-hour pass to visit London.

Now to bed, wherein I'll read Harold Nicholson's "Why Britain Is at War." Meanwhile, eating an orange and a Lyons fruit pie (these pies, by the way, grow emptier and emptier of fruit). More of my potty poetry:

---

* The German pocket battleship *Graf Spee*, which was patrolling the Atlantic, was a grave threat to Allied shipping, having already sunk eight merchant vessels in three months. The Battle of the River Plate was fought in the South Atlantic on December 13, 1939. In the ensuing action, HMS *Exeter* was severely damaged; HMS *Ajax* and HMS *Achilles* suffered moderate damage. Damage to *Graf Spee* was critical because her fuel system was no longer functional. *Ajax* and *Achilles* shadowed the German ship until she entered the port of Montevideo, Uruguay's capital, to effect urgent repairs. That neutral nation's authorities informed *Graf Spee*'s skipper, Hans Langsdorff, that his stay could not be extended beyond 72 hours. Believing that the British awaited offshore with a superior force, he ordered the ship to be scuttled. Three days later, Langsdorff died by suicide. Victory in the Battle of the River Plate, the first major naval engagement of World War II, greatly boosted British morale.

† Guildhall is the iconic medieval town hall municipal building in the Moorgate area of London.

> Does Stalin think
> He can conquer Helsinki?
> They've been fighting in
> the Karelian Isthmus
> Since Christhmas

Monday, March 18. Seems only yesterday that Reggie Metcalf came up and told me I was posted. A fortnight, Friday, actually. Since then, been in hospital.

Bidding goodbye to Legs King was a wrench, also to Champ, Wilfie, etc.

Spent the first weekend in Manchester lodging in civvie digs. The Coopers. A childless couple. He's a bus-driver. Enjoyed the comforts of home—fine meals, mornings in bed, bright fire in the grate.

A radiogram with records varying from Ellington's "East St. Louis Toodle—OO" to [Nikolai] Rimsky-Korsakov.

Ringway* aerodrome. I saw the latest fast bombers—Beauforts [torpedo bombers], also American Lockheed Hudsons [light bombers]. Here are tested Fairey's latest craft.† Jim Mollison is around here daily, though I don't know what he's supposed to be doing—test pilot, I suppose. When I saw him, he was unkempt, unshaven, and turning over a DH Puss Moth [high-wing monoplane].

We are forming an anti-aircraft cooperation unit. I'm in No. 6AACU.‡ Kites are civilian type—Monospars [touring and utility aircraft], Dragon Moths [commercial light aircraft and military trainers], other DHs [de Havillands]. I gather that when we are fully operational, our work will be to give the Army's AA [anti-aircraft] gunners a bit of practice. Apparently, they aren't getting enough of the real thing.

Our CO is Sir Nigel Norman, some say the son of the Bank of England chief [Montague Norman]. He seems likeable enough, lectured us on our first day here.

A week after I arrived, German measles hit me and I was rushed by ambulance to Monsall, an isolation hospital outside Manchester. It's actually a venerable mansion. I was there six days.

---

* RAF Ringway was a Royal Air Force station in Ringway, Cheshire, near Manchester. It was operational from 1939 until 1957. The site is now occupied by Manchester Airport.

† The Fairey Aviation Company Limited was a British aircraft manufacturer of the first half of the 20th century based in Hayes in Middlesex and Heaton Chapel and RAF Ringway in Cheshire.

‡ Anti-aircraft Cooperation Unit, part of the Royal Air Force.

Sunday, March 24, Easter morning. Barrage balloons* glinting in the early spring sunshine... "Dig for Victory" posters... Some Easter. But at least I'm home in Cardiff for the holiday. Good Friday morning heard the hot cross bun sellers shouting along the streets, just as in peacetime.

Saturday night, I donned uniform, thinking it would be more effective at the dance than civvies. But with Tom, I got to drinking ... at the Taff Vale, the Tivoli, the Griffin. And forgot about the dance. Met Pat of the Bute Street episode last year. She was with an even prettier girl, named Maureen, with whom I spent much of the remaining evening, yet somehow wound up taking Pat home.

Friday, March 29. That was a happy week at home. Heard lots of jazz, ate plenty of food despite rationing. By the way, going down home in the train last week I had a fair companion, Doreen Wallace, who said she is Victor Sylvester's niece. We met at the Manchester railway station where she asked me, "May I travel with you?" Some very nice moments with her in the blacked-out train corridor.

Wednesday, April 3. Grand weather. Quite a bit of flying goes on daily here, mostly the Monospars, Rapides [short-haul passenger biplane] and other assorted DH's, still with their old civvie markings and bright colours. But we generally pack up before five.

Paddy Brazier has asked me to spend next weekend with him at his aunt's home in Liverpool.

Saturday night in Manchester, saw "The Stars Look Down," based on [A.J.]Cronin's novel, which I've read twice. Afterwards, Paddy B and I to the George and Dragon where the beer is served amid loud music from a hot little trio (drums, piano, accordion) perched up on a wall. Picked up two girls one of whom, Cynthia, I took out Sunday. Nothing more romantic sitting with a girl on a park bench in the blackout watching the searchlight beams play tag across the sky. Or is there?

Well, things aren't so bad. Even with a war on. Seems to be a lull in it anyway.† Something brewing?

Tuesday, April 9. 7 pm. Memorable days these. Heard this morning that the Navy is sowing mines in Norwegian waters—and soon thereafter

---

* Large hydrogen-filled balloons attached to steel cables that hung over British cities to discourage enemy aerial bombing and low-level strafing runs. The balloons were 62 feet in length and achieved altitudes as high as 5,000 feet. In 1940, 1,400 barrage balloons hovered over England, one-third of them over London. These defense balloons were under the authority of the British Balloon Command.

† The Phony War was described by journalists as the period with little military action from early September 1939 to the German invasion of France, Holland, and Belgium on May 10, 1940.

that the Germans have invaded both Norway and Denmark. Tonight the news is Copenhagen occupied, Oslo bombed.

All these events were building up as I enjoyed a pleasant weekend with Paddy Brazier in Liverpool.

Tuesday, April 16. Battles in Norway and the Scandinavian seas. Neutral Holland and Sweden fear invasion. British troops landing in Norway.* The Second Great War is speeding up all right.

Well, I've had a battle-scarred Fairey Battle to look after these past two days. I don't know quite what action it has been in before coming to Ringway. Believe this type aircraft hasn't been much of a success as bombers in this war. Anyway, while being refueled tonight following a flight down to Castle Bromwich [a village in the West Midlands], it was damaged when a petrol bowser [fuel tanker] backed into it. So I'm without a kite again.

Up near the civilian airport watch-tower and café is a hangar whose doors are almost permanently shut. Inside—I've spotted them once—are two hush-hush Manchester bombers [medium bomber], whose performance is expected to be phenomenal.

April or no April, it snowed this morning.

Sunday, April 21. Warm and sunny Sunday, I've just woke up from a pleasant nap. Big battle for Trondheim [Norway] imminent.

Hitler's birthday yesterday, and to celebrate it we torpedoed two Norway-bound Nazi troopships.

"Gone with the Wind" drawing crowds in London—also drawing criticism that the film is too long. The book certainly was, for me. I gave it up when halfway through. Maybe the fault was mine. Still, I never gave up Cronin's "Stars Look Down."

Friday night crossed the square to the concert hall. One of the biggest RAF camp dances, surely. The band (one Jerry Dawson and his Boys) was large and lifeless and a floor show from Manchester not much better. Bottles of sherry and meat pies we swiped from hapless bartenders and real pandemonium broke out after "The King," when the cloak room arrangements collapsed and coats, hats, umbrellas were simply hurled willy-nilly into the tightly packed and mostly inebriated mob. On the way out among the dispersing crowds, I heard someone growl "I know the Army is inefficient but God knows the Air Force has got 'em beat."

Well, not the Army now landing in Norway. Nor the Air Force bombing Stavangar.

---

* Bergen, Stavanger, Egersund, Kristiansand, Arendal, Horten, Trondheim, and Narvik were also attacked and occupied within 24 hours.

Tuesday, April 30. Some while ago I sent a short story to Lilliput.* My first submission. Also, my first rejection. The story returned today and in the same mail delivery I received a parcel from home—containing a volume entitled "The World's Greatest Short Stories."

Thursday, May 9. Left-wing papers cried jubilantly this morning, "Now He'll Have to Resign." All carried accounts of the fierce debate. Attack after attack hurled at the pale Premier, shouts of "Resign!" and "Go! Go! For God's Sake, Go!" from socialist benches. But Lloyd George† was also among the attackers. Chamberlain won the vote of confidence but by such a small majority it left him shaken. All this because of his handling, or mishandling of the Norwegian episode. Because of overwhelming German land forces and superior air power the British had to withdraw. They did so, said Chamberlain trying to make victory out of retreat, "successfully, without a single loss."

Now the only British left in Norway are fighting near Narvik. Frances Smith accompanied me to see "Chu Chin Chow"‡ in Manchester. She told me her mother received a telegram saying that Ron, Frances' brother, was forced down in Belgium, interned. No news since that telegram and the family worries. What if Belgium is invaded next?

Saturday, May 11. At 7:40 pm yesterday morning out in the wash-house, I heard that Belgium is in the war. Thought it a rumor. Glorious sunny morning. Bought a newspaper, read that Chamberlain will probably resign, likely to be replaced by Churchill.§ In a late news column, a bulletin that phone communication with Holland cut off. 8:30 am on parade, and our CO, Sir Nigel Norman, confirmed the reports. Said all leave is likely to be stopped. He hoped we will take this in the right way. He ended: "The balloon has gone up now allright."

At 9 am, I was working on the brakes of my Battle 5208. We were ordered to fall in. Men with Vickers [water-cooled machine gun] or Lewis gun [light machine gun] experience were singled out, volunteers for ground defence called for. No one stepped forward, so men were detailed. 10:30 am in the NAAFI: heard Luxembourg also invaded, Antwerp, Rotterdam, bombed.

Excitement mounts all day. In the afternoon, our machines are

---

* *Lilliput* was a British monthly magazine specializing in short stories, the arts, humor, and photographs.

† David Lloyd George was Prime Minister from 1916 to 1922.

‡ "Chu Chin Chow" was a musical comedy that premiered in 1916.

§ Winston Churchill became Prime Minister on May 10 after Chamberlain lost a vote of confidence in the House of Commons. Churchill had previously been Lord of the Admiralty from September 3, 1939, to May 10, 1940. He had also held this post from October 1911 to May 1915.

started up, taxied across the drome and picketed [securing parked planes to restrain movement]. Work in dusty spring sunshine. Hangar space left by our Battles now occupied by a KLM Douglas air liner, one of only two (I heard) able to escape from Holland. I saw its crew, a tired haggard bunch in dark blue uniform.

I was tired too, by 5:30 pm. All leave cancelled. Paddy Brazier made frantic efforts to secure at least a 48-hour pass. He has spent so much time and money planning his wedding for Monday. Finally, wearily, he sent a telegram to his Wiltshire bride-to-be cancelling the wedding. The last straw—on what would have been his wedding night. Paddy is posted for guard duty.

All this was yesterday. Paddy last night managed to get out of camp into Stockport. Got drunk, missed the last bus, walked seven miles back and, two hours adrift, [absent without leave], placed on a charge, which, mercifully, was dismissed this morning.

Meanwhile, I had gone into Gatley last night, had two beers, and saw "French Without Tears."

AA Coop [anti-aircraft cooperation unit] seems at a standstill. Only one of our Battles took off today. Two fighter squadrons expected here within 36 hours. I'm staying in tonight.

Final note—Thursday night, I listened to The Ramblers, fine Dutch band, broadcasting from Hilversum [southeast of Amsterdam] and relayed by the BBC. Announcer finished: "We have enjoyed playing to you, are looking forward to broadcasting again for our English listeners next Friday." The band faded out, playing its signature tune "Farewell Blues."

Sunday, May 12. Greatest war in history raging with a vengeance. BEF is in Belgium. Dutch have recaptured Rotterdam. Churchill is at the helm here, with Eden, Attlee, Sinclair in the new cabinet.* Another sunny day today. I walked along a country lane bordering the drome, came upon a Lewis gun in a sandbagged nest, one of a series surrounding Ringway aerodrome. Each gun manned by a tin-hatted soldier. One said to me, "I'll give 'em bloody 'ell if they come this way."

Headline in today's Sunday Pictorial: "Now We're at Their Throats." And in other papers, "Belgians Halt the Invader" "Allies Advance into Holland" "The War Now Only 90 Miles Away."

Wednesday, May 15. Bad news. Holland capitulated. I'm not surprised. Parachute invaders dropped in swarms behind Dutch lines, major

---

* Anthony Eden (Secretary of State for War). Clement Attlee (Lord Privy Seal). Archibald Sinclair (Secretary of State for Air).

Dutch cities cruelly bombed. In Belgium, Liege has fallen though her forts still blaze away at the Nazis.

In Gatley the other night I met a girl who introduced me to a soldier friend who looked at me in quite a hostile fashion. Turned out he was in the King's Own Yorkshire Light Infantry, had been in Norway, saw comrades killed. He said, "You chaps were supposed to be coming to our rescue. The RAF. We needed you. But you let us down." He said only eighty survived of a thousand men in one sector. All I could do was argue lamely that we'd had no bases but he brushed that aside. "There was an aircraft carrier in the North Sea." With not enough aircraft, I presumed. Was relieved though, with a vague guilt feeling, when we parted.

Thursday, May 23. News slowly improving. Arras [northern France] recaptured, the French closing in on Amiens [southwest of Arras]. Things looked bad this past week, and Raynaud spoke of bridges that weren't blown up, of "incredible mistakes." Gamelin* sacked, Weygand supreme war chief. Here at home, the guns can be heard along the South Coast. Yesterday's bill giving the government wartime controls means virtually a dictatorship. Still a fear of parachute invasion. Here at Ringway, sixty Manchester Corporation buses are lined up near the Fairey's workshops ready to be driven out on the field to prevent enemy landings. Yesterday and today I've been filling sandbags. Pilots from here left hurriedly in old DH Dragons, flew south to Boscombe Down, I hear, from which they ferried Hurricanes and Battles across to France.

Some Tank Corps men here with a couple of tanks, and guns are mounted around the drome and on the watch office roof. Paddy Brazier got three days leave for his wedding.

Sunday, May 26. A curtain of silence over the huge battles believed raging across the Channel. Last real news was Churchill's grave announcement that the Germans have captured Boulogne [northern France on the English Channel]. Sir Oswald Mosley† arrested, also Captain Ramsey, MP and other potential fifth columnists [subversives].

Some 200 weary and weather-beaten men in mud-stained uniform, with tin hats and gasmasks, reached here Thursday night and slept in

---

* Commander-in-chief of the French Armed Forces at the start of the war, Maurice Gamelin was relieved from his post by Paul Reynaud, who had replaced Édouard Daladier as Prime Minister in March. Gamelin was replaced by Maxime Weygand.

† Oswald Mosley was prominent in the 1920s as a member of Parliament. He later became leader of the British Union of Fascists. Archibald Ramsay was a British Army officer who later went into politics as a Scottish Unionist Member of Parliament. From the late 1930s, he developed increasingly strident antisemitic views.

the Drill/Dance Hall. Remnants of an army cooperation squadron* just back from France. Spoke to a few of them, learned they'd had two hectic days in Belgium, saw air dogfights, had to fall back across France, stopped at ten different places snatching rest where they could. Once they were aroused and told the advancing Germans were only three miles away. On the move again, left kits and personal belongings behind. They had seen their aircraft, Blenheims [light bombers], destroyed.

Three of their Lysanders [special mission aircraft] escaped, reached here last night. These fellows have seen war at close quarters. Wonder how long before I do? National Day of Prayer today. We assembled on the square, where a chaplain read prayers from a paper he held. More effective, surely, if prayers come directly from the heart.

Coward, skunk, traitor, Judas ... some of the names flung at King Leopold† by our newspapers. One exception, Daily Express, suggests we should withhold our judgement and reserve our hate for Adolf Hitler.

Summoned to the guardroom, there was a phone call for me. From Frances, so I visited her at home, met her brother Ron, home on 48-hour pass. He had crashed in Belgium, his pilot killed. Ron was freed from internment [had been interned and freed while Belgium was still neutral] when the Germans invaded and he rejoined his squadron, returned to England. All this was told me quietly by his father, because the family had decided to avoid discussing the war in his presence while he was home. Even so, Ron had little to say, seeming emotionally drained.

Fighting continues at Calais and Zeebrugge [Belgian port], but the BEF is falling back on Dunkirk, the only [French] port available. The French hope to form a rearguard, covering the BEF's withdrawal.

Sunday, June 2. Glorious weather. Stirring news that all the BEF but one division have been successfully withdrawn from Dunkirk.‡ All sizes and shapes of boats and ships have been crossing and recrossing the Channel, bringing home thousands of weary but indomitable Tommies.

I was on guard last night at the barrier on one of the roads adjacent to the aerodrome. With a rifle and five rounds. We have tons of ammo here and hundreds of men, including the Army Co-op men who were bombed and chased out of Lille and across to the coast. They and their

---

* The RAF Army Cooperation Command was a short-lived major command of the Royal Air Force comprising the army cooperation units of the RAF. The command was formed in December 1940. Its role was to provide air support to the British Army.

† Belgium's King Leopold III (who reigned from 1934 to 1951), was greatly criticized for surrendering his country after the Germans invaded it on May 10, 1940.

‡ About 340,000 BEF, French, and Belgian troops were stranded on the beaches of the French seaport. A large armada of mostly privately owned boats evacuated these Allied troops to England from May 26 to June 4, 1940. This massive rescue, formally called "Operation Dynamo," has come to be known as "The Miracle of Dunkirk."

Lysanders are here. We'll be able to put up a good show, I think, when the Nazis arrive over Ringway. But now I'm off for a walk in the setting sun, will call in a pub. Beautiful weather. Saw James Stewart in "Mr. Smith Goes to Washington" the other night. Best film I've seen all year.

Some sections of the British press have criticized British film actors who apparently prefer to stay in Hollywood instead of coming home to join the fight. No names mentioned. Well, we could do with Errol Flynn, perhaps. His old "Dawn Patrol" chum, David Niven, has returned via Italy and is in the Army.

Friday, June 7. Tomorrow I leave this dusty, gun-infested, sundrenched and overcrowded camp, head for Wales with a 48-hour pass.

German bombers over the southern counties last night. Working on a Fairey Battle in the cool of the hangar today. When electrically operated doors of another hangar slid open, I glimpsed the two brand-new Avro Manchester heavy bombers inside. They soon go into general production.

Our handful of Battles keep up the Army Coop work over Manchester and Liverpool. Last Saturday I flew with F/O Dendy, flight commander, my first flight in a Battle.

Dunkirk episode over. Glorious evacuation of some 335,000 troops.

Tuesday, June 11. Italy is in the war. Typical Mussolini move, waiting until the British had retreated and the French are prostrate, then delivers the stab in the back. He'll regret it. We'll make him wish he had never been born.

Bleak news, though, for the Allies. Loss of the carrier Glorious* with over a thousand men returning from Norway. Cobber Kane,† this war's first air ace, reported killed.

Thursday, June 13. Il Duce's air force has bombed Malta and Aden. Our RAF and South African squadrons have attacked Libyan and Abyssinian [Ethiopian] bases, also Northern Italy. Glad to see we took the initiative following Italy's declaration of war. But grave danger now is position north of Paris. Germans have captured Reims and Rouen, crossed the Marne, the Seine. Paris being evacuated. Disturbing outbreak of senseless anti–Italian violence in many British cities. Men and women acting like some American lynch mob.

---

* Aircraft carrier HMS *Glorious* was sunk on June 8, 1940, in the North Sea by two German battleships.

† Edgar "Cobber" Kain, a New Zealand fighter pilot with the RAF, was killed on June 7, 1940, at age 21, in north-central France. Kain allegedly shot down 17 German aircraft and was Britain's first recipient of the Distinguished Flying Cross. He died while performing a non-combat and unauthorized low-level aerobatic maneuver.

Home last weekend, found a 22-year-old Belgian refugee and her 2-year-old son. Her husband is a Flemish fisherman somewhere at sea. Their home in Ostend was left in ruins. About all she and the child escaped with was the clothes they wore. And a doll. Folks get 29 shillings weekly to take care of them. Hardly enough, Ma says. Old man working hard helping care for the wounded from Flanders.

Long hot spell ending, cooler since my return to Ringway.

Sunday, June 16. France in anguish. Reynaud has appealed to Roosevelt. Couple of days ago the Germans entered Paris, swastika flies from the Eiffel Tower. American intervention is vital, I think. This should be their war as much as ours. At least they should send over aircraft, hundreds of them.

The weather has been in Hitler's favour. Now at last some rain might hold up his advance. Certainly, it's high time the Almighty quits His neutral stance. Not that I'm doing all that much. We have half a dozen Battles, four ex–Dutch DC-3s, and assorted De Havilands, Percivals [low-wing wooden planes], etc., but we are No. 6 AACU. Many similar outfits have been disbanded and AACU work is at a standstill. So we do nothing but small maintenance jobs, also do guard duties and man machine gun posts. I almost feel guilty.

Further up the aerodrome are five of the hush-hush Manchester bombers. Avro's people are working on them day and night. But our routine seems sluggish, unproductive. "Dig for Victory," [grow your own garden] "Go to It," mean little to us. Nothing morally uplifting about this existence. I go out, get drunk, make numerous dates. But fighting the war? The Air Ministry seems to have forgotten us.

Friday, June 21. I hear South Wales was among last night's Luftwaffe's targets. Cardiff bombed. Great shock when word came that France has asked Hitler for armistice terms.

I was on duty flight Wednesday night. We started up a Battle at 11:30 pm, it taxied out for takeoff, came trundling back and Sgt. Pilot Jenkins (shot down in France earlier in the war) yelled above the Merlin's* roar for me to find out why the Control Tower wouldn't okay takeoff. I sped away to the Duty Pilot who told me to dash back and get the Battle's lights out and engine stilled. Same moment, out went aerodrome's flarepath lights. By the time I reached Jenkins again, he had already cut his motor, notified by Tower that enemy aircraft were heading our way. Night-flying canceled, I tumbled into bed at 2 am. An hour later, camp sirens and all those in Manchester vicinity howling away. Up

---

* The Rolls-Royce Merlin engine was a liquid-cooled V-12 engine that powered many British aircraft during World War II.

went the blackout screens—rooms in darkness anyway, men chatting, laughing. No excitement. No bombs either, and all-clear sounded at 3:40 am. Odd feeling of exhilaration when that steady all-clear sounds as you realize that during the alert your stomach has tensed up in a knot.

Sunday, June 23. Last night France signed acceptance of Hitler's terms (still undisclosed). So the waiting, the suspense is over. British uncertainty as to whether France would sign replaced by "grief and amazement." Italy in on the kill, too, completing France's humiliation. Questions abound. What will America do? Will Japan grab IndoChina? What will happen to the French Navy? As for our little island, it's now a fortress braced for onslaught. Could come from several directions, from Norway, Denmark, Holland, Belgium, France.

Well, I escaped, to some extent from all this Thursday night at the Odeon in Manchester seeing "Of Mice and Men," a movie with no really big names, chiefly Burgess Meredith and Lon Chaney, Jr., but superior to many films that feature box-office favourites.

All our Battles are going, including my 5208 on which I've worked since March.

Tuesday June 25. The Germans were over here again last night. George Cleves and I had spent the evening at the George and Dragon in Manchester. Took home two married women, caught the 1:40 am Wythenshawe bus, and when it was two-thirds into its journey, the bus stopped and out we got. Sirens were wailing. A lonely road bathed by fitful moonlight and the glow from dozens of searchlight beams above. George and I loitered outside an air raid shelter that had quite filled up. Along the road, LDV* men were stopping strollers and motorists and cyclists, checking identification cards. Those who confessed to having left their cards at home were shepherded to a hut near the ARP [Air Raid Precautions] shelter and held for further checking. They were still there when the all-clear sounded.

Back at camp I hear that S/Ldr. Ivens, in Battle 5206 (which I'd DI'd [Daily Inspection] the previous night) was in flight when the alarm came. He was picked out by our own searchlights and back he headed for Ringway in a hurry, landing on the completely blacked-out field.

So I got in at 3:15 am and up again at 7:30, wearied by the beer drinking, the pub's hot music, the demands of my female companion, the raid-imposed delay, and a three-mile walk. And tonight I'm on a gun-post crew.

---

* Local Defence Volunteers or (LDV) was an armed citizen militia supporting the British Army during World War II.

Sunday, June 30. Warm and sunny. George and Dragon packed, band on the wall battering one's ears with bouncy jazz. Plenty of uniforms in evidence. Odd feeling of security seeing all this manifestation of military and knowing we are all concentrated on this island to face Hitler's next move.

Met old Welsh pals Jack Morgan and Will Price in the pub. Same Price with whom (also Sandy Powell) I had ridden in his Morris Minor* down to Cardiff from South Cerney last year.

Will was in France with a Hurricane squadron but after a week there the whole damn outfit was retreating to Lille, then to Arras. Will saw six or seven Messerschmitts strafe the Lysanders and "we dived under the mainplane of our Hurricane, we could see the distant grass flattening out under the Messerschmitt's bullets." And Fifth Columnists. "You wouldn't believe it, Len. We were followed by Jerry [Germans] everywhere and bombed. See, we had to mix with all kinds of French civilians."

I heard the same sort of thing from 4 Squadron chaps. Torch signaling, revealing the squadron's position.

Paddy Brazier tells me South Cerney was attacked last week and Block 50—my old barrack block—got hit.

Broken relations with George Cleves owing to my failure to join him on a date with those married girls. (Their husbands are on the Mediterranean front, I believe.) Fact is, I don't feel comfortable about pursuing that affair. Went to the movies instead. Cagney in "The Roaring Twenties." I funked telling Cleves my feeling, so I'm partly at fault. So, dead silence between us two.

Tuesday, July 2. 8 pm. In bed early. Little sleep last night I was one of six manning a gun post. There we were, with machine gun, bandoliers of ammo, rifles, ammo drums, and Verey pistol [signal pistol], in sandbagged enclosure. Raids somewhere in Northern England but not in our vicinity. Dozed on ground-sheets, pestered by insects.

Hore-Belisha says we should act firmly with Ireland now to make sure Hitler doesn't get at us through that "neutral" land.

Letter from Cardiff says that in a recent all-night raid most of Jerrys' bombs fell in the Bristol Channel mud. (Germans, though, claim they hit Cardiff oil tanks.) "Raid Saturday morning about 10. The gunfire was just over our house. Your ma says she is not panicky." Enclosed was a <u>South Wales Echo</u> clipping, account and photo of a 17-year-old

---

* The Morris Minor was a four-seater car originally manufactured by Morris Motors Ltd. from 1928 to 1934. A newer model was introduced in 1948.

WAAF,* engaged to marry former Welsh boxing champ Jack Peterson, but killed in a raid last week.

Six Dutch DC-3s still here, also three Spitfires drop in each night to help defend Manchester if need be. But so far, no raids in this neighborhood.

Thursday, July 4. Fire picket tonight. I hear we sank the French fleet.† Meanwhile, country [Britain] still awaiting invasion.

Sunday, July 14. Don writes that Cardiff raided fourteen times in ten days and nights. Strange feeling to know your hometown is regularly under attack. I remember when the Anderson shelters‡ first arrived, and on all sides could be heard a confident "I don't suppose we'll ever need them." I've said the same thing about gasmasks, but there is a rumour circulating that the Germans might use some colourless, odourless, near-invisible gas called arsine.

At long last our military bigshots have decided on a parachutist force. Here at Ringway, men have been detached from A and B flights of 6AACU (whose activities remain stalled), and will work with the "Central Landing School" [CLS] being formed here to train soldiers for parachute attack. The trainees—tough-looking, I saw them on PT [physical training] today—will conduct drops from Whitley [medium] bombers, two of which have arrived. Cleves and Paddy Brazier are among my friends (former friends in Cleves' case) posted to CLS.

Sunday, July 28. Out on the 'drome today, and nearby Len Maine was swinging the prop of a DH Dragon, Sgt. Pettit in the cockpit. Engine didn't start, Maine called "off." Pettit apparently didn't hear and failed to reply. Maine swung the prop, as, of course, he shouldn't have, the engine started, the blade slicing Maine's wrist. He screamed rolled backwards. Tonight, his arm is in a sling but he has gone out anyway to meet his date.

Talking of accidents, CLS had its first fatal one—a soldier jumped from a Whitley, parachute didn't open. (The drops take place at Tatton Park.)

---

*The Women's Auxiliary Air Force, whose members were referred to as WAAFs, was the female auxiliary of the Royal Air Force during World War II.

† On July 3, 1940, the British Navy sank (by air and sea) the French fleet at Oran, on the coast of French Algeria to prevent the Germans from making use of the French ships. Results: 1,300 French servicemen died, one battleship sunk, and several others destroyed. France had signed an armistice with Germany and Italy on June 25, 1940.

‡ Anderson shelters were named after Sir John Anderson, Lord Privy Seal, who was in charge of air raid precautions in 1938. They were made from corrugated iron or steel panels that formed a semi-circular shape.

Wednesday, July 31. Invasion now thought inevitable. Meanwhile RAF constantly attacking German ports, airfields, invasion barges, and enemy bombers by day and night raid Northeast and Southeast England, also South Wales. General population seems calm and busy. Cinemas and theatres still crowded. Radio and newspapers feed the up-beat mood. Non-war items still fascinate. Three dead women found on lonely farm, widow arrested for murder. In USA, Roosevelt nominated as Democrats' candidate for third term president. Lots of criticism leveled at BBC for Charles Gardner's sporty commentary on an air fight off southeast coast last Sunday.* Most people thrilled and delighted by it.

Yesterday, Saturday, I lay flat on my belly gazing through the large round hole in the fuselage floor of a Whitley bomber while we flew 6000 feet over Lancashire and Cheshire. These Whitley bombers belong to CLS [Central Landing School], parachute training squadron. The Army trainees have to get so many hours in. Having nothing to do in 6 ACCU's B Flight, I and two companions sauntered up to the Whitley, pulled down the door that forms steps and climbed in. No one stopped us. We had no parachutes. Our coolness was rewarded with a 20-minute flight while through the hole—site of the old "dustbin" [retractable belly] gun turret, we viewed the fields, roads, streams, and railway lines drifting beneath. Third type of aircraft I've flown in, the others being Airspeed Oxford and Fairey Battle.

Letter from home says a bomb hit a ship in Cardiff Docks, killed seven. Old man, being in Red Cross, among those on the scene, he praises rescue work of my old schoolmate Billy Allen in Red Cross since his release from RAF on health grounds.

Though no Gene Krupa, I gave hot drumming support for Ozzy Osborne, trombonist (and no [Jack] Teagarden) over in the Drill Hall. There's a good trick drummer, by the way, at the Britannia, a Manchester pub, which I frequent these nights because my former favourite haunt, the George and Dragon, has lost its fine accordionist to the RAF. Also, the G and D is usually packed with too much uniform—French, Australian, Polish etc.

Friday, August 2. Air raids, occasional naval action, African skirmishes. But, as yet, no invasion of Britain. And now a new rule—we have to carry rifles and ammo whenever we go out of camp. But (presumably to give as many possible a break before the Big Battle) generous leave is

---

* On July 14, 1940, pioneer BBC broadcaster Charles Gardner stood on the White Cliffs of Dover to do a live report on an aerial dogfight over the English Channel between the RAF and German dive-bombers attacking a convoy. His reporting turned controversial when his commentary seemed to make it a sporting event. The broadcast caused an uproar at all levels.

available. My application is in for four days beginning August 15. This is the day Goebbels has broadcast his boss Hitler will announce the end of the war from London. One of us is going to be disappointed....

Sunday, August 4. Twenty-sixth anniversary of Britain declaring war on Germany ... 1914. Heat wave still on. Last night I was on gun-post duty, conveniently near an air raid shelter. Sirens sounded after midnight. Nothing else for a while except chattering of distant soldiers. Then the thrumming of the bombers overhead. Searchlights weaved aimlessly. Down the road, sentries called challenges. The searchlights snuffed out. Silence, and I went back to my ground-sheet in the tent.

Monday, August 5. Seven Defiants [interceptor turret fighters] arrived this morning, bristling with guns. I worked all day in the fresh and cooler air fitting a new radiator to my Battle which should be serviceable tomorrow.

Tuesday, August 6. He hasn't been in the RAF more than a few months. Married, highly educated, he could have claimed exemption and remained a civilian. Joined up instead. Told yesterday he was to be a permanent room orderly, i.e., floor-sweeper, lavatory-cleaner, wash basin-scrubber—he said he'd desert before taking a charlady's job and that wasn't what he enlisted to do. But he will have to. He is up against a typical service mentality which could lose us this war.

Thursday, August 8. Still no invasion. I go on leave Saturday. Had to go out to Barton last night, on the other side of Barton, to my Battle, which had come down with slight engine trouble. With me was Sergeant Crispin, Doug Pratt, and my fitter Bowden. We fixed the kite and the sgt.-pilot took off, giving us a farewell scare with a dive almost into the deck. We stopped in Manchester on the way back for a few pints. And just after midnight, bombs fell not far from Barton, the AA guns were in action.

Letter from home says a bomber shot down in the Bristol Channel.

Cassandra,* in today's Daily Mirror, calls [actress] Gracie Fields' Italian husband a "swarthy-faced wop," and also lashes Noel Coward for hiding out in the USA on "MOI [Ministry of Information] work."

Wednesday, August 14. Bombs on Portsmouth, Southampton, Dover, and elsewhere. Opening rounds in the Battle of Britain.† All this going

---

* Sir William Neil Connor (1909–1967) was an English newspaper journalist for *The Daily Mirror* who wrote under the pen name "Cassandra."
† From July 10 to October 31, 1940, the RAF and the Fleet Air Arm of the Royal Navy fended off air attacks by the German Luftwaffe over the United Kingdom. The RAF prevailed over the German fighters and bombers. From September 7 to May 11, 1941, the Germans intensified their bombing raids over the UK, a period known as "The Blitz."

on—and I think I've fallen in love. Rex Bowden and I met them in the Britannia in Manchester, Saturday night. Her name is May, has a dazzling smile, the first thing I noticed about her. Rex's choice is a pretty number named Geraldine, who sings—she did "Don't Ever Pass Me By" and, accompanied by a hot drummer, Mama Mia. Met them again last night. May's smile disturbingly attractive. Drummer meanwhile taking rhythmic breaks and occasionally yelling, "And another Messerschmitt bit the dust," the patrons cheering each outburst because the RAF had downed 78 enemy aircraft over southeast England. At 11:30 pm, I was kissing May in a blacked-out side-street when the sirens howled. She clutched me, I struck a protective attitude. She was chiefly worried because her mother was home alone. But the all-clear soon sounded.

Thursday, August 29. Have had seven days' leave in Cardiff. Nightly raids. Daytime alarms, too. Schoolteachers and shoppers hurrying through the sunlight to the nearest shelters. Puffs of smoke among the barrage of balloons against the deep blue sky. The raids, of course, tediously dominated conversation. Evident the moment I arrived. "He'll be over tonight all right ... dropped most of them in the mud yesterday ... one fell on City Road ... no, I didn't get out of bed...." But the chatter was reassuringly unconcerned and you only sense the underlying fear toward evening as people hurry their footsteps homeward.

Got little sleep. Night after night the shellbursts and "flaming onions" [tracer rounds] blaze in the sky, and the air reverberates to the thud and crash of guns and bombs. The first night home, seized by the novelty of it all, I lingered in the garden looking upwards until Ma implored me to join her in the backyard shelter. The old man is on Red Cross duty. I met Tom Parry (on the railway, still not called up), and Billy Allen (doing sterling work on his motorbike for the Red Cross), and went drinking with Don (whose marriage to Queenie is shaky). Also spent a night with George Cleves and his future wife. Caught in a raid, we crossed from the pub to one of Cardiff Castle's* shelters and sat out the noisy hours.

Saw bomb wreckage off Bute Road and over in Penarth. Slum homes mostly. Gawkers with nothing better to do around one ruined home whose resident, an old lady, said to me, "I wish they'd go away. I do wish they would." But they seemed as if wanting to help, some offering words of sympathy. And I heard that the authorities were trying to remove the old lady from the shattered walls and piles of debris (a

---

*Cardiff Castle is a medieval castle located in the city center of Cardiff. Norman invaders built the castle in the late 11th century atop a 3rd-century Roman fort.

battered sideboard still stood upright, on it a faded photo of the Forth Bridge),* but she refused to leave.

These slum houses should have been knocked down years ago, but to their dwellers they are, of course, home.

Passed a bomb-gutted warehouse with a signboard saying, "Anyone found damaging or defacing these premises will be liable to prosecution."

A woman nearby collected pennies for Cardiff's Spitfire fund. Billy Allen's house had all its windows blown out by blast.

When I left Cardiff at 4:55 pm Saturday afternoon, the sirens wailed to let citizens know they were in for another lively deadly time. Five hours later, I arrived at Manchester's London Road station—to be greeted by shrieking sirens, and I spent the next two and a half hours in the air raid shelter...

Last night, Wednesday, at a cinema in Manchester, followed by a snack at the Services Canteen, then caught the 10:40 bus, but immediately, despite drizzling rain and a black starless sky, sirens wailed, buses and tramcars halted, emptying themselves of passengers who straggled through the wet blackness to street shelters. The one I found had the usual "grin-and-bear-it" crowd, except for a girl of about 20 who whimpered incessantly, bursting into sobs each time the gunfire or bomb explosions sounded a bit close. I went outside for a hand-shielded smoke. Odd—no searchlights. Sporadic gunfire, and to the south, the fitful glow of a distant fire. Raid over in an hour, but once back in camp and in bed I could hear, above the spattering of now heavier rain against the windows, some low-flying aircraft and guessed it to be German, doubtless lost in the storm.

Most of the activity these nights is west of us. The bombers pass over Manchester to concentrate on Liverpool, and we can see the continuous flashing, hear the endless rumbling, of what must be a fearsome barrage indeed. Like a distant thunderstorm of great intensity.

This afternoon we had a mock air raid and gas attack. Morgan's Battle dive-bombed so fast the sliding window was torn out in midair. Manchester's ARP [Air Raid Precautions] cooperated, sent along ambulances for "casualties." On arrival here, they found a real "yellow" [ambulance] in action so tore back to town without any [mock

---

* The Forth Bridge was a railroad bridge across the Firth of Forth in eastern Scotland, nine miles west of Edinburgh. Opening in 1890, it was longest single cantilever bridge in the world at that time, and became a symbol of Scotland. On October 16, 1939, the Rosyth Naval Base near the bridge became the Luftwaffe's first bombing target six weeks into the beginning of World War II. RAF Spitfires shot down the first German raider aircraft during the war. The bridge was undamaged during this air battle.

casualties]. I was one of the "walking casualties," my injury, "a cut above my right eye." They bandaged me for a broken jaw.

Last Tuesday I was 22. More significant anniversary today is the first of that memorable Friday when the Germans crossed into Poland and started it all.

Tomorrow I'm best man at George Cleves's hurried-up wedding to a Cardiff brunette who is seeking a new life up here near Manchester far from the scene of an unhappy life with, I'm told, an unpleasant mother. Wedding will be quiet in a Registry Office at Cheadle, with a binge afterwards in the George and Dragon.

May is still on my mind. Haven't seen or heard from her for a fortnight and I've forgotten her address. So I can't write. And maybe she has lost mine.

Wednesday, September 4. In bed after attending a concert party called "In Camp Tonight." In attractive scanties, WAAFs pranced about the stage, one or two sang (?) and nearly all were easy on the eye. Not so easy on the ear, a corporal who tried to sing like John McCormick, and Ozzie Osborne took two so-so trombone solos. These concerts are held earlier these nights because of raids. I spent two hours in a Northenden shelter last night while the guns rumbled westward. This shelter had seats, unlike the cold tomb-like shelters in Manchester's Piccadilly.

Warm today, Spitfires up in the blue frequently, and we've had three daylight warnings, the most so far.

Couple of days ago Churchill revealed that 1222 houses and shops wrecked in one violent Ramsgate raid. Portsmouth suffered about 100 casualties, a cinema and crowded shelter hit.

Last Saturday, George Cleves wedded to Olga in Altringham. Being best man, I had to rush hell-for-leather to get there by noon. Got a lift on a dusty brick truck. (Damn! Sirens wailing, lights out, writing this in the bloody dark.)

Thursday, September 5. I slept through three local raids last night— well, gunfire awoke me once. To continue with George's and Olga's wedding—Bridegroom had borrowed my shoes. As I wrote last night when Jerry interrupted, I got to the registry office on a brick truck. We adjourned to the George and Dragon in Cheadle afterwards where George's first meal as a husband was eggs, chips, and Welsh rarebit. Then we drank. I took too many Benedictines and whiskies, an explosive mixture. As soon as we left, I collapsed in the fresh night air. A middle-aged couple, who had watched us celebrating, kindly took us to their home. I dimly recall being sick, hearing distant sirens. Awoke at 6 am in a comfy chair. Tie and shoes had been taken off. Our host came downstairs, prepared a nice breakfast. George and Olga joined us. They had also occupied an upstairs room, their wedding night (will they ever forget it?) in a stranger's home. A very kind stranger, who wrote a note saying he had befriended us during the raid. I presented the note, checking in at the guardroom 8½ hours late. No trouble.

Hush-hush Short Stirlings on the drome. Huge well-armed bombers. Also, a Spitfire squadron, very busy these days.

On "duty crew," so no sleep for me tonight.

Sunday, September 8. Yesterday a memorable day. Five hundred German planes over London all day, raining bombs on the world's largest city. Hundreds killed.*

Beautiful moonlight right now.

Two letters from Cardiff telling of heavier raids, on Swansea as well as the Welsh capital.

So, following Hitler's frenzied outburst last week when he threatened to rain terror on Britain as reprisal for RAF bombing of Berlin, we now bear the brunt. Whether he will succeed in shattering us may be gauged from the fact that the country carries on—and 99 Nazi bombers downed in the latest raids.

Tuesday night. Raids on London continue, day and night. 306 reported killed in the first big raid, 265 in the second.

[**LFG notes here**—*"Orig. diary late Sept. early Oct. missing? (if there was one)"*]

Monday, October 14. Yesterday morning attended compulsory church parade. Incredibly boring service. Rev. Chrissop is a genius at organizing debates and concerts but no great shakes as a padre. Why does he insist on choosing little-known hymns for his services?

Well, now living four to a room in two-story flats on Cross Acres estate. Still lack beds and for a while without coal, light, blackout screens, hot water. When our CO, W/Cdr. Blackford, discovered these deficiencies, he promptly sacked the civilian barrack-warden whose job it was to provide our necessities. We are also promised radio sets.

Recently spent a week at Leamington Spa, in civvie digs while attending a course in hydraulics at Lockheed's.† My landlady was an

---

* On September 7, 1940, 300 German bombers raid London, in the first of 57 consecutive nights of bombing. This signified the beginning of the "Blitz."

† Automotive Products or Lockheed Brakes was a factory in Leamington that worked continuous shifts during the war making parts for armaments and aircraft. It employed nearly 10,000 people, including many women. The factory was a primary target for German planes and was bombed several times.

odd forty-year-old widow who didn't like my late hours, and who one night told me she didn't agree with the verdict of suicide a coroner had passed upon her husband's death. She lives alone, "except for you boys whom I often have in," and is writing a book of her life, which she calls simply "47," the street number of her house.

At Lockheed's, I made several friends. Altogether new experience, seeing all the girls at the machines in noise-filled workshop after workshop while the loudspeakers blare "music while you work," ranging from Handel's "Largo" to "Begin the Beguine."

I returned to Ringway with some slight knowledge of hydraulics, a set of blueprints, a pack of aircraft identification cards, and two snaps of myself taken by the strange landlady. During my Leamington stay, enemy planes passed over daily, heading for Coventry. In a Leamington pub, I was told that a Dornier [German medium bomber] had dropped bombs near the gasworks, and by the time the local ground-gunners got themselves organized, the German bomber had left, to be replaced by a British Whitley [medium bomber] stooging on to the scene. Yes, the gunners shot it down.

Back in the Manchester vicinity, found Jerry had been active in my absence. Gaping craters and wrecked buildings at Northernden, Gatley, Cheadle and a time bomb believed not far from where I am writing this. Fellow Welshmen back from leave tell me bombs struck Constellation Street in Cardiff, which worries me for our back gardens are up against those of Constellation Street. One of the fellows says a "Mr. and Mrs. Price" killed or injured, and I wonder if it's old Ted Price, a good singer, lame, in whose house we lived in rented rooms six years ago.

Tuesday, October 29. Yesterday morning Italy opened war on Greece. One more nation added to the already long list of victims to aggression. But I do hope Greece doesn't become another Norway.

Sunday night, walking with Rex Bowden from the bus stop up to Cross Acres estate, where we are billeted. Heard the thrum of enemy bombers between the thud of AA gunbursts. Also, the dull roar of exploding bombs westward. Familiar sounds now. Almost every night last week while I was home, the South Wales AA barrage opened up on enemy aircraft that crossed often in several waves. Flashes lit the blacked-out streets like lightning bolts. Our old house on Constellation Street, where we lived eight years ago, was destroyed. Lots of damage along Albany Road. The folks have a dog. Which slightly eases mam's loneliness when the old man is on a late shift with the Red Cross.

Saturday night went to a dance at Belle Vue after attending a swing record recital at the YMCA in aid of the Spitfire Fund.

A colleague from Liverpool tells me that in a Merseyside park recently, where a German bomber had forced-landed and burst into flames, crowds gathered about the wreck and no one lifted a finger to help save the Germans they could see struggling within. And heard screaming. Liverpudlians have been so frequently bombed, this sort of thing may be understandable.

Tuesday, November 5. Election fever in the USA. A tight fight, by all accounts. Both FDR, seeking a third term, and Republican Wendell Willkie* promise more aid to Britain if elected. Both hate Hitler. But it's been a smeary campaign with Roosevelt supporters making an issue of Willkie's German blood and the latter's supporters attacking Mrs. Roosevelt and calling her sons cheats.

Anger in places here—Manchester among them—against bus drivers who refuse to carry on their work during night raids. "We refuse," they say, "to risk our lives carrying pleasure seekers and pub-crawlers." Well, many of the latter happen to be war-workers, soldiers and sailors and airmen. And I've had more than one exasperating experience of being turned out of the bus into a cold rainy night while the bus crew stayed aboard or parked themselves in a nearby café. This when there hasn't been a sound of aircraft or gunfire.

Last Friday one of our Short Scions [light transport], old ex-civilian aircraft, crashed killing its Polish crew. Their comrades here at Ringway sad-eyed. A Polish pilot escaped when his Leopard Moth [high wing monoplane] glided under telegraph wire and sheared off a wing on a tree. We—Sgt. Williams and nine of us—had to go out to the wreck 30 miles away. Worked there until 3 this afternoon dismantling the remaining wing and tail unit. Lifted the fuselage bodily aboard a trailer and brought it in.

Not as hot as I'd hoped was a concert at the Odeon Sunday night featuring the RAF Squadronaires.† This is Corporal Jimmy Miller's crew, including such fine men as George Chisholm, trombone, Tommy McQuator and Al Craig, trumpets, Andy McDevitt, clarinet. But they played too many pop tunes. High spot was a rousing rendition of "Copenhagen."

Tuesday, November 12. Another Sunday night jazz concert, again at the Odeon. Nat Gonella's New Georgians. A showman as always,

---

* In 1940, Wendell Willkie was the Republican nominee for President of the United States running against Franklin Roosevelt's bid for a third term.
† In 1939, the RAF devised a plan to raise morale and entertain the troops during wartime. The Squadronaires was one of the bands organized as a result. The band drew from some of the best musicians of the day.

Gonella treated us to "One O'Clock Jump," "Woodchoppers Ball," "In the Mood." Then came an air raid warning but the concert continued until an hour after the all-clear.

Neville Chamberlain died Saturday night. He worked hard for peace, had finally to declare war. I believe he meant well, was short-sighted in dealing with Hitler, gave this country a year during which we ought to have prepared more vigorously for war. Well, history will be the best judge of Chamberlain.

We still live in billets three miles from the drome and there is inadequate transportation, so we line up each dark morning often in pouring rain and icy wind and thus we are in an ugly unpatriotic mood when we finally reach the hangars. This is no way to win a war. And too often, when we finish work, we are served cold ham, rancid butter, or a roast apple and more rancid butter. The only transport back to the billet is 5:45 pm and to get it means sometimes missing a meal. And, God help us, the service police still act like a little Gestapo, bullying men who dare turn up their greatcoat collars against the wind or sling their gasmasks over the shoulder instead of across the chest. Some of the NCOs around here are petty tyrants.

Some more choice items, while I'm in the mood... Read of a man who, off his own bat, removed a heavy time bomb from a house. He was fined a hundred pounds with the option of a three-month jail term. Somewhere else, people waited an hour for a bomb-disposal squad to show up and deal with a delayed-action bomb. Presumably unwilling to risk a fine or three months in the cooler, they did nothing about it. It exploded before the squad arrived and killed eight.

Been raining incessantly the past five days and nights. The Poles are now flying our Battles. Polish equivalents of names of controls and instruments are painted on the panel. We now also have a Blenheim and four Westland Lysanders.

Monday, November 18. 6AACU now has four Battles, two Blenheims, five Lysanders and an assortment of former civilian aircraft. Lots of rumors flying around of postings and detachments. Some fellows have left for Yorkshire. Hope I don't go for I've seen May only once lately and want to see her again.

A terrific raid on Coventry* last Thursday night. The city centre destroyed, likewise its ancient cathedral, and hundreds killed. King and Queen visited the stricken city. London heavily bombed the following

---

* On the night of November 14–15, 1940, 300 German bombers dropped explosives, incendiary bombs, and parachute bombs on the industrial city of Coventry. More than 500 civilians died in this raid.

night. Guns active around here, but no attacks. It's a quiet misty day today. But somehow the atmosphere feels tense.

I read that a 40-year-old man, unable to bear the sight of his 71-year-old mother shivering on the Underground steps in London during the raids, strangled her with a radio cord. Found guilty of murder but judged insane. Other murders have preoccupied police and public these blitz weeks. A soldier hunted in a Liverpool case, the victim a 15-year-old girl found strangled in a blockhouse. A widow battered to death in Bristol. These private tragedies occur within the great tragedy of war that envelopes us all.

Wednesday, November 20. Received a bit of a shock tonight. Rex Bowden, who has been going around with Gerry, May's friend, told me that he had learned May is married. A blow, this, for I've recently renewed our acquaintance and I'm very fond of her. Seems Gerry is married, too, but she left her husband years ago and plans divorce. May's husband is in the Army. She never told me the truth, apparently because she and her husband are not estranged. Rex also says she has a child.

Went to a movie last night, saw Bob Hope in "The Ghost-Breakers." Came out into semi-deserted streets that quivered to the shock of overhead gunfire. Gunbursts blazed all over the sky.

A dance at the camp two nights ago, the RAF Squadronaires, this time in fine form. Lots of hot choruses to which even our revered CO danced vigorously while our engineering officer, Sqdn. Leader Bloodworth, winced and covered his ears. Morgan and I hung around the bandstand. The likeable Pole, Sqdn. Leader Grynzpan, who we affectionately call "Whizzbang," danced a slow foxtrot with comic dignity to each and every number including a hurricane-tempoed "I Got Rhythm."

Monday, November 25. Spent the past weekend down at my friend Jack Morgan's home at Mumbles Swansea. We journeyed down and back in another friend's Standard Ten [Standard Motor Company's small car] through Shrewsbury, Ludlow, over the Brecon Beacons. Driving down coincided with a terrific battering of Birmingham and elsewhere in the West Midlands. As we sped along deserted blacked-out Welsh highways, far to the left the sky flashed and sparkled, with now and then the bigger glare of a bomb explosion.

Swansea's commercial centre badly ravaged. On Saturday morning, the guns banged away. Out in the bay, a gunboat passed the upturned keel of a mined vessel. Anti-invasion concrete blocks lined the shore, and troops were encamped everywhere. At night we danced at the Pier Hotel and I met a charming girl named Anita. Morgan's parents excellent hosts, they made me feel very welcome.

Saturday, November 30. A Saturday night but I'm in early. Went to town, saw "Mayerling" (Charles Boyer) and bought a copy of Daphne du Maurier's "Rebecca." A quiet night, quite a contrast to Thursday's eight-hour blitz. I was at the Odeon watching a Hollywood version of "Tom Brown's Schooldays" when the sirens sounded. Gunfire heavy when I left the theatre about ten. Piccadilly packed with stalled trams and buses. I stood near a bus stop. Shellbursts far above, heavy drone of bombers. Wavering searchlight beams. I struck up a conversation with a smartly dressed blonde. With a backdrop of gunfire and distant bombing and in the occasional glow of descending parachute flares, it lasted until 4 am, the site of it shifting from bus-stop bench to air raid shelter to the sidewalk to a stationary bus. And covered a wide range of topics. I learned she had owned two flats in London, been engaged twice, once in love, was on the stage, is twenty-six. We made a little mild love towards dawn as the raid petered out. Her name is Joan Wilson, she is very attractive, leaves shortly for Scotland, and I'll probably never see her again.

I got into bed at 5:10 am. Up, feeling very tired, an hour and thirty-five minutes later. Heard that the raid, involving 200 bombers, had largely concentrated on Liverpool. But three unexploded bombs somewhere around Ringway, one near the petrol dump.

Last night I took the delightful 17-year-old Doreen Kelly to see "The Mortal Storm" (James Stewart, Margaret Sullivan, and a fine performance by Frank Morgan).

Sunday, December 8. Churchill has refused to consider proposing a Christmas truce. Yes, it would, I think, be a mockery to call off the bombings just for one day and a night to commemorate the birth of the Prince of Peace. No enemy aircraft reported over Britain last night though. Brief relief for London, Liverpool, Southampton, Birmingham and Coventry.

I have half a crown in my pocket. Would have had less if I'd seen Doreen as arranged Friday night. I turned up half an hour late and of course she wasn't there. Reason? Sqdn. Leader Ivens, after a day too gusty for flying, decided to fly Battle 5011 at 4:50 pm when the wind had died somewhat and wanted the fitter and rigger to accompany him. Morgan, the rigger, was absent. So I had to do harness, climb into the gunner's seat, and endure half an hour's bumpy flying. Thus, I left camp late.

Thursday, December 12. After a cold and hard day's work, damned angry at being rewarded for supper one solitary bone-filled kipper [herring], two pieces of dry bread, a pad of rancid butter. Rarely do we see bacon and eggs now. Well, cheering news on the radio. Sidi Barani* recaptured by our chaps. Next stop, Tobruk [port city in Libya].

Monday, December 16. 9:30 pm. All-clear just sounded. During the ninety-minutes alert as the bombers passed over through a heavy AA barrage I stood at our back door and heard the whip of falling shrapnel.

Sunday, December 22. Cardiff. It's midnight, and they've droned to and fro over the city since seven. Endless gunfire all over the sky, with the closer rattle of shrapnel on roof tiles. Unable to concentrate on Damon Runyon. I walked out with the old man to a nearby ARP post where wardens off duty played billiards and a pretty blonde served us tea. Returned home, found Ma chatting at the fireplace with the evacuated family from London now staying with us. A couple with two kids; they lost their home and all belongings. The woman still jumps fearfully at the slightest thump of distant gunfire.

Despite the nightly alerts, Christmas shopping crowds heavy as always.

Wednesday, December 25. Last night they stayed away. All was calm and notwithstanding the blackout, all was bright. Shoppers laden with gifts and often somewhat inebriated, cannoned into each other on the dark and crowded streets, but good humor seemed to prevail. Uniformed men with mistletoe springs in their forage caps and glengarries [traditional Scottish cap].

Newspapers report Greek celebration of the capture of Chimara,† BBC broadcasts from English Channel minesweepers, Coastal Command flying-boats, troops at home and abroad, evacuated kids in America and their sadly cheerful parents here at home. The King, his voice halting yet clear and deliberate.

But I appear to have left Manchester just in time and am genuinely grateful. For Manchester was heavily bombed Monday night. I wonder anxiously about Doreen. About my friends who didn't get leave. Of the pubs and cinemas where I've spent many a happy hour.

I bought a doll and toy farmyard animals for the evacuated London kids here. Model searchlight and guns for Ray and Freddie. Toy soldiers are scarce this year. Food much dearer than usual. Bananas almost unattainable also apples, oranges. I bought records of Woody

---

* A British victory over Italian forces in western Egypt and eastern Libya. This action was the first large-scale effort by British forces to engage the Axis in North Africa.

† From December 13 to 22, 1940, the Greek Army counter-attacked the Italians on the Greek-Albanian border. Himara is on the coast of the Ionian Sea.

Herman's "Woodchoppers Ball" and Deanna Durbin singing "Ave Maria" (Bach-Gounod).

(Return to a madly bombed Manchester)

Came out of London Road Station* at 8 pm, headed for the Piccadilly bus station. Smotheringly dark, streets deserted but for tin-helmeted police and wardens. Smell of burning on the night air. Police and barriers blocked my path to Piccadilly. I didn't know then that Piccadilly no longer existed.

By a roundabout route, I walked through streets slick with water and flanked by burnt-out shells of buildings. At St. Peters Square I tried to go up Mosely Street. Blocked by more police and wooden barriers. Heard the hard rasp of water under pressure. A bus passed, quickly swallowed up in the blackout. I felt uncannily alone in a city that had teemed with life when I last saw it. Relieved to find a pub, its interior brightly lit and crowded. Ran into Frank Barrett, like myself, also just in from Christmas leave.

In the grey light of next afternoon, 72 of Manchester's bomb victims were buried in a cemetery desecrated by a 30-foot-wide crater. I went into town on the No. 46 bus. Along the five-mile ride into Manchester, hardly a window unshattered (the result, I afterwards learned of our own heavy AA barrage). The centre of the city is devastated. Tall buildings, the business heart, now hollow and blackened shells or towering piles of rubble. Free Trade Hall in ruins. Woolworths, Deansgate, still smoldering. Manchester Cathedral shattered. My favourite CWL [Catholic Women's League] Canteen on Mosely Street, where friendly women had served the troops hot suppers, is demolished. Death toll estimated at 500—including presumably Salford, which suffered terribly. Where Doreen lives.

(Never saw or heard from Doreen again. Almost immediately on my return from that New Year's week I was posted to Wittering,† a night-fighter station. Was there, catching up on this diary, describing Manchester after that Christmas blitz, when lights snuffed out.)

Tuesday, December 31. New Year's Eve in Stamford. We attended the Farmers Dance. Rather snobbish affair, retired colonels and tired squires. But the beer was free and so, in their deportment, appeared some of the sundry wives and daughters with whom I danced. But after "Auld Lang Syne" at midnight, I took home a WAAF.

---

* During the war, Piccadilly was the principal railway station in Manchester. Originally named Store Street in 1842, it was renamed Manchester London Road Station in 1847.

† RAF Wittering, a Royal Air Force station near Peterborough, Cambridgeshire.

1941

Thursday, January 2, 1941. Wittering (snowbound). Seems a long time since my last entry. Here I am with AC2 Evans, Corporal Trueman, and a Lysander piloted by Sgt. Harris, on Army Cooperation—none of which carried out since I got here. At Wittering, besides us, are fighter squadrons, with Spitfires, Hurricanes, and the new twin-engined Beaufighter night fighter. The latter took off last night when a raider came over (glim lamps [runway lights] switched on but cannot be seen above 2000 feet) and met no AA gunfire. The raider dropped four bombs on this area. We heard them falling and dived under our beds. About then the Beaufighters took off. Shortly afterwards, snow began to fall. I hear today that the bombs did little or no damage.

Food here is little above average. Corp. "Tubby" Trueman and I walked into Stamford on New Year's Eve, had a few drinks, looked about the old place for a dance hall.

(Speaker from operations warns of enemy aircraft ten miles away.) Okay, lights back on. On this highly operational station all rooms, billets, NAAFI, dining hall, have loudspeakers, all hooked up to control operations room. Thus, warnings, standbys, and other orders reach everybody.

Tuesday, February 4. A cold clear Tuesday night. Almost nightly German aircraft pass high overhead, coming and going. Last night heard bombs drop somewhere.

Versatile and really rather spicy Ralph Reader "Gang Show"* entertained us last night. Reader is quite a winning personality. Show was in the camp cinema. A copy of Tatler† found its way into our barrack room last night, Each week you see it in the camp canteen, damned if I know why. It has the same silly peacetime smugness, same footling [trivial/irritating] pictures of society figures, debutantes and the like, on war work, at charity parties, but still reeking with snobbery. This crowd is still with us despite the war, and I suppose always will be. But then, are we taking this war seriously? I've just read that a question will be asked in the House of Commons about the use of lipstick in the women's

---

* Ralph Reader produced the variety entertainment "Gang Show," featuring many Boy Scouts. RAF Intelligence used Reader and his shows as a cover for intelligence gathering in France. The "Gang Show" was later expanded to be a "USO" type of entertainment to travel around the world during the war to visit military bases. One of the Boy Scouts who was part of the early "Gang Show" troupe was actor Peter Sellers.

† Tatler is a British magazine, first published in 1901, which features articles on lifestyle, fashion, high society, and politics.

services. Ships are sunk and cities bombed, yet some people still seem all wrought up over women's nail varnish, Sunday cinemas, and alleged immorality in air raid shelters.

Wednesday, February 5. Outside, a fierce blizzard howling across the camp, snow piling in heaps. Last night was moonlight however, and ten miles from here one of 151 Squadron Defiants attacked a Dornier until it blew up in midair. All told, six Nazi bombers have been brought down in the past twenty-four hours. Raids were widespread, though not heavy.

Wendell Willkie over here, visited Bristol today.

Monday, February 10. 9:40 pm. Completely crowded canteen silent for the past forty minutes, everyone listening to Churchill summarizing the war situation for us. Talked mostly of Africa, where the main fighting goes on.* Paid tribute to Wavell, Wilson and their startlingly rapid advance, scooping up Sidi Baranni, Solum, Tobruk, Benghazi, 150 miles or more in three days. This is even more remarkable than the German sweep along the Channel ports last summer. Churchill revealed that Wendell Willkie had brought him a letter from Roosevelt. In reply, Churchill has told FDR that we can get along without American soldiers, but with a German invasion attempt still possible, we need all the weapons and technical equipment we can get. He ended his speech with the words in his letter to FDR: "Give us the tools, we will finish the job" [February 9, 1941, radio broadcast].

I was in the station armoury today with a friend, an armourer, who showed me the twisted wreckage of the armament salvaged from the Dornier recently shot to pieces near here. A Verey pistol seemed intact and presented an unexpectedly sickening sight, for the burned remains of a human hand still adhered to it. My companion told me that the gunner of the Defiant that scored the kill had snatched an Iron Cross off what was left of one of the bodies. "Don't mention this to anyone for he'll be on the carpet." The dead Germans will be buried tomorrow, a detachment from here going out to give the military salute.

The armourer also told me that a wallet had been found belonging to one of the Germans, and it contained a photo of a beautiful girl, presumably his wife or sweetheart.

---

* In Operation Compass, from December 9, 1940, to February 9, 1941, British forces pushed back and defeated the Italian Army in North Africa. Field Marshal Henry M. Wilson served as General Officer Commanding-in-Chief of British Troops in Egypt. In that role, he launched "Operation Compass," attacking Italian forces with considerable success. Field Marshal Archibald Wavell counter-attacked the Italian army in North Africa, first in Libya in 1940, and then in Eritrea and Ethiopia in 1941. By February 1941, Wavell had overrun the Italian Tenth Army, capturing 130,000 prisoners, and driving nearly all Axis forces from North Africa.

Last night, I was at the Embassy in Peterborough where the stage show, featuring Maurice Winnick and his band and a chorus line called the Dorchester Lovelies, wound up with "There'll Always Be an England" and then "Land of Hope and Glory." The Lovelies in full undress shouldering flags of Australia, New Zealand, Canada, and other dominions. Everyone was cheering and singing. Not quite everyone, I sat unmoved in my one-and-ninepenny seat, and couldn't help thinking of what I'd seen and heard in the armoury.

Has anybody thought of this? So many military experts and strategists writing about the different methods Der Fuehrer might use to invade us, surely they've given him quite a few—even he and his generals haven't thought of. So are these people, by wracking their brains to tell the world of different ways to invade England, unwittingly acting as Fifth Columnists? I'm only asking.

Wednesday, February 12. Sgt. Harris brought back the Lysander yesterday, was posted to Hatfield this morning, and a Polish sergeant arrived to take his place flying the Lizzie on Army Coop. He knows a smattering of English and is quite a charming chap. I suppose the Lysander will get in a few more flying hours now. Harris flew infrequently, spent most of his time in Nottingham, leaving the machine at nearby Hucknall, supposedly weatherbound. From our standpoint, that was nothing to complain about, we had little to do but lounge and read over the stove-fire in the little office adjoining the 151 Squadron hangar here at Wittering.

Into Peterborough last night, saw "Foreign Correspondent," an Alfred Hitchcock film with good performances by Joel McCrea, Herbert Marshall, and George Sanders. Lively, topical ending, McCrea broadcasting from London as the bombs fall... "Hang on to your lights, America.... They are the only ones left in the world." Perhaps Joel, they will be out soon....

Willkie is back in the States, testifying on the Lease-Lend Bill. Newsreels I saw showed him before he left Britain. Surrounded by grinning Londoners, he was saying, "I have been in four or five air raid shelters. I have seen perhaps a thousand people. I have not seen anyone—afraid. If Hitler thinks he is going to beat this gang, then he is kidding himself." And the crowd in the shelter, on mattresses and bunks, sang "For He's a Jolly Good Fellow," as he left.

Quite a while since the last heavy raids on Britain, but the RAF bombed Hanover last night. The Greeks are hurling back Italian counter-attacks, Germans are swarming across Bulgaria. And Time, as they say, Marches On.

Thursday, February 13. Sgt. Harris left here yesterday and Sgt.

Bakanesh (or so it's pronounced) arrived. He flew a bomber in Poland before that country was defeated, speaks fairly good English. Has had great difficulty finding sleeping accommodation and the higher-ups (including the inevitable SW), did their damndest, it seems, to make things difficult, and he is sleeping tonight in the office.

My work today consisted in doping two patches on the Lysander.

Food is worse here than at Ringway. Breakfast this morning was Weetabix [packaged breakfast cereal] swamped by watery milk, and a piece of shriveled bacon with a small heap of dry brackish mashed potatoes, weak tea, and bread and margarine. Still no chocolates in the NAAFI, few cigarettes, plenty of meat pies, their contents generally regarded with suspicion, twopence-halfpenny each.

Tuesday, February 18. Thick damp clinging fog… Around the roaring fire in the barrack room, ten of us discussing the war, the Balkans* situation mostly, and most of us pessimistic about it. Only Bill Worth, a former market gardener, insisted that the Balkan mess won't outweigh our African successes, and that we are bound to win in the end. Personally, I fear there is too much complacency at large. Our midday discussion was broken up by the welcome arrival of mail, but while all the others present got letters and parcels, I didn't get a thing and I cursed out loud.

But was very pleased indeed by the unexpected appearance in the dining hall yesterday of a fine little dance band, and we ate our fried fish and dry cake to the strains of "That's Aplenty" and other jazz hits. This is really a good innovation. Each Monday the band will play at our dining-hall and on other nights in Sgts.' mess, officers' mess, WAAFs, etc. Some cynics say the whole idea is to take the men's minds off their lousy grub. But the effect on me is exhilarating.

Stibbington (5 miles from Wittering)

Saturday, February 22. 9 pm. In this "hospital"—converted old manor—with severe attack of the old complaint, tonsillitis. It started creeping up on me earlier this week. Tried to ward it off with gargles of Milton† and long periods in bed, hoping for a cure in time to visit (with McCall) Northampton for a weekend, which would include a Joe Loss [dance band leader] concert. Instead, my throat grew worse. I held out until yesterday morning, went sick, ambulance took me out on to the

---

* From October 28, 1940 to June 1, 1941, the Balkan Campaign, at this point in February 1941, consisted of Greek forces pushing Italian forces back to the Albanian border.

† Milton sterilizing fluid was produced for sterilization of babies' feeding utensils, including baby bottles. The fluid has been used in endodontics to irrigate an infected root canal, although it was not medically licensed for oral use.

snowy North Road. Am in a bare-walled room containing five beds and no radio. Newspapers come by rarely, but I've heard that Tuesday and Wednesday nights Swansea [in Wales] was severely bombed. Swansea raided again last night, and as I write this I can hear the bombers passing overhead. My temperature is about 100, was 102 yesterday.

Since I'm the only rigger in our Army Coop detachment, Corporal Dugmore will either have to do the daily inspection himself, borrow a rigger from one of the squadrons, or arrange for Sgt. Bakanesh to operate from nearby Hucknall until I get back.

Monday, February 24. Much better, though still shaky and my tonsils remain slightly swollen. The MO [medical officer] who came around this morning was S/Leader Walker, RAFVR [RAF Volunteer Reserve], a London specialist whose uniform hasn't robbed him of a genial bedside manner. He seemed infatuated with my over-large tonsils and breathed as he examined them, "How I'd love to take them out...."

This makeshift hospital is an old house, with an equally old stable that now serves as temporary morgue for victims of downed aircraft and even of crashes on the Great North Road. Last night Goering's bombers nullified the good effects of the two sleeping pills the medical orderly gave me. I started off well with a promising doze, only to spring awake sweating with the bang of a bomb explosion not very far off. Wasn't fear that made me sweat—I'd intended to sweat as part of the cure. Others in the room slept soundly, as did I, finally, but only after another bomb burst had set a dog barking. I learned today the bomb had fallen on a nearby village, killing one, injuring ten.

Swansea has been getting nightly raids, from what I hear, in a reported attempt to deliberately destroy that Welsh port. Why destroy a town? What is the mental make-up of a man who gives such an order? Why does God allow him to live?

Tuesday, February 25. Only two patients now in this room. The other chap with me is a soldier married to a French girl sixteen years his senior. He rather bores at times but he's a link with the early thirties, remembers all the dance tunes of that time.

Faint wail of sirens half an hour ago, and over go the bombers again. Swansea had a weekend's respite, allowing the city to clear debris and bury its dead. I feel terribly helpless and useless here. I wish I was in Swansea. (Hell, that soldier is boring again, he delights in reading out loud, quite oblivious to my obvious lack of interest.) I haven't seen a newspaper all day and don't know how the war is going. I feel vaguely as if everything is suspended, arrested in movement, frozen into still-life—until I come out of hospital.

Wednesday, February 26. At least I think it's Wednesday. One loses all track of time in this bare-walled cell. I've played Lexicon [word game], read Flaherty's* "The Assassin," gargled and swallowed tablets today. Cold and sunny outside. The windows fail to keep the cold out, the walls succeed in keeping the sunshine out. Last night, three bombs fell within a mile or two of here, big ones, evidently for they shook this building to its venerable foundations. In the post today, with newspapers from home that tell me little more about the Swansea raids than I already know, came my book club choice, David Garnett's collection of T.E. Lawrence's "Letters."† Look forward to reading it. Plenty of time for reading and would be more if my Army friend in the opposite corner would keep quiet. Still, I'd feel damn lonely if he left and I remained the only occupant.

One feels quite detached here. I've hardly given a thought to Dugmore, Evans, the Lysander, or 6AACU. If I were a wholly conscientious airman, I suppose I would worry a little. Then how foolish it is to be wholly conscientious! I learn that this place, Stibbington House, is in the county of Rutledge.

Thursday, February 27. Utterly bored. Thank God for the few magazines, a pack of cards, and "The Letters of T.E. Lawrence." They save my sanity. But I should be out of here in a couple of days. Daily Express landed on my bed. Main war news seems to be our victory in Italian Somaliland.‡

Friday, February 28. From my window I can see short green grass, hedges, trees, and a deep blue sky flecked with hastening white clouds. Seems mild and blustery out there. I'm still shut in. My talkative soldier and Lexicon companion has gone, leaving me utterly alone. I feel a desperate longing to get outside. I feel fine, as if I could leap a dozen five-barred gates at once. Expect to be discharged Sunday.

Not left alone long. My companion is an airman from Wittering, who has stomach trouble. He says he has seen the Lysander flying, which means they are carrying on quite well without me. Fine. Let them continue to do so when I'm on sick leave—I hope—next week.

Saturday, March 1. I was allowed up today and walked the grounds

---

* Liam O'Flaherty (1896–1984) was an influential Irish short-story writer and novelist.

† The book *The Letters of T.E. Lawrence*, edited by David Garnett, was published in January 1941. T.E. Lawrence was popularly known as "Lawrence of Arabia."

‡ The East African Campaign (also called the Abyssinian Campaign) lasted from June 10, 1940 to November 27, 1941. In February 1941, British forces forced Italian forces north from Mogadishu.

of this decidedly old house. Stibbington Manor, its oak-paneled interior containing (so a medical orderly tells me) at least one underground passage.

Well, I found the secret passage but as I was about to enter, through its small door, an orderly approached and told me I wasn't permitted to go down there. He didn't say why, but I suspect the orderlies have a secret liquor supply stored there.

This room now full again, laryngitis, tonsillitis, and ear cases having arrived. The ear case is an old soldier with a foul mouth and a belief that the war will be over by September.

St. David's Day [patron saint of Wales] today. Exactly a year ago I bade farewell to Johnny "Legs" King and left South Cerney for Manchester and Ringway. And so began my Army Co-op work. Yanks were still calling this a phony war when I dumped my kit at Ringway's rambling guardroom. Spent a sunny weekend billeted at Mrs. Cooper's house on Garland Road. Such a hell of a lot has happened since.

Read vol. one of F.L. [Frederick Lewis] Allen's "Only Yesterday" today. Damned fascinating account of the twenties in the USA. Must get vol. two from somewhere; can't find it here.

Halfway through Lawrence's "Letters." How he hated the Army! He was still sore at his dismissal* from the RAF in which he was so happy. In a letter to a friend, he complained of the other men in his hut, their filthy talk, and lack of either culture or enthusiasm. I know what he is talking about, a little of what he suffered. Thing is, though, he didn't have to suffer. Yet he was determined to, until "the burnt child no longer feels the fire...." I don't think I can completely understand Lawrence even from his letters. I fervently agree with his remarks about Uxbridge [RAF training base].

Sunday, March 9. Quite an unusual week. Have been home in Cardiff five days. I say "home" but not once did I go into our house. Discharged from hospital a week ago with a recommendation by the MO for a spell of sick leave, I had returned to Wittering to find two Lysanders, one Blenheim and fresh crews—all ex–Ringway men, including none other than Sgt. Harry Williams, my old NCO. I had no time to ask questions but rushed through a 295 (leave form) and was out on the road hitch-hiking by early afternoon. Got to Peterborough, then to London and by train west. The train made good time through the blackout, but

---

* Thomas Edward Lawrence, AKA "Lawrence of Arabia," changed his name—to remain anonymous—when he enlisted in the RAF in 1922. Aircraftman "John Hume Ross" was discharged after his real identity was discovered. In 1925, he enlisted again in the RAF under another assumed name "T.E. Shaw," and he remained with the RAF until February 1935. Three months later he died in a motorcycle accident.

after going through the Severn Tunnel and approaching Newport, the already dim lights went out, I put aside the <u>Lilliput</u> I'd been reading and cursed the Germans.

At Newport the sound of guns grew louder. "They're giving Cardiff hell," said a porter. The darkened corridor of the train was pierced by the lightning flashes of distant AA guns, and a couple of searchlight beams stabbed the night sky. The train slowed to a stop two miles from Marshfield. We passengers crowded the corridors, heads bobbing out of windows. All eyes turned westward towards Cardiff. It was a sight to behold. The sky above the city seemed to shudder with gun flashes. Our train shook with the reverberations of shell and bomb burst. A woman near me said something about "the futility of it all, men killing each other. I mean it <u>is</u> the twentieth century." A man in her party said he had once seen Hitler and Goebbels at a Nuremburg rally. Heavier crashes shook the train, and we could hear the pulsating drone of aircraft not so very high overhead. Now there were searchlights all about us, beams crisscrossing. And the flak going up from in and around Cardiff, was as hundreds of fleeting red gleams, and suddenly a crimson glare spread from below and some of us cried, "A fire.... He's started a fire." Five flares appeared, hovering above the city. Red streaks—tracer shells—flew up at them and they disintegrated one after another into flaming fragments. A little cheer went up from those of us watching. A girl said to a friend, "Are you afraid?" He replied, "No, of course not." My own anxiety was for my people in that hell. There seemed no letup in the thunderclap of explosions or the brilliance of that deadly fireworks display.

After three hours, the train rumbled back into Newport. Here, railway officials were in a bewildered daze, waiting for instructions as to what to do with a trainload of passengers for Cardiff and the West. I went into a station canteen, drank tea, talked to a soldier who expressed fears about "my wife and kid." I snatched some sleep in a train. At 3 am, it started moving. Via Caerphilly, a slow little-used route, it rumbled into Cardiff. I awoke from a doze as dawn streaked the sky, now peaceful, and the train pulled into Queen Street Station. I walked out into the street and the first thing I saw was a blackened, fire-ruined house.

Walked home avoiding the broken glass and slates that littered the ground. Firemen were still spraying water on the smouldering shell that had been the Blind Institute. The back of the Infirmary was wrecked, too, and every shop along Clifton Street seemed windowless. Iron Street was deserted. A tin-helmeted ARP warden told me the area was evacuated because of time bombs. So I went to Queenie's and found her dazed from lack of sleep. She did not know where Ma was.

Later that morning, Ma came in looking pale and haggard. She had been at the Salvation Army, which had sheltered hundreds with homes menaced by unexploded bombs. She told of how policemen had banged on the door after the raid, and told her to pick up her valuables and leave. Our bedroom windows are out. Ma cried and kissed me.

The old man came in after a very busy night. We shook hands, then he asked, "Where's Pat?" Olwen didn't know where her friend and hairdressing partner was. "Oh, my God," he exclaimed. "Poor Pat." "The house, the shop, it's all gone." Along with two other buildings on Broadway, Pat Greedy's home and the shop her mother kept were destroyed. Pat was safe, her father injured, a friend killed.

All my leave we stayed at Queenie's. There were minor discomforts, I slept on a settee next door at Mrs. Taylor's. Walked around battered Cardiff. Kids searched excitedly for shrapnel. The old church on City Road corner was a burned-out shell, as was the Post Office and many houses along Newport Road. Moorlands Road School, the first I attended, was hit by bombs on two successive nights. Several streets in Splott flattened. The Dutch Café, the Carton, and other buildings on Queen Street were in ruins—Queen Street, St. Mary Street, and other main shopping throughfares were roped off. Unexploded bombs. St. Davids Cathedral, Marlborough Road, Howards Gardens, [Eglwys] Dewi Sant Church, burned and devastated. Out in the Bristol Channel were two downed German bombers. I was told that, during a raid last Wednesday, an orphanage on Penylan Hill burned like a beacon. God knows how many people have been killed in all this nightmare.*

Tuesday evening, with Don's brother Stan, I went down Bute Road to where Pat was staying. More ruins on the road to the docks. We hurried back to the Great Eastern, that pub being near my temporary home, arrived just in time. The sirens howled, the bombers droned overhead, the guns opened up, we heard the bombs. This raid was less heavy than last night's but the pub quickly emptied, leaving the only occupants, a sleep-starved barman, Stan, and myself. Slightly drunk, Stan and I walked unsteadily home through a blackout pierced by the lightning bolts of the anti-aircraft shellbursts. Everyone at the Taylor's were out the back in the air-raid shelter, which is where Stan and I made for. Stan was the only one who slept, his snoring keeping everyone awake until, as

---

* During 1940, the Luftwaffe targeted Cardiff in July and August. This was followed in 1941 with three massive raids in January. Bombers dropped high explosive bombs, incendiary bombs, and parachute mines. In one raid, more than 165 people were killed and 427 more injured, while nearly 350 homes were destroyed or had to be razed. Further raids followed on February 27, and on March 1, 4, 12, and 20. and on April 3, 12, 29, and 30. Raids continued from May 4 through 11. Between 1940 and the final raid on the city in March 1944, approximately 2,100 bombs fell, killing 355 people. This period came to be known as the "Cardiff Blitz."

if by unanimous consent, some of us pushed him outside into the blitz. He staggered indoors and spent the rest of the night under the stairs. I finally dozed until the all-clear sounded.

The remainder of my leave was raid-free. I slept nightly in my trousers—well, hardly slept. Twice went to the cinema. Met Billy Allen, who related his blitz experiences, not sparing the grisly details. Pat's reactions are intriguing and may be typical. She seems not to realize that there actually lived and breathed a few men, German boys, directly responsible for her homeless plight. Not once did I hear her mention Hitler or Nazis or even German. It was as if no one was to blame, an act of God perhaps. There was no "if only I could get my hands on Hitler" attitude.

Left bomb-battered Cardiff pm Saturday. At London, I noticed St. Pancras Station, half-destroyed. And I left London as dusk fell, just before the first big fire raid in several weeks.

Tuesday, March 11. 10 pm. Aircraft droning high overhead, bound inland.

Wednesday, March 12. 9:40 pm. Almost full moon. Sparklingly clear night, Beaufighters, Spitfires, and Defiants patrolling overhead. Today, a sunlit Wednesday, our Blenheim flew to Cottishall on army cooperation with our CO and a Polish pilot-officer as passenger. We spent much of the afternoon kicking a rugby ball about the field while Spits and Defiants in smart formation, sped across a cloud-flecked sky. Yesterday Roosevelt signed the Aid-for-Britain bill.* Hitler is sure to make some big move against us before the full weight of American help is felt. There was much wrangling in the United States Senate before the isolationist front collapsed.

For the past few nights, we in this hut have listened to some propaganda broadcasts from an unknown location. Apparently, some Red calling voluntary fire-watchers "poor duped buggers" and urging workers to strike. This is nothing like the silky toned William (Haw-Haw) Joyce and is essentially communist rubbish.

Thursday, March 13. Full moon. Enemy aircraft passed over an hour or so ago.

---

* With President Franklin D. Roosevelt's signature, Lend-Lease was enacted on March 11, 1941. This program enabled the United States to supply Britain, the British Commonwealth, Free France, the Republic of China, and later the Soviet Union and other Allied nations with food, oil, and other matériel. This included warships, planes, and other weapons. The aid was free, although some hardware, such as ships, were returned after the war. In return, the U.S. obtained leases from Britain on several army and naval bases in the Western Hemisphere.

Sunday, March 16. Will never forget what happened Friday night. With three friends I had gone into Stamford where, over beers in a pub, we discussed forming a station rhythm cub. Returned to Camp at eleven, booked in at the guardroom. The countryside was bathed in moonlight. Near the moon could be seen the familiar white streaks, vapour trails of high-flying aircraft. We turned past the cookhouse, walked the remaining dozen yards to hut 9, my billet. It was warm and nicely lighted inside and we talked idly before undressing for bed. A thunderous bang shook the hut. I dived under the bed, froze face down, and frantically chewing a wad of gum. A louder crash rocked the hut, glass shattered, and the blackout screens toppled from windows suddenly ablaze with a blue-green glare. Someone had the presence of mind, and courage, to make for the light-switches. The hut remained lit with that strange and frightening glare. A third bomb exploded nearby, I heard shouting outside, an ambulance starting up, the crackle of flames.

Dazed and still chewing that infernal gum, I filed with companions to the shelter where we cowered for twenty minutes but no further bombs fell. Sid Heiger, former West End dance-band drummer, worried about his drum kit stored in the camp cinema, which someone shouted was on fire. With Rhodes, I walked over to the cookhouse. It was half-wrecked, and smoke and the reek of gunpowder filled the night air. Officers and men, some tin-hatted and others half-dressed, picked their way over debris. There were pools of blood at the wrecked entrance to the dining hall where an airman had his legs blown off and died almost immediately.

We walked along to Block 2, once my quarters. Firemen on 50-foot-tall ladders fought a fire devouring the roof. On to the cinema, a gutted shell. Met our Polish CO and accompanied him to the officers' mess, also shattered with cars on fire nearby. Our CO's quarters were uninhabitable and we helped him salvage some of his belongings.

Next morning. Breakfast (bread and corned beef, smoky tea) served to long queue by sleepless cooks and WAAFs. No. 25 Hanger was wrecked, two new Beaufighters written off—inside rested an unexploded bomb, 50-yards radius from it roped off. Out on the field our Lysanders and Blenheim were untouched, though shrapnel lay not far from them, and dozens of burn patches showed where incendiary bombs had exploded.

I've heard so far that three were killed, over 30 injured. Last night a number of men left the camp for safety, but fog descended, ruling out further attack. There are shrapnel holes in the wall three feet from where I write this.

Wednesday, March 19. 8:45 pm. Planes flying overhead. Night-flying means flare paths, hangar lights, which mean danger, but the risk must be taken, I suppose. Sergeant Harry Williams, NCO in charge of this detachment, told me that I have been recommended for promotion to corporal. The news was pleasant, though I have no military aspirations. I am happy enough out on the green turf working on the "Lizzie," gazing at squadrons of Spitfires, Defiants, and Beaufighters winging across the deep blue sky. The food here is substandard, this camp too far from a big city, but, all in all, I am content here (or is it the mood that I'm in?)

Bombs on Kiel [German port on Baltic Sea] and Wilhelmshaven [port on the North Sea] last night. Heavy enemy attack on Hull [port city in eastern England].

Mother's 55th birthday yesterday. I sent a pink RAF-crested table runner and a letter ending "what with bombs and guns, this must be the noisiest birthday you've ever had."

Our camp cinema being charred ruin, the "Witterbugs Concert Party" held its show in Stamford instead at the Oddfellows Hall. As usual, Tiny Winters (former bassist in Lew Stone's band) provided most of the fun. Some pretty members of the 157 WAAFs on this station sang and danced. Talking of numbers, there are 1275 airmen and over 200 soldiers also here. This is the base for three fighter squadrons, Nos. 25, 151, and 266.

Sunday, March 23, 7:40 pm. From the small radio on a wooden locker halfway down the smoky hut issues a hymn, "Fight the Good Fight." The hut is practically empty. It's a cold clear night outside, with our own aircraft thrumming far aloft. Something comforting about old hymns. My favorite is "Jesus, Lover of My Soul." But nothing lasts. Two of my colleagues just walked in, cursing and laughing, and one switched the radio off. I might have protested. But these are men I work with, and I'll be travelling with one of them on my next leave.

Today the King has called a National Day of Prayer. Letter from home tells me the old man has chucked his FAP [First Aid Post] job, for reasons he doesn't give beyond a cryptic "I refuse to be treated like a dog." He is now fire-watching nightly on the roof of the Kardomah Café, Queen Street.

I was surprised to see so many young men of obvious military age in civilian clothes thronging the bars of Peterborough pubs. I suppose they are all on war work.

I have almost fallen for a WAAF who works in the dining hall and can be sighted most days performing glamourless tasks that range from dabbing butter on rounds of bread to slapping meat out of a steaming tray on to one's proffered plate. She _is_ pretty.

Monday night, March 24. Rain all day. With its bomb-wrecked cookhouse and drab huts, this is a depressing place in wet weather. The RAF bombed Berlin and Hanover last night—10,000 incendiaries on the German capital. Germans attacked Malta, lost thirteen aircraft according to our Air Ministry. Raids on the Clydeside area were described to me by Jock Rundell, who was on leave in his hometown of Glasgow. He says 14 of fifty Argentinian foodships in the harbour were destroyed. The official Glasgow death toll is about 500.

Tuesday, March 25. Heavy rain. Just back from the barrack block where I took a bath. Military band played in the dining hall this evening at teatime (pilchards) [sardines].

Thursday, March 27. A detachment now tours around, weekly, other AACU detachments, providing some relief from work. So a bunch of old Ringway comrades are down here for a week and they include my old friend Arthur Wilson. Very pleased to see him again. He was a work-mate of mine at Ringway, and before that, he was on a Fairey Battle squadron in France. He watched the fliers take off on that suicidal mission to destroy the Maastricht Bridge.* Leaving behind their equipment, also the squadron's collection of Bing Crosby and Deanna Durbin records, Wilson and the rest of the outfit fled before the advancing Germans—he was among those evacuated at St. Valery after Dunkirk. Wilson tells me that our mutual friend, Rex Bowden, was posted to Driffield, in Yorkshire, and that Rex's girlfriend in Manchester has sung on the radio with Billy Cotton's band. This news set me thinking of May and stirred my emotions.

Amy Johnson took off from Squire's Gate on her last flight.† That's near Blackpool. Wilson's travels with his detachment took him to Squire's Gate where a mechanic, who claimed to have seen Amy J's take-off was prepared to swear there was nobody on board the plane except herself. Yet the body of a mysterious person, name not disclosed, is said

---

* As German troops advanced through Holland toward Belgium, the RAF sent Blenheim bombers to destroy the intact bridges in southeast Netherlands at Maastricht on May 12, 1940. The operation ended in seven of the nine bombers being shot down by German fighters. Another 24 Blenheims, were also sent to destroy the bridges but almost half of these aircraft were then lost to ground fire, 10 of the 24 failing to return to base. Of the 96 bombs dropped, all missed their targets.

† Amy Johnson was a well-known British aviator. Early in the war, Johnson joined the Air Transport Auxiliary (ATA), which transported Royal Air Force aircraft around the country. On January 5, 1941, while ferrying an Airspeed Oxford, Johnson went off course in adverse weather conditions. Reportedly out of fuel, she bailed out as her aircraft crashed into the Thames Estuary. Rescue attempts failed and her body was never recovered. In 1999, an RAF veteran claimed to have shot down Johnson's aircraft when she twice failed to give the correct identification code during the flight.

to have been picked out of the water with Amy's. Talking of mysteries... Near Liverpool, a 19-year-old girl waiting for a bus in the blackout, was fatally stabbed in the back. Murderer unknown.

And did Sir Delves Broughton* murder Lord Erol in Kenya?

Tuesday, April 1. Asmara, capital of Eritrea, surrendered to the British.† More good news, six Italian warships sunk by Admiral [Andrew] Cunningham's force with no losses to our side.‡ This in the Mediterranean. It is being described as the most amazing British naval victory since Trafalgar.

While such momentous events under way, I try a hitch-hiking experiment. Soldier's pay being what it is, men in uniform depend on the generosity of motorists and truck-drivers to travel long distances to home or camp. Having no more "warrants" [vouchers] for this year, I must hitch-hike home or pay the railway more than 30 shillings. So with Evans, I carried out a dress rehearsal for next Friday week when (I hope) I go on leave. Hitched all the way—170-miles—and back. Brief surprise visit to Cardiff. Weather was warm. Took thirteen lifts going down and fourteen coming back. Most were in private cars. Four in commercial or army trucks. Conversations with drivers were less cheerful going to Wales than returning, when the defeat of Mussolini's navy was generally known. Journey down—via Stamford, Kettering, Northampton, Oxford, Cheltenham, Gloucester, Newport—took 9½ hours. Found on arrival that Mother has bought a second piano for me. I cannot play it but would love to.

Friday, April 4. Tonight, trying to concentrate on Charles Morgan's "The Fountain," but the noisy barrack-room chatter, cursing, and guffaws of card-players, scrape of beds on the floor, din of a badly-tuned radio, make close reading all but impossible. Wish I had a room of my own or, like T.E. Lawrence, when he served in the ranks, a cottage nearby to which I could escape periodically for study and contemplation.

Last night I accepted McCall's invitation to form a foursome with two young married women. My spirits, cool at first, mellowed when I

---

* Sir Henry John Delves Broughton was a British baronet was tried for the January 1941 murder of Josslyn Hay, 22nd Earl of Erroll. The event was the basis of the film *White Mischief*.

† As part of the East African Campaign, February 3 to March 27, 1941, Italian-controlled Asmara in Eritrea (north of Ethiopia) surrendered to British forces at the Battle of Keren.

‡ At the Battle of Cape Matapan, fought from March 27 to 29, 1941, south of Crete, the Royal Navy defeated the Italian fleet, sinking the heavy cruisers *Fiume*, *Pola*, and *Zara*, and destroyers *Vittorio Alfieri* and *Giosuè Carducci* and damaging one battleship and a destroyer. More than 2,300 Italian sailors were killed and another thousand captured. Cape Matapan was Italy's greatest naval defeat of World War II.

saw their good looks—and their care. The night proved highly enjoyable, I felt no twinge of conscience kissing my date, and if she did, it was quite evidently stifled.

Palm Sunday, April 6. Germany attacked Yugoslavia and Greece this morning. Italy has declared herself at war with Yugoslavia, which gives the latter's army a good chance to strike the Italian left flank in Albania and drive it into the Adriatic.

Listened to Lord Haw Haw tonight spouting Hitler's "justification" for this latest aggression. American help for Britain is imperiled by strikes over there—labour strikes, that is. The Battle of the Atlantic* continues with the RAF bombing German ports, the Luftwaffe bombing ours. That's how things look on a cold windy Sabbath before Easter.

Wednesday, April 9. 9:30 pm. The drone of aircraft is all I can hear (from my bed and above the music of [Bert] Ambrose and his band on the radio) of the second night of a moonlit battle. Last night's, score of victories was seven—five by Hurricanes and Defiants of this station. But Coventry was heavily bombed. Tonight, raids will be widespread. There is a magnificent full moon. Samford's sirens have already sounded. Germans are sure to pay us back for our two smashing raids on Kiel.

On the Mediterranean front, things don't look well. British army troops have been withdrawn from Libya to help out the Greeks, whose forces in the east are cut off. Salonika [Greek port city on the Aegean Sea] is in German hands.

Our solitary Lysander flew this afternoon on Army Coop, piloted by our new CO, a Polish officer, in peacetime a doctor.

Thursday, April 10. The few men in this hut (including myself) climbed somewhat uneasily into bed last night as the roar of night-fighters drowned the deeper thrumming of German aircraft. I slept fitfully, awoke in pitch blackness to the heavy bump of exploding bombs. We were out of and under our beds in a hurry. I groped for my tin hat and shoes, which I tugged on to the wrong feet. Wilson, under the next bed, wondered out loud if the chances of being hit by a bomb equaled those of winning the Irish Sweepstakes. At 4 am, we crawled back in our beds.

The attacks were mainly on Birmingham. Ten bombers were downed, two by fighter planes from this station. Skies cloudy tonight, things should be quieter. Tomorrow, perhaps, I'll hitch-hike home.

---

* The Battle of the Atlantic lasted from 1939 to 1945: German submarines, warships, and the Luftwaffe fought against the navies and merchant vessels of Britain, U.S., and Canada.

Sunday April 20. A twin-engined Whirlwind, new RAF fighter, landed here this morning. We clustered around it. After a spell to stretch his legs, the pilot re-entered its cockpit and took off again. We watched. And I wish I hadn't. The pilot wished to impress our Spitfire and Hurricane men with a Whirlwind's capabilities. The plane flew off some distance, then turned to come back at the field at a terrific speed at low altitude. It spun into a fast roll—too fast, and its second roll may not have been intentional, the pilot without control. It flashed low across the airfield upside down at over 400 mph. Howard and I, at a corner of the hangar, watched it arc downward, vanish beyond distant trees. "He's had it," some shouted.

I can't remember hearing the sound of the crash but will never forget the sight of that machine twisting in midair, hurtling to its doom only a mile or so away on the other side of the North Road.

Had a good Easter leave at home except for a touch of the flu. Managed to attend a dance at the Capitol where I met old workmates "Slim" Morgan and Jack Kelleher. On the way home, I had spent an hour in Coventry, which had been heavily bombed the previous night. This was Good Friday. Whole blocks were in smoking ruin, townsfolk, carrying what they could of their belongings, trudged in a daze along what remained of their streets. This was how I got into Coventry. Hitched a ride from Leicester in a lorry [large transporting truck]. Had already heard of the Coventry raid and that no one was allowed in the stricken city.

Six miles short of it, we were stopped by police. The lorry driver pleaded frantically with them, his wife and kids were in Coventry; he lived there. They finally let him through, with myself still aboard, on the back. Within the city we saw little traffic except military and ARP. Mobile canteens served food and drink to the homeless and to weary firemen, black-faced and red-eyed, who still managed to joke as they sipped tea. The ground was carpeted with broken glass and a smell of gas mingled with that of burning.

I jumped down from the truck and wished the driver good luck. His face was anxious as he drove off. Maneuvering amid the rubble, women pushed perambulators [baby carriages] laden with what possessions they had salvaged. Tired kids trotted alongside. I found a packed bus bound for Birmingham, was allowed aboard. The man I sat next to said the raid had been hell, "Jerry hit all the buildings he'd missed last November. Must have killed hundreds."

(It was on this occasion, while roaming Coventry's wrecked streets, that I'd glanced up and saw a great wooden face staring down on me from an upstairs' window. It was an effigy of the Peeping Tom, the Lady

Godiva* voyeur, blasted or otherwise removed from its pedestal and because of its size, thrust halfway out the window at its hastily chosen place of safe storage.)

Birmingham, too, had been attacked but the trains were running and I boarded one for Cardiff.

Thursday, April 24. Clear cold night. News is of serious [British] withdrawals in Greece. Some people saying we shouldn't have transferred troops there from North Africa when the Tobruk garrison is only barely holding out.

Tuesday, April 29. We have two Lysanders here engaged on Army Cooperation. On one, the inner tubes of the undercarriage burst. No tubes on this station so Sgt. Williams phones the nearest Lysander station—Hucknall. Yes, they have tubes of the required size and will send them over. That was Friday. Now it's Tuesday. Exasperated, Williams asks one of our Polish sergeant-pilots to fly the serviceable Lizzie over there. An hour later he returns and we pounce on the boxes, only to discover that Hucknall has sent tubes of the small, tail-wheel size. Off goes the Lizzie again. Now Hucknall says, sorry—they haven't got the tubes—which arrive finally, by mail. But lo, these are also tail-wheel size. An almost speechless Sgt. Williams this time sends to Ringway for the tubes. Much petrol and time wasted on account of someone's incompetence.

Thursday, May 1. We are pulling out of Greece. And Tobruk is under attack. Depressing news. CO back from Ringway—with the inner tubes, which we promptly put in the wheels, putting us back to full strength—with two Westland Lysanders. Letter from Frances Smith, now a nurse at Melton Mowbray, suggests we meet in Nottingham. Her brother is reported missing in action.

Monday, May 5. Saturday night went to a dance in Peterborough. Widespread raids, and about midnight I stood in the blackout listening to the familiar pulsating hum from far above where searchlights probed a starbright sky.

Last night I heard Lord Haw Haw say Churchill was a drunkard who would be court martialed for his blunders in any country but Britain. And quoted his boss Hitler as saying that he has no territorial ambitions in the Balkans. Same old song.

---

*Lady Godiva is remembered for a legend dating back to the 13th century, in which she rode through the streets of Coventry naked, covered only by her long tresses. Later versions of the legend refer to "Peeping Tom," a man who observed her and was struck blind or dead.

From home, a parcel, with cigarettes, cake, Oxo's* and a letter telling of more bombs on the city. From the roof of the Kardomah Café (says the old man) "It was a fine sight." With Sergeant Williams on leave, our CO up at Ringway, and just a single unserviceable Lysander down here, little to do but relax in the May sunshine.

Hitch-hiking from Peterborough at 8 Sunday morning. I felt glad to be alive. Vaporous clouds flecked a deep blue sky, the deep green grass sparkled with frost crystals, a dazzling sun made up in brilliance what it lacked in heat. The previous night, death had fallen across the land in large steel containers, and though it had left its mark upon cities, the countryside was peaceful, quiet enough to make you hold your breath. I had broken out of camp and re-entered the same way through an unguarded gap in the hedges that flank this camp.

Wednesday, May 7. Evening. Last night a sudden bang sent me leaping from bed. I struck my head on the hard floor. Learned later that a German bomber had dived low over the flare path, cannon firing.

Just finished reading "How Green Was My Valley," and am left in a vaguely nostalgic mood.

Thursday, May 8. 9:45 pm. Just finished rigging up my bed down in the air raid shelter near this hut. So has Wilson. And Rhodes. Others of this hut, off to Peterborough, will stay there overnight. For last night was hellish. We were bombed and machine-gunned.

Wilson and I had not long returned to camp from a visit into Stamford. We were in our beds and I dreaming—of fire. I awoke to an awful bang followed by a heavy clatter—a bomb burst and cannon-fire. I heaved out of bed, still sandwiched in blankets, groveled in the dark and yelling, aware that my head throbbed from striking a bed-leg. Aware too that my bed frame was no protection against bombs and 20 millimetre cannon-shells. The blackout screens had tumbled down. I braced for steel thudding into my back. Panic had only been momentary. I crawled, as did my comrades, from under useless shelter and groped for the door, outside of which I eventually stood under a cold moonlit sky, my only attire boots, a shirt and shorts—and a tin hat. Emitting curses and nervous laughs, I went back for my trousers ducking futilely as more aircraft sounded above.

Once outside again I saw incendiaries burning on the square and two men, one supporting the other, staggering from the opposite end of our hut. Blood ran from both shoulders of one man. The time was 2 am.

---

* A brand of food products, including bouillon cubes, herbs and spices, dried gravy, and yeast extract.

An hour later some of us grouped around the stove in the middle of the hut. Occasionally we heard short bursts of machine gun fire from far above in the night sky. [Fairey] Battles raged up there.

Learned later that ten bombs had struck this camp. Two hit a barrack block not far from my hut, killing five personnel, injuring eight. This hut narrowly escaped—at the opposite end of the hut from where I sleep stands now a blood-soaked bed, and the walls and roof there are riddled with holes. The papers say twenty-four enemy bombers were downed in widespread heavy raids across the country.

Tonight promises again to be cloudless. Station headquarters personnel, their living quarters wrecked, are evacuated to the Stamford Hotel. Wish I could join them but am really too sleepy to feel apprehensive.

Saturday, May 10. 1:20 am. The last two nights have brought more high-explosive, incendiary and cannon-fire blitz upon us here in Wittering. I suppose other night fighter squadrons are getting the same attention. During last autumn's Battle of Britain, fighter squadrons in southern England were daily targets. Now, with Beaufighters and other night-fighter craft downing raiders in record number, the Luftwaffe has evidently launched a second B.O.B. [Battle of Britain] night version—while still attacking metropolitan centres (Nottingham, Derby, Hull on Thursday). And on that Thursday, I scarcely dozed. Wilson and I, in the bomb shelter, had been reading by flashlight—his book was a C.S. Forester's "Captain Hornblower" yarn, mine a collection of Damon Runyon short stories. We had then closed our books but sleep was impossible—certainly for me. I sweated under the blanket and tensed at the slightest noise. It was about 2 am when bombs shook the shelter, with once more that vicious clattering. The bomber must have come in quite low, thundering across the living quarters, offices hangars, and airfield. Wilson was awake. We exchanged weak jokes. We heard the grinding of gears as ambulances moved off from the sick bay.

After daybreak, I saw the results. Craters surrounded the gunpost near the watch-office. Ground defence men at this post had fired their twin-barreled Lewis gun as the attacker streaked overhead. Across the airfield, eight bombs had fallen, killing at least one man, wrecking vehicles, and setting a parked Hurricane on fire. The grass I trudged over was littered with metal fragments, pieces of clothing. Our army coop Lysander is badly damaged by shrapnel. I will work on it today. And what bright sunny day it is, but serving more to emphasize the grimness of events rather than lighten it.

Coming back from Stamford last night (Friday) following a movie visit, I couldn't help noticing how unusually quiet were the airmen and WAAFs with whom I shared the bus. We all knew that the attackers would return. And they did, about 3 am. In the dark of the shelter, I heard the all too familiar thrumming. They were searching for their target. I felt slightly sick with suspense. The thrumming increased to a steady roar. All hell broke loose. The crash of bombs punctuated that hideous yammering of cannon-fire, and to the enemy's din was added the punch pom-pom-pom of new Bofors guns [40mm anti-aircraft] deployed around the airdrome. At 4:30 I fell asleep, awoke three hours later.

Tonight, I am off-duty, will head for Peterborough, reportedly itself hit by fire bombs last night, but that's where I intend to stay until tomorrow morning. Enough is enough!

Sunday May 11. 9:45 pm. So I spent last night in Peterborough. So, in fact, did virtually all 6AACU detachment and doubtless many more Wittering personnel, three nights in a row of bombs and machine gun strafing quite sufficient, thank you, so it's out of camp without authority by way of the sports-field, and hitch-hike into Peterborough. I stayed at the Services Club, sixpence a bed, two blankets. Night of the full moon, and I learn today that Westminster Hall, House of Commons, set on fire,* other venerable London buildings damaged in a fierce all-night raid.

Tonight, thank God, clouds are spreading across the sky. I had hitch-hiked back to Wittering with Corporal Doug Irwin, and perhaps tonight will be quiet. Last night's raids cost the Germans 33 bombers. Stevens, an ace from this station, downed two. Well, it might be quiet tonight, but few are taking any chances. Chaps have already been trudging from billets to shelters. I and other 6AACU members will be in one of those dugouts shortly.

Tuesday night, May 13. HESS!† His dramatic arrival by Messerschmitt 110 and parachute is considered one of this war's biggest sensations. Rudolph Hess is in a Glasgow hospital with a broken ankle!! Incredible but true.

Last night and tonight, cloudy skies give us some peace.

---

* During World War II, the Houses of Parliament buildings were bombed 14 times. On the night of May 10–11, 1941, the seat of government suffered the most damage following an attack featuring both incendiary and high explosives.

† On May 10, 1941, Rudolf Hess, a member of Hitler's inner circle, flew from an airfield in Germany flying a Messerschmitt Bf 110 fighter-bomber. Displaying considerable skill and evading British air defenses, he reached Scotland. Out of fuel, he bailed out and was captured shortly after reaching the ground. He hoped to contact high-ranking British officials with a proposal to make peace with the Nazi government. His self-described mission was unsuccessful, and he was held as a POW for the duration of the war, after which he was tried by the International Military Tribunal at Nuremberg. Hess died by suicide in Spandau Prison in 1987 at age 93.

Wednesday, May 14. The world still speculating on the significance of Hess's flight into Britain. Has he fallen out with Hitler? Or is this a part of some trick? Is Hess insane, as some Germans allege? Would be something if he has actually defected—and may soon be broadcasting to his country over the BBC! Still, we mustn't forget that he is as much a liar, a thug, and a murderer, as any other of the Nazi gang.

Sunday night, May 18. Warm day. Little flying. Much sunbathing on the airfield, reading the Sunday papers, some of which criticize the government for mollycoddling Rudolf Hess.

Sky cloudless tonight. I hope this doesn't mean a resumption of those raids. A Beaufighter crashed on the airfield last night.

Monday, May 19. Evening. Rain all day. Two airgunners posted abroad, so Howard and I collared their beds in one of the big and relatively sturdy blocks. Among other advantages they have over the wooden huts are indoor plumbing, hot water, and central heating. Moving into blocks from the huts is all the more welcome since sleeping in shelters is now officially forbidden as "unsanitary," and renders one liable to "severe disciplinary action!"

Wednesday, May 21. Settled in a block, and sharing a room with Howard, two SHQ [sector headquarters] clerks, and two very pleasant Poles. Right now all is quiet save Chopin coming from the radio, and the scratching of my pen. One of the Poles, named Josef, is reading a Polish-English dictionary. Earlier he played whist with Rhodes, Howard, and me. He likes telling of life in Poland, seems to prefer Germans to Russians, and has bought a motorcycle.

The other night, idly turning the radio, I came upon the strains of reasonably good jazz. When the band faded out with "Farewell Blues," I realized it was the Ramblers coming from a German-occupied Dutch radio station.

Thursday noon, May 22. Britain is at grips with the most monstrous armed force ever known. From Narvik [Norway] to southern France, the European continent is under Hitler's tyranny. The British are fighting for their lives. Well, not all of them. Two rather unhappily looking RAF men, with armbands marked SP [Service Police], are standing in the sunshine outside our dining hall, and their sole contribution to the war effort is to intercept men from the flights, the squadrons, the ground crews from the Beaufighters, Spitfires, and Defiants, and order them to go all the way back again for their hats. It's a fresh sunny day, yet no one is allowed to go in the open air without that damned silly glengarry perched on the right side of one's head. I was among the intercepted, stopped en route to lunch by an SP corporal who asked if I had a hat, and to my affirmative, gave a sickly smile and murmured, "Well, go back and get it."

"Good God," I said. "Do I have to wear a hat for only a 20-yard stroll?" His face going red, his stammering of "twenty yards is twenty yards," rather moved me to pity and with a shrug I retraced my steps.

Friday, May 23. Like the Joads in [John Steinbeck's] "The Grapes of Wrath," I'm on the move again. Via phone from Ringway we heard this morning that 6AACU, in fact all remaining Anti-Aircraft Cooperation Units are being disbanded. Flight command is taking over their work. We have been recalled to Ringway. We leave Sunday or Monday. As far as possible, Sgt. Harry Williams is trying to keep this detachment together and remaining with him, including Wilson and myself. So far, we haven't quite placed the camp we go to from Ringway. Sounds like Babbington, and I hear is somewhere near Birmingham and Coventry. Ringway—it will be good to see Manchester again, if only briefly. I suppose our future work will be the usual army cooperation stuff, but not under Army Cooperation Command. We expect to have a Blenheim and two Lysanders—as of now.

Sunday, May 25. We leave at 7 am tomorrow for Manchester. Spent all last night at Peterborough. After a movie (Ray Milland and Claudette Colbert in "Arise, My Love"), we ate somewhere then drank at the Bell and Oak where I wished the pretty barmaid Rose goodbye. On to a dance, from which I took a girl home. After leaving her about 11:30 pm, I fell in with another two, one of whom, named Rita, particularly attracted me and after a happy two hours I hated leaving her. I will write to her.

Big battle raging in Crete.* Our chances of holding the island look good, seems to me. But shocked to hear that the Hood† is no more, sunk by the Bismarck.‡ Terrible loss of life, a handful of survivors out of more than 1200 men.

9:15. From the radio news, seems a big naval engagement is brewing in the North Atlantic. The hunt for the Bismarck is intensifying,

---

* The Battle for Crete took place from May 20 to June 1, 1941, resulting in a German victory. Paratroopers conducted the initial stage of the invasion, the first such assault in history.

† On May 24, 1941, early in the Battle of the Denmark Strait, a 15-inch shell of the German battleship *Bismarck* struck HMS *Hood*'s main magazines, almost instantly destroying the pride of the Royal Navy. The battlecruiser's sinking and the loss of 1,416 crewmen (only three survived) was a devastating blow to British morale.

‡ Three days later, on May 27, Hood was avenged when *Bismarck* was sunk after being cornered by 13 capital ships of the Royal Navy.

following her destruction of the Hood. As for Crete—an island only 150 miles long, 40 miles wide—fighting is fierce, many of the Nazi paratroopers and other airborne invaders killed the moment they touch ground. Difficult to imagine all that hell as I snuggle down here between the sheets, listening to Vernon Bartlett's* Sunday night radio postscript. Dugmore packing his kitbag for tomorrow's journey (I've packed mine). Howard writing a letter. Josef Nowataski's laying quietly on his bed, perhaps thinking of his Polish homeland. Me? I just feel tired. Tomorrow, up early and on to blitzed Manchester.

Of this camp at Wittering, I will miss the relatively easy duty schedule, the little swing band—and will never forget those nights of the full moon. I am the only one left of the original small 6AACU detachment that arrived here the first of January. Hope someday to return to Peterborough and see Rita.†

Each week, one reads in the papers that the enemy is short of some commodity. This week it's leather. When I read of the Germans being short of breath, I'll sit up and take notice.

Saturday, May 31. Honiley/Baginton‡ near Coventry. Eventful week. Cheerful news following the Hood disaster and our imminent loss of Crete is that the Navy has destroyed the Bismarck. And Dublin in neutral Ireland has been bombed by German aircraft.§ This even ought to induce De Valera¶ to at least let us use his ports.** [It didn't. Ireland stayed neutral throughout the war.] **(Notation from LFG 1992)**

Well, here we are at a new location—new to us anyway—Wilson, Paton, Sgt. Williams, Dugmore, etc. Last night went into Leamington with Wilson and Sgt. Williams. Coventry is also nearby. When our pilots arrive, we will continue the usual routine of army cooperation. Baginton is a dreary airfield and the tea we drink here is lousy because the water used is chemically treated in consequence of the bomb damage to Coventry's water system. Coventry—I was there Thursday—defies

---

* A British journalist, politician and author, Vernon Bartlett served as a Member of Parliament from 1938 to 1950.

† I never did—LFG,1992.

‡ Honiley, a village in Wroxall, Warwickshire, is seven miles southwest of Coventry. An RAF station was located there during the war.

§ Several German bombings of the Republic of Ireland occurred during the war. The first took place on January 2, 1941, and another early the next morning. On May 31, 1941, four more bombs fell on north Dublin. This attack left 28 dead and 90 injured. Approximately 300 houses were destroyed or damaged, leaving about 400 people homeless. It is believed that navigational error was responsible for these attacks.

¶ Eamon De Valera served as Prime Minister of the Republic of Ireland from 1932 to 1948, 1951 to 1954, 1957 to 1959, and president from 1959 to 1973.

** Ireland remained neutral throughout the war. In wartime speeches, De Valera repeatedly stated that small states should stay out of big power conflicts.

description. People there laugh, drink beer, dance, visit what cinemas still stand (actually I saw only one) carry on some semblance of normality, but all among entire blocks of gutted buildings and hills of debris.

This morning, I was assigned the unexpected task of taking a group ten miles away to collect an ancient pipe-organ, donated by a generous old lady. Paton enjoyed himself playing "Begin the Beguine" on it repeatedly all the way back to camp.

I have a 48-hour pass as from tomorrow and intend hitch-hiking home.

Thursday, June 5. Dreary, desolate scene, our camouflaged huts under a lowering sky. But last night was moonlit and those same huts trembled (as did some of its occupants, including myself) to the roar and bang of uncomfortably close anti-aircraft fire, also bombs. The heavy drone of bombers above seemed never to cease. Main targets were doubtless Coventry and Birmingham.

Today as yesterday, a tender* took us from Honiley into Baginton at 9, brought us back at 5:30 pm (12 miles each way). No work yet, nothing to do but combat boredom with a book inside a drafty tent pitched inside a no less drafty hangar. Wilson is home on 48-hours pass, checking on his parents' safety following Manchester's raid last Sunday, the heaviest since that of Christmas Eve. On my brief visit home that same Sunday, I dozed in the Anderson shelter while Cardiff's guns barked at the raiders heading north.

Growing criticism over our withdrawal from Crete. Evidently our men were not adequately supported, but most serious was the apparent failure to effectively fortify the island before the Germans attacked. Why are we so lacking in foresight? Norway, Dunkirk, Greece, now Crete. One retreat after another.

Our people here at home are taking the new clothes rationing program stoically, some perhaps with a secret pleasure for it especially affects the wealthy who will henceforth have to content themselves—the men that is—with one suit per year, like the rest of us.

I danced at the Connaught Rooms the other night and got some perverse pleasure out of pulling the leg of a totally drunk and undignified army captain.

Pat and Stan, Don's brother, get married June 15.

Saturday June 7. Spending a warm Saturday night in this most depressing camp. Why? Well, I want to make sure of seeing the RAF Squadronaires in Coventry tomorrow and I have little cash. Something

---

* A vehicle used in mobile operations by a public service or the armed forces.

happened to make this evening more irksome, Wilson and I, after showering, had adjourned to the almost deserted canteen to eat sausage and mash [mashed potatoes], then we relaxed, smoking, all unaware that a man who quietly sneaked out was some swine of an SP off duty. He reported us to the orderly sergeant who appeared in the canteen and rather apologetically asked us to go and put on our collars and ties that we had been reported for not being properly dressed. Wish I could get my hands on that SP creep who made such a trivial "complaint." What happens, God help us, when men with such mentality acquire positions of high authority? It's that sort of mentality which has come close to losing us the war.

Tuesday, June 17. Prolonged sun-bathing on the Baginton 'drome, my skin is flaming red. Flying for us had ceased at 4 pm, but a 25-year-old squadron leader, with a DFC [Distinguished Flying Cross] and no Lysander flying experience, sauntered up and said he wished to fly a Lizzie after tea "to see what they are like." Corporal Dugmore, in charge of us since Harry William's departure, timidly acquiesced. So our return to Honiley was delayed. Petrol and aircraft flying hours were wasted. Too hot to write further. Besides, Wilson wants his pen back.

Thursday, June 19. War between Russia and Germany a growing possibility. Troops on each side of their frontiers massing. As for us, the RAF is well on the offensive, bombing the Ruhr [Valley] and invasion ports. Revived feeling that an attempted invasion of Britain is imminent. At the local village of Knowle last night, the war seemed remote as I watched a fine movie version of Steinbeck's "Of Mice and Men."

Sunday, June 22. Churchill announced tonight that we are allied with Russia. This upon the news that Germany has attacked the Soviet Union.* We heard the news sprawled half-naked on the grass alongside our Lysanders and single Blenheim. Heat wave continues. Civilian workers outside our huts listening with us to Churchill [in a radio broadcast on June 22, 1941], broke into cheers when he called Hitler a "bloodthirsty guttersnipe." But his declaration offering Stalin all possible aid was greeted with silence. Still, as Churchill went on to say, though he still abhors communism, the main enemy is Hitler. The Nazi gang must be smashed, and in this endeavour, we and the Russians are now comrades-in-arms.

Odd questions remain or rather loom. The Finns, whom we helped fight the Russians, are allied with the Germans. The Poles, our allies, are

---

* On June 22, 1941, the German Wehrmacht launched "Operation Barbarossa" to invade the Soviet Union.

Interior of Hut 79 Honiley Camp, Wroxall, Warwickshire, August 1944.

still technically at war with Russia. And will the BBC broadcast on Sunday night the "Internationale" [Soviet workers' anthem], along with the anthems of other allies? Will British communists, like Willie Gallagher, continue to encourage opposition to the war?

Yesterday, I flew for 2½ hours in the Lysander, mainly over Birmingham and got air-sick. May be the continuous heat.

Monday, June 23. No big battle yet along that 1500-mile [Russian] front, but Germany claims penetration of Russian defenses at several points.

Our Poles have received the news with apparent impassivity. Once more their native land is a battleground. Cooler today but not much.

Tuesday, July 1. Just returned from the NAAFI cinema show on the camp. [I saw] an old film, "Follow the Fleet," with Astaire and Rogers, one of my favourites. How I remember those Depression years, when a bright spot in my otherwise fairly drab life was dear Ginger. Hell, in those days I fell madly in love with her, used to pray that one day I would go to the USA and meet her.

This Honiley. Sunbaked and dreary. No radio in our hut, just sweating cursing men with their uniformly neat beds, wooden benches and tables. Up at Baginton, lots of flying these days. Our CO now is a temperamental officer named Da Costa.

Friday, I hitch-hiked home. Spent brief weekend in Cardiff. All night Saturday alongside the Canal with a girl whose name I've forgotten. A brief air raid that morning but otherwise little enemy activity on the home front.

Notation from LFG: No entries for next half year or so have survived.

Notation from LFG on back of a page of the 1941 diary section:
Favorite Pubs, 1940–1942
Kenilworth: Virgin and Castle (where I was given a send-off party, March 1943)
Birmingham: Golden Eagle: Castle (especially its lounge)
Manchester: George and Dragon: Brittania
Closest pub, and most favorite, to Honiley (288 Squadron AACU) was the Tom O'Bedlam, on the main Birmingham-Stratford Road (or Birmingham-Warwick!)

1942

Monday, February 2. Cold and damp after yesterday's heavy snow. Am trying to rid myself of a hangover from last night's binge at the Tom O'Bedlam with Wilson, Twiss and Mansell on the solicitors Robertson and Pearce,* during which beer-swilling orgy I lost my gasmask. If it doesn't show up, I fork out 29 shillings and two pence for a new one. All in all, last night's excursion into the deep snow was hardly worth the effort. But I was the ass who suggested going out in the first place. Big question these days—will Singapore† hold out?

Wednesday, February 4. Was in Coventry on Monday night, saw Humphrey Bogart and Sylvia Sidney in "The Wagons Roll at Night." Story unconvincing, some hackneyed situations. Am on the lookout for "Citizen Kane."

Thursday, February 5. Snow most of the day. Tonight, read another chapter of Churchill's "Great Contemporaries"‡ and waded through the statistics in Barbara Ward's interesting little work, "International Share-out." Ate a supper of liver, mashed potatoes, and onions at the NAAFI. Wrote a letter home, telling them to expect me and ordering a record of the Boston Promenade Orchestra playing "Dance of the Hours."

---

* Robertson and Pearce was a law firm in Cardiff.
† Churchill called the fall of Singapore (the "Gibraltar of the East") to the Japanese as the "worst disaster" in British military history. On February 15, 1942, General Arthur Percival surrendered more than 80,000 British, Indian, Australian, and Malayan troops.
‡ Published in 1937, Churchill's *Great Contemporaries* profiles figures ranging from Franklin Roosevelt, Adolf Hitler, T.E Lawrence, Leon Trotsky to Charlie Chaplin, H.G. Wells, Rudyard Kipling, and George Bernard Shaw. Written in the inter-war years, the essays focus on statecraft and contemporary culture.

Wilson and I discussed plans for our Birmingham visit tomorrow. Plans may be upset by improved weather and resultant flying. At lunchtime Wilson and I went to stores to get new gasmasks—Wilson had lost his as well. We found the place unlocked and absolutely deserted, with gumboots [rain boots], clothing, aircraft spares, etc. quite unguarded, open to petty thievery. Wilson took an old tunic which, though "unserviceable," he will exchange for a new one at the next clothing parade.

Saturday, February 7. Very cold. More snow. Yesterday, Wilson and I hitch-hiked into Birmingham. Ate at the Services Club, browsed in a bookshop, an essential feature of our afternoons out, and bought Everyman's Library editions of, in my case, Vols. 1 and 2 of [Samuel] Pepys "Diary," [Daniel] Defoe's "Moll Flanders," and [Ernest Rehs's] "British Historical and Political Orations, Twelfth to Twentieth Century." A literary treat. Feeling cheerful and content we went to the Paramount Cinema and saw Barbara Stanwyck and Joel McCrea in "The Great Man's Lady."

Night continued without a snag. Wilson doesn't dance so we drank at the Golden Eagle. Headed for New Street Station when our good time ended. Or almost did. We had missed the last train. Fortunately, we availed ourselves of the excellent services of the Voluntary Transport people, whose business it is to help stranded military personnel. We got a ride to Knowle, from which we walked the four miles to camp, made the right excuses at the guardroom, and climbed into our beds at 3 am.

Rommel's armies are reported advancing in Libya, our forces in retreat.[*]

According to the Vicar of Aldershot, "A picture of a woman in the nude, or semi-nude, does encourage immorality among young people." He should see the interior of this hut. Pictures of half-naked beauties all over the walls. And contrary to the vicar's pronouncement, such pictures don't put any ideas in my head that aren't there already.

Sunday, February 8. On the news tonight, soap is to be rationed. Also, I see that a secret court-martial concerning the sinking of the aircraft carrier Ark Royal[†] is to be held. Wonder if the findings will be made public?

---

[*] From June 11, 1940 to February 4, 1943, the Western Desert Campaign (the "Desert War") was fought in the desert sands of northern Egypt and Libya. The Afrika Korps under Field Marshal Erwin Rommel's Afrika Korps pushed the Allied forces eastward back into Egypt.

[†] On November 13, 1941, a torpedo from the German submarine U-81 struck the aircraft carrier, *Ark Royal*, killing one sailor. All crewmembers were evacuated before the ship capsized and sank southeast of Gibraltar. A post-war investigation concluded that a contributing factor in the sinking was inexperience and poor judgment on the part of the damage control party.

Tuesday, February 10. The expected Jap attack on Singapore was launched yesterday. I don't give much for Singapore's chances, considering how easily, without opposition, the Jap invasion barges crossed the Johore Straits [1-3-mile-wide strait between Malay Peninsula and Singapore Island]. Have we no RAF bombers out there at all? Does air bombing have much significant effect at all? The Daily Express seems to doubt it, arguing that if the Germans' offensive against our comparatively tightly-packed industrial area failed, there is even less chance that our air attacks on their widely dispersed centres will do us much good. Personally, I suspect that the huge output of big bombers to bomb Germany was the Air Ministry's response to the popular clamour for revenge. Now, because of the Russian front, the Luftwaffe's attentions on Britain have almost ceased. Our Blitz casualties have been avenged. But we continue to bomb Germany—to what avail? Yet, on reflection, we must continue to maintain a huge striking force, necessary for our coming invasion of Europe and in case Hitler, even yet, contemplates an invasion of Britain.

With Wilson in Birmingham last night, saw "Tom, Dick and Harry." Not a great film but it rekindled my old spark of love for Miss Ginger Rogers.

Monday night, February 16. Quite a weekend just ended. The Scharnhorst, Gneisenau, and Prince Eugene [*Prinz Eugen*], long bottled up in Brest harbor by our bombers, managed to slip out into the English Channel, and with a protective screen of minesweepers, aircraft, E-boats* and destroyers, they steamed northward into safe waters. Our own heavy force of ships and aircraft failed to stop them in large part due to filthy weather. We lost 42 planes in the attempt. Grim news this, coming at the same time as reports of Singapore's last hours, that key base's surrender [February 15, 1942] announced last night by Churchill. I spent most of the weekend in Cardiff, took out Eileen Allaway.

Tuesday February 24. Last Friday attended a large 285 Squadron binge at the Tom O'Bedlam, also present our CO Flt. Lieutenant Da Costa. Next night, dancing in Coventry, and Sunday saw Gary Cooper in "Sergeant York." But today (and tomorrow), much work, fitting a new tailplane, yet another having cracked. Rest of the week, I will be on a backers-up training course.

Funeral in Coventry today of Flt. Lieutenant Mayhew, killed in a crash at Baginton. His father, Sir Basil Mayhew, came from London to

---

* E-boats were fast attack craft of the German navy similar to the U.S. Navy's PT-boats. Heavily armed with machine guns and torpedoes, they could achieve speeds up to 50 mph.

attend the rites. One of our Lysanders flew up over Baginton, and Mayhew's ashes were scattered over the airfield.

Monday, March 2. Total eclipse of the moon tonight. Yesterday into Coventry with Paton to see the RAF Squadronaires. A fine swinging band of former West End musicians. Paton, a bit of a drummer himself, got Jock Cummings, the band's percussionist, to autograph his drumsticks. Wilson, back off leave in Manchester, brings Communist literature clamouring for the ban to be lifted from the Daily Worker.

Thursday, March 5. In Birmingham last night and saw "Citizen Kane." Weird. Orson Welles's film demands concentration, got instead from some in the audience, oddly nervous giggles. But taken all around, this is startlingly new cinema, acting and photography especially notable. Two sergeants took us on the backers-up training. I fired 15 rounds of ammo, threw a hand-grenade, absorbed information on tommy guns and anti-tank guns. Also included some bayonet practice. Present much of the time was an army lieutenant, who seemed contemptuous of the RAF, and clearly felt that its value in "backing-up" the army should invasion come, would be negligible.

The Air Minister, Sir Arthur Sinclair, says our bombing offensive will continue with even greater severity. We are still getting a holiday from the Luftwaffe, thanks in large part to Russian operations.

Tuesday, March 10. [Foreign Secretary] Anthony Eden reveals shocking atrocities by the Japanese in Hong Kong. British soldiers were bound hand and foot then bayoneted to death. Perhaps the worst mistake the Western World ever committed was to teach Japan the arts and crafts of modern warfare.

Bill Twiss and I were in Birmingham yesterday and saw Glenn Miller's orchestra in "Sun Valley Serenade." It features this season's most popular hit "Chattanooga Choo Choo." We ate a good meal at Woolworth's cafeteria. Met up with two nice girls at the Golden Eagle, finally slept (without the girls) in bunks at the Services Club.

Rangoon [Burma] has surrendered to the Japs. Are we witnessing the decline and fall of the British Empire?

Wednesday March 11. It is announced tonight that after Easter, no white bread will be available in Britain. Also, that the maximum penalty for black marketeers is fixed at fifteen years jail. Should be the death penalty.

As Ted Mansell and I walked back from the NAAFI tonight (where we had eaten roast spuds and steak and kidney pie), we talked of Drake's

Drum.* Ted said he believed strongly that the spirit of our warrior ancestors actually does return to infuse us when we are hard-pressed. I told Ted of a story, said to be true, of a bomber pilot who ran into a hot area of flak over enemy territory. The pilot saw a Hampden dive straight into a cone of searchlight beams. The Hampden, thus drawing all the ground fire, enabled the bomber to make its escape. Back at base, the intelligence officer, after hearing the pilot's account, checked and discovered that not only were there no Hampdens in that vicinity, none had been over the continent that night. Quite appropriately, as Ted and I stumbled through the blackout, we reached our barrack, but with a bit of glimmering help from two searchlight beams that slowly crossed the overcast night sky.

Sunday March 15. Spent the afternoon reading newspapers. Big feature, the Java Seas battle† of a fortnight ago. Our losses, twelve allied warships, including the Exeter of River Plate (Graf Spee) fame, were heavy, as were also, however, the Japanese. Also read of a young Home Guard who, disgusted with pikes as weapons, built a perfectly serviceable Tommy gun from spare parts. He was arrested for illegal possession of firearms and fined one pound! Crazy!

Thursday, March 19. Feeling hangoverish from last night's Birmingham visit with Bill Twiss. Saw Tyrone Power and Betty Grable in "A Yank in the RAF." Well-meaning Hollywood nonsense. Then met two girls at the Golden Eagle and probably drank a bit too much.

Wednesday, March 25. Last weekend quite memorable, spent in London with Arthur Wilson. We hitch-hiked down on Saturday, found digs at the Gordon Services Club near Vauxhall Bridge, took a bus to Piccadilly and after a few beers found Jigs Club. We had read about this night-spot in an issue of the Melody Maker. Located on Warndon Street, it was said to be a haunt for London dance musicians when they quit their regular work. Wilson and I failed to get in at first, but on Sunday night were admitted with a nod of approval from the club's white boss. Most males present, including those on the bandstand, were black. As far as we could see in the smoky gloom, we were the only uniformed customers. The music was wonderfully torrid, the hottest live jazz I had

---

* After Sir Francis Drake's death, a legend arose involving a drum with his coat of arms that he supposedly took with him at all times. On his last voyage and near death off the Panamanian coast in 1596, the legend said that Drake ordered the drum to be returned to his home in Devon—Buckland Abbey. If the kingdom were ever threatened and the drum was beaten, he vowed to return from the dead to defend England.

† On February 27, 1942, Allied naval forces were defeated by the Japanese Imperial Navy. The Japanese were then able to occupy the Dutch East Indies.

ever heard. We got into the place on Monday night as well. How we ran short of cash, lied to the RTO [Railway Traffic Officer], and secured railway warrants to head back to camp late Monday night is another story. But Jigs Club is a real find, and I hope the police don't close it before I get another chance to visit. Cops raided the place only last week.

Palm Sunday, March 29. A dull church service on the camp today, the padre stammering and less than forty—WAAFs predominating—in attendance. These Church of England services don't appeal to me, and I couldn't obey the padre's exhortation to "pray for our enemies."

Lots of flying these days by our 285 squadron. We now have four Defiants and an Oxford and work late every night, the weather being consistently fine. I did manage to get out Friday night into Birmingham where I kept a date with Margaret, a pretty blonde eighteen year old.

Shook me to read last Wednesday, in William Hickey's column (Daily Express) that Jigs Club, which had apparently also attracted Hickey, was struck off for serving "nonmembers."

Poignant moment in crowded, sunny Trafalgar Square last Monday morning beginning Warships Week fund-raising. From the bridge of a huge model ship, Lieutenant Esmond Knight, R.N. [Royal Navy], ex-actor, urged the crowd to "Look up, look up, at the monument behind you." Thousands of eyes upturned in the direction of [Admiral Horatio] Nelson atop the column. Knight's eyes, too. But he saw nothing. He was blinded last year in action during the pursuit of the Bismarck.

Tuesday March 31. Saw [Disney's] "Fantasia" in Coventry yesterday after spending the afternoon looking over Kenilworth Castle, to which somber ruin Ted and I had walked the four or five miles from Honiley camp. Took a bus from Kenilworth into Coventry, which also has its share of ruins, thanks to the Luftwaffe.

Easter Sunday, April 5. But no eggs. No hot cross buns. No holiday. Just hard work as Defiants and our single Oxford are pushed into the hangar for periodic inspection. Our sole serviceable Defiant flew most of today between heavy April showers. I spent this afternoon cramped in a painful position within a Defiant fuselage, aft of the front cockpit, my legs in Boulton and Paul's one-time hush-hush gun turret. Attachments and fittings dug into my torso, an air-bottle containing 200 pounds per square inch pressure hung a couple of inches above my head. I cursed sweated, and groaned. Wilson prevented anyone from revolving the turret, which would have torn my body in half, grinned and made humourous remarks. Flt. Lieutenant Da Costa prowled around the hangar, his scowling face bearing a scarcely healed scar, result of his Canadian WAAF girlfriend's apparently unintentional assault. In fun it seems, she threw a glass of water at him. The glass went with the water and gashed his face.

Don writes from a camp near Stratford-on-Avon that he is "fed up with this bastard war." Last night, I went with a crowd to the Tom O'Bedlam. Had a good time singing and drinking, but on the 2½ miles walk back I got thoroughly rain-soaked.

Wednesday, April 15. Alternate days we work until 9 or 10 pm, other days until 5 pm. One half-day free each week. The weather continues fine and we are short of men.

Lots of fresh grumbling by civilians following government's announcement that tobacco, cigarettes, beer will cost more.

Shocking accident last week on Salisbury Plain when a Hurricane, instead of diving as planned on an enclosure full of dummies, swooped instead at a booth filled with Army and Home Guard officers. The plane's machine guns killed at least 25 of them.* I hope for a week's leave beginning next Monday.

Wednesday, April 22. Instead of leave, yesterday I was one of a party driven to an anti-aircraft gun emplacement near Birmingham. The idea was Flight Lt. Da Costa's. The weather turning bad, he thought it a good opportunity for us personnel of 285 squadron pilots as well as ground staff, to get a close-up look at the guns and soldiers for whose practice we fly our aircraft. We were shown over four big Armstrong Vickers batteries, watched the firing teams at work, had the predictor, range-finders, and other complicated systems explained to us. The technicalities are pretty awesome and mostly beyond our comprehension. But we were well received, as sort of guests, and served tea. Chatting with a sergeant, I learned that the men, and ATS woment get only one night free in ten, and that recently they were given the stupid order to polish all the brasswork on the guns, this for a visit by the Duke of Kent [Prince George, the King's younger brother]. Another source of grousing are the route marches the gunners have to make after a long day's practicing on the guns. Strikes me the Army authorities seem sometimes to go out of their way to create apathy and dampen patriotic ardor.

---

* On April 18, six Hurricanes and six Spitfires were demonstrating ground support operations at a British Army training ground on Salisbury Plain in Wiltshire. The event, unfortunately conducted in hazy conditions, was a dress rehearsal for an upcoming visit by Winston Churchill and General George Marshall, Chief of Staff of the U.S. Army. Five of the Hurricanes hit the correct targets—several armored vehicles and mock tanks. The pilot of the sixth Hurricane mistakenly opened fire on the spectators, killing 25 and wounding 71.

† The Auxiliary Territorial Service (ATS) was the women's branch of the British Army during World War II.

Our own work schedule has resumed. We are still short-handed. Wilson is on leave, two more are serving a 28-day prison sentence for stealing a wheel from a flight-sergeant's car. I worked until 9 last night, 8 tonight, will work yet again tomorrow night—but Monday I hope to go on leave.

Wonder which historic town will be bombed tonight? When we bombed Rostock [port city in northeastern Germany] recently, Hitler said we deliberately destroyed that city's historic buildings. So as reprisals, his planes have struck twice at Bath, then attacked Norwich, and last night hit another cathedral town, York. The latter raid cost the Luftwaffe five of the 20 bombers. I suppose Stratford-on-Avon and Warwick are the closest places of historical significance to this camp. Kenilworth, with its crumbling Elizabethan-era castle, is nearer still but smaller, and its centre lies already shattered by a misdirected German aerial mine.

We share this RAF station with Boston Havocs and Hawker Hurricanes. Night fighter squadrons, that were here when our little outfit arrived last year, have since departed for overseas and according to news filtering back to us one of them, 605 Squadron, was headed for Singapore, redirected to Java when Singapore fell, but met with bad luck anyway by getting caught up in the Japanese invasion. Most personnel were killed, wounded, or taken prisoner.

Wednesday, May 13. Yesterday, returned from seven days' leave. Saw Eileen Allaway a few times. Also bought a nice new blue civilian suit for three guineas. Populace appeared, I thought, more optimistic than usual, buoyed, I suppose, by Churchill's latest speech* in which he warned Hitler not to start using gas. My moments with Eileen were of little account for I have a rival, a sailor who has visited New York, among other romantic places, and who presented Eileen with such niceties as a powder compact embossed with the Statue of Liberty. I can't compete with that sort of thing so many of my hours in Cardiff were spent alone. Anyway, no air raids occurred to spoil my leave, and I can't say I'm glad to be back at camp.

Tuesday, May 19. Wilson, Twiss, and I went into Birmingham the other night, saw and enjoyed Mickey Rooney and Judy Garland in "Babes on Broadway."

Russians are slowed on the Kharkov front and the Nazis in their Kerch offensive [peninsula on eastern side of Crimea].

---

* In a radio broadcast on May 12, 1942, Churchill warned Hitler that if he deployed chemical weapons against the Russians, the RAF would retaliate by using poison gas on Germany.

Sunday, May 24. Quite some fuss in today's papers over the War Office order that Army training instructors must stop saying or doing anything designed to stir bloodlust in the hearts and minds of trainees. Officers and NCOs must quit shouting such things as "Kill that Hun," "Get the bastard," "Stick your bayonet in his guts," etc. Well, maybe they can use such utterances in order to evoke the required "offensive spirit," but such reported techniques as daubing men with sheep's blood, [and] marching them to a slaughter-house so they can get used to the sight and smell of gore must henceforth cease.

Wednesday, May 27. 8:30 pm. According to the 6 o'clock news, the lid has blown off in Libya and it's an Axis offensive, not ours.

Sam Kirvin, married and over thirty, learns that he is on PWR's [orders] for overseas posting. We hear many from our HQ, at Wrexham, are on the boat! One of our armourers recently departed on a "hush hush" trip, he has returned and tells us he and many other armourers from all over were rushed to a northeastern port where lay the U.S. Aircraft carrier Wasp. The men were engaged replacing guns with cannon on Spitfires the Wasp carries. One of the carrier's officers was recognized as Douglas Fairbanks, Jr.* The Wasp sailed off for Malta.

I have a huge boil on my leg.

Saturday, May 30. With Wilson in Birmingham last Thursday night. Missed the last train by five minutes and hitch-hiked fourteen miles in the moonlight. We got into camp precisely 74 minutes late, as recorded by an over-officious SP. Our CO, Tony Da Costa, as disgusted as we were by the consequent waste of time and paperwork over a trivial charge, merely admonished us.

Big battles in Libya. In Russia, the Red Army is furiously shelling Von Bock's forces entrenched in Kharkov. A terror wave sweeping Czechoslovakia in the wake of an unsuccessful assassination attempt on "Butcher Hedrick [Reinhard Heydrich]."†

I've been reading "Anzacs in Battle" about the Australians and New Zealanders at war. I've managed to keep up some good reading despite circumstances. Of course, the inevitable paperbacked lurid novels come my way. Is there a barrack-room in all England that hasn't seen a copy of "No Orchids for Miss Blandish?" James Hadley Chase's latest is

---

* The famed Hollywood actor, as an officer in the U.S. Navy Reserve, was aboard USS *Wasp* delivering British aircraft destined for embattled Malta.

† On May 27, 1942, Reinhard Heydrich, de facto Nazi ruler of occupied Czechoslovakia, was wounded in an attack planned and executed by the Czech government-in-exile. He died of his injuries on June 4. His death led to a wave of reprisals by SS troops, including the destruction of villages and the mass killing of civilians.

something called "Lady, Don't Turn Over." Another is "Road Floozie" in which a truck driver seduces a half-drunk girl and says, as he fumbles beneath her dress. "Bit sheeted up this end, aren't you honey?" To which she sleepily retorts, "Take 'em off."

But I hear that author Chase (an ex–RAF pilot officer?) and his publishers were fined last week for producing indecent material.

Tuesday, June 2. On Saturday there occurred history's biggest air raid—1036 bombers attacked Cologne.* Last night another four-figure raid was mounted with Essex† the target. A few German planes carried out a Baedeker raid on Canterbury.‡ From the two big raids, we lost 79 bombers, a loss of some 500 men. Tragic, all this killing. Churchill threatens continued heavy air attacks on German cities. They are justified only if they shorten this war.

Weather here is very warm. Not much work, we have only one machine serviceable. 1456 and 257 Squadrons (Havocs and Hurricanes) leave this weekend, are staging a dance tomorrow night—with free refreshments ("no glasses, bring your own mugs").

Thursday, June 4. Continued heat wave. In Czechoslovakia, the man once described as the "mildest man who ever cut a throat," Heydrick [Heydrich] died "in great pain," the papers say. But the Nazis are wreaking vengeance, killing hundreds of Czechs. Our Home Secretary [Herbert Morrison] refuses to lift the ban on the publication of the Daily Worker, also refuses to retract his warning to the Daily Mirror. The squadron farewell dance last night was a huge success. Hundreds of airmen and WAAFs crowded into the dining hall with mugs, for an orgy of drinking and eating of sandwiches and Swiss rolls. The floor was soon slippery with spilled beer and crushed food, the smoke-filled air vibrating to joyous chatter and shrieks of laughter.

Sunday, June 7. On the way back from the Tom O'Bedlam last night, an ugly situation developed involving three civilians, one of them claiming

---

* On May 30–31, 1942, Bomber Command of the RAF conducted the first "thousand-bomber raid" in which 1,047 aircraft attacked Cologne, dropping 1,455 tons of ordnance on the city. More than 3,000 buildings were destroyed and another 9,000 damaged. One aim of the raid was to overwhelm the Cologne fire brigades and cause fires similar to those inflicted on London by the Luftwaffe during the Blitz.

† Essex is a county in southeast England between London and the North Sea.

‡ The Baedeker raids were carried out by the Luftwaffe on English cities. The name came from Baedeker, a series of German tourist guidebooks containing maps that highlighted designated bombing targets. The raids were in response to the RAF's bombing offensive, which began with the bombing of Lübeck in March 1942. The German aim was to force the RAF to reduce attacks on German cities. To increase the effect on civilian life, targets were chosen for their cultural and historical significance. The Baedeker raids began in late April 1942, and wound down by the end of May.

to be a wing commander in mufti, a dozen Irish workmen and four airmen including myself. All involved had had more than a little to drink. Setting was a lonely country lane, night was sultry, thundery. A brawl was only narrowly averted. Those three civilians strike me, on reflection, of being a Fifth Columnist.

Tuesday, June 9. Often justifiably criticized, the NAAFI can sometimes put up a good show, as here at Honiley. I've just enjoyed a meal of two sausages, fried onions, Yorkshire pudding and chips, followed by an apple tart and custard, bread and butter, cup of tea, all for only eleven pence.

In London an unexploded bomb hidden beneath homes near the Elephant and Castle [Underground train station in southeast London] exploded and killed eighteen people including children.

I went to the dentist this afternoon, had two teeth drilled and filled.

Thursday, June 11. Startling announcement on tonight's radio of the Anglo-Russian Treaty and the well-kept secret of Molotov's* London and Washington visits. How fervently Wilson and I agreed, as we listened to his hut's wireless, with Lloyd George [elder statesman] when he said that had we entered into a close collaboration with Soviet Russia ten years ago, this war might never have been. The pact is good for twenty years. We are treated to the amazing spectacle of Churchill and Stalin exchanging good wishes, King George VI cordially greeting President Kalinin† of the Soviet Union, and of Molotov personally calling on the King! Well, I am all for this. I hope and believe that Roosevelt, Churchill, and Stalin, after the fighting stops, will do their utmost to outlaw for all time the attempted solution of international problems by resort to war.

And the time for a Second Front seems close. Eden tonight promised it for some time this year. I believe it is a matter of weeks away. Several members of this outfit are standing by for overseas posting. For France? If so, Wilson and I want to be among them.

Sunday, June 14. 8:30 pm. A quiet, warm, hazy day ending with a distant rumble of thunder. Out of the clouds yesterday swooped a lone Heinkel which flew low over Leamington and dropped three bombs on Lockheed Automotive Works, injuring some female employees. I was, just then, on my way to Coventry where I spent the afternoon, mostly at

---

* Vyacheslav Mikhailovich Molotov served as the Soviet Minister of Foreign Affairs from 1939 to 1949 and from 1953 to 1956.
† Mikhail Ivanovich Kalinin was the Soviet Union's formal head of state from 1919 to 1946.

a cinema—Robert Young in "H.M. Pulham, Esq.," based on the John P. Marquand novel (which I haven't read).

Corporal Paul Gibson, orphan but far from penniless, leaves tomorrow for a pilot's course. Until his mother died last autumn, Paul was pretty much tied to her apron-strings then, though, he came under the pernicious influence of Eric Hobson (now overseas), a caddish darling of the ladies. Little by little, this mob is disintegrating. Among the original diehards of 9 Group Flight still remaining are Wilson, Twiss, Valentine, Protheroe, Bruchez, Mansell, Paton, Prior, Wrentmore, and myself. Dugmore is still NCO in command, Da Costa is in hospital having that facial scar patched up, and P/O [pilot officer] Ben Lynes is acting CO.

Thumbline sketches: Bruchez ("I say wipe out every bastard German"); Ted Mansell (clerk on Washington, Durham, Council); Wrentmore (illiterate Welshman, dance-mad); Valentine (illiterate Londoner, dance-mad and without a clue what we are in the war for); Prior (fat, greedy Scot); Paton (orphan and would-be Gene Krupa); Protheroe (Welsh, sex-crazy, twice VD victim); Wilson and Twiss: book-lovers, music-lovers (especially jazz), film fans, interested in politics, possessors of a crazy sense of humor—my two best friends.

Wednesday, July 1. On leave last week in Cardiff, spent two pleasant evenings with a pretty red-head named Pat Morris, who works in a cake shop on Clifton Street. Took her dancing and for a ramble in the country side. She failed to keep a third date because, I subsequently learned to my relief, her sister had injured a leg accidentally, and Pat, in the absence of their mother, was required to act as nurse.

Saw the film "Johnny Eager" with Robert Taylor, a luscious Lana Turner, but acting honours go to Van Heflin, a newcomer.

In pubs I heard a lot of depressed talk concerning our defeats in Libya, fall of Tobruk,* etc. Gloom not lifted even by news of another 1000 bomber raid—this time on Bremen [northwest Germany]. But everyone applauds the defenders of Sevastopol [Crimean port city], and tributes to Russia formed much of the speeches at an open-air rally outside Cardiff City Hall. Chief speaker was Arthur Horner, chief of Welsh mineworkers union, and a Communist who made the expected demands for a Second Front. The Hammer and Sickle [Soviet] flag flew alongside the Union Jack, and the rally ended with renditions of the Welsh, British, and Soviet national anthems.

---

* On June 21, 1942, the 34,000-man British garrison at Tobruk, Libya, surrendered to Erwin Rommel's combined Italian-German force. This was one of the worst British defeats of the war.

Not long ago, we received various items of clothing knitted by American well-wishers, whose names and addresses were attached. My randomly picked gift was a pair of woolen stockings. I wrote a thank you letter, and the result is a letter from a 22-year-old Helen Kidwell. She is a secretary at the U.S. Navy Department, and she tells me, "You write things that are so well-thought!"

"William Hickey" my favourite (Daily Express) columnist, proves to be Tom Driberg, and he is now a member of parliament, having won the Maldon bye-election. Beaverbrook's Daily Express takes pains to declare that "we do not agree with the political views of Mr. Driberg," and "Hickey" replies in that paper that he disagrees with many of its opinions.

Sunday night at home, my windows shook to the sound of bombs and gunfire, mostly across the Bristol Channel. Our Cardiff guns opened up as well. I got out of bed, stumbled downstairs in the dark followed by Ma, and headed out back to the air raid shelter. The old man stayed in bed. So should I have, for there was no danger. The target was Weston-Super-Mare or Bristol, it turned out. But how the hell was I supposed to know?

Sunday, July 5. Wilson and I read "How Green Was My Valley" a year or so ago. Now we have seen the film version. Hollywood's version, even with John Ford directing, of Richard Llewellyn's best seller, might have been a disaster. Far from it. Despite some uncertainty with accents, the film is emotionally gripping with excellent performances from Walter Pidgeon, Maureen O'Hara, and especially Donald Crisp as the father, and Roddy McDowell, the young Hugh Morgan. Will see this film—and read this book—again.

The Germans are only 60 miles from the Nile. And in Russia they [Germans] have taken Sevastapol. Had a strange letter from—Pat [Morris], accusing me of being married. She says she knows my wife by sight! I've written asking her what my "wife" looks like and do I have any children? After all, I should know...

To continue a 30-hour inspection on a Boulton and Paul Defiant, I needed a torch [flashlight]. We have torches and 4-volt batteries. But the bulbs are 2-volt, each lasting scarcely three minutes before burning out. I complained to Sergeant Dugmore. "For Pete's sake, hasn't Main Stores any 3- or 4-volt bulbs?" All Dugmore could do was shrug. Somewhere, I suppose, on some RAF station, men are in a similar dilemma, only with 2-volt batteries and 4-volt bulbs.

Another example of silliness—. As "punishment" for some trivial offence, Underwood was taken off maintenance work and told to walk around the airfield perimeter carrying a parachute! He did so and decided to take the rest of the morning off! Valuable man-hours wasted! And it seems there had been some misunderstanding, Underwood wrongly charged so he received a half apology from our C.O., Tony Da Costa.

Monday, July 13. Russia's position precarious. Now, more than ever, appears need for a Second Front. I think it will come before winter, and I hope I'm in on it. From Pat—"My informant is sure you are married. She has letters of yours—you were out with her nine months ago."

A Beaufighter from this station crashed into an Insane Asylum six miles from here. The plane's two occupants were killed, no one in the mental home hurt. Am reading John Buchan's "Greenmantle."

Tuesday, July 14. Cool, showery. Letter from home says Bridgend Hospital was hit in a recent air raid.

Friday, July 17. 10:30 pm. Yesterday, Leamington received another surprise visit from the Luftwaffe—a Dornier 217 bombed Lockheed's, killing four. Today, Ted Mansell and I were in that same attractive town, saw Fred Astaire and Rita Hayworth in "You'll Never Get Rich!" Story frail, but Fred's footwork and Rita's curves are good enough for me.

Thursday, July 23. Cardiff.

A sleepy afternoon. On the carpet in front of the fireplace, a black kitten drowsing. Clock ticking. Radio lazily playing Tchaikovsky. On the table "How Green Was My Valley," waiting for me to take around to Pat Morris when her shop shuts at 5 pm. I saw her yesterday morning, proved to her that I wasn't married. It seems a girl I once knew, an ex-barmaid now ATS, to whom I wrote one letter and never did take out, told Pat I had a wife and child.

Saturday, July 25. Returned to camp yesterday morning after an all-night train journey. Yesterday afternoon Ted Mansell, Bill Twiss, and I took a momentous step. We each made out an application for overseas service. Our CO, Tony Da Costa, spent most of an hour trying to talk us out of it. Comical really, a commanding officer attempting to discourage his men from volunteering.

The Second Front is bound to open soon before Russia collapses—already the Germans are in Rostov and threatening Stalingrad. Wilson is also keen on getting involved in the Second Front but thinks volunteering now for overseas service might bring a posting to the Far East instead. Wilson has already sought to get on a pilot's course, but is discouraged by the lack of response. Personally, I wouldn't mind a posting to South Africa, even India, or Canada, especially Canada.

Now I'm wondering if I've done the right thing.

Sunday, July 26. While Russians are dying by the thousands, defending their homeland, here in Britain a controversy rages over whether sentimental love songs via the BBC shouldn't be replaced with more zestful martial airs. Personally, I'd like to hear a little more classical music, but generally this is a broadcast on the BBC Home program, and the majority of my hut-mates prefer dance bands or atrocious "Old Mother Riley"* shows. So much dance music these days tends to bore me, I don't get enough real jazz.

A lot of reports lately of Yanks and British soldiers brawling with each other. Some of the stories are believed untrue and spread by Fifth Columnists. Still, most of the airmen I meet do not seem to like Americans. Envy and jealously are the reasons, I suspect when Americans, so much better paid than their uniformed English counterparts, are seen walking with English girls.†

Monday, July 27. Hamburg well and truly battered last night. Moonlight illuminated the city as RAF bombers dropped 180,000 incendiaries first, then when vast areas of the seaport were on fire, hundreds of tons of high explosives. We lost 29 aircraft.

Here at the odd hour of 7 am, some German bombers made scattered "breakfast" raids. Our sirens sounded, our Beaufighters took off in cloud and pouring rain, returning—as I headed for work in the hangars—without having found a single bomber. One of the Beaufighters crashed a few miles away, killing its crew.

Tuesday, July 28. After midnight last night, 70 German aircraft (or 200 if Goebbels is to be believed) flew over different parts of the country, heavy attacks on Birmingham. Our sirens joined others at 2:10 am, and as the wailing died away, the night sky throbbed with the sound of the bombers' engines. Beaufighters took off and all the AA guns in this neighborhood banged away. My bed trembled, the very hut seemed to shiver with every roar of gunfire or thud of distant bombs. Ted Mansell and I, sleep being impossible, stepped outside the hut and watched the flashing and fitful glow and sky-high bursts of flame, all in the direction of Birmingham. Occasionally we could see a string of fiery blobs, like fairy lights, suspended above the city. The noise kept up long after we returned to our beds. The camp loudspeaker system announced in quite

---

* Old Mother Riley, a fictional Irish washerwoman, was portrayed by Arthur Lucan. His daughter was played by Lucan's wife, Kiitty McShane. From 1934 to 1954, the couple performed in music halls and theaters, broadcast on British radio, and appeared in films.

† A popular expression at the time among British servicemen, when confronted with increasing competition by arriving U.S. troops was "overpaid, oversexed, and over here."

unemotional tones that "a Beaufighter from this station has shot down one enemy bomber." (I heard it since it fell six miles from here. And that a total of eight were destroyed.) Cox came in late, said a "time bomb" on the railway had held up his train, that earlier he'd been busy extinguishing incendiaries. Paton, returning from Birmingham, said a bomb exploded right near the Services Club where he was spending the night.

Thursday, July 30. Yesterday I was informed of my promotion to the rank of corporal. This is probably due to my long service and First Lt. Da Costa's recommendations. And it won't alter my attitude towards friends of lesser rank. What I most appreciate, anyway, is the increase in pay. And since my promotion is with effect from February 1, I can expect a few quid in back pay.

Last night another noisy raid lasting two hours, the target again Birmingham. Throughout the bump and thunder of explosions, cattle in nearby fields lowed continually. I heard someone on night duty whistling the "Lincolnshire Poacher [folk song]," and uneasily I dozed....

Saturday, August 1. Much work today, corporal or no corporal. Change oleo-leg [strut on landing gear] on a Defiant and begin a 30-hour inspection on an Oxford. Hot, sweaty, unglamourous work. But essential. Last night, a thousand bombers struck at Dusseldorf. Thirty failed to return.

Tuesday, August 4. Photos in the press show great damage to Dusseldorf, bombed by 700 aircraft.

I see the Australian troops have a pay increase. Debate on British army pay and allowances will occur when Parliament reassembles, and MPs are expected to demand higher pay, more generous family allowances.

The old man writes that he agrees "How Green Was My Valley" is one of the best films, and also recommends "Reap the Wild Wind." With Ma, he is getting to be quite a movie fan.

Thursday, August 6. In the NAAFI an hour ago, I ate kidneys on fried bread, sausage, potatoes, jam tart and custard. Nice, now, to lie in bed listening to dramatized stories from the war fronts.

The military has quickly followed on Herbert Morrison's announcement that civilians need not carry their gasmasks everywhere. We are now told ours are only to be carried during leave periods longer than 24 hours. Thank heaven! The bulky, clumsy things thud against you should you run, are easily left behind in pubs, and knock people's hats off when you grope for your seat in the cinema. More of a nuisance than they are worth.

Saturday, August 8. Clocks turned back one hour. Weather far from summerlike, is cold and it's raining. Last night in Birmingham, Bill Twiss and I took a tramcar out of the town centre to the Burnt Oak pub. After six pints, enough to make me drunk, we went to a dance hall where we met two girls whom we later took home. I was quite befuddled and had, quite unromantically, to interrupt my blackout love-making with an alcoholic vomit. All very regrettable. But I walked with her through the vast Bournville* estate whose atmosphere is heavy with the smell of chocolate. The girl is an ex-employee of Bournville's and she praised the amenities—educational programs, social recreation, swimming pools, and golf links—provided for the firm's workers. If only all employers were so considerate. Walking back towards Birmingham at about 1 am (later caught a taxicab). I thought I saw a ghost, at least a white-faced motionless woman, at a bombed house. Can't say for sure— after all, I *had* been drinking. I was still walking when an air raid siren sounded, but the all-clear came only fifteen minutes later. Dozed at New Street Station amid the clatter and hiss of trolleys and locomotives' steam. Reached Berkwell Station, in pouring rain, and rejoined Bill Twiss there, agreeing with him that while we'd had a good night, what future girlfriends we acquire must live closer to Birmingham's town centre.

Sunday, August 9. [Mahatma] Gandhi, his wife [Kasturba], [Jawaharlal] Nehru and other Indian leaders arrested yesterday.† Riots throughout India. Gandhi's campaign to free India of British rule, stepped up at this point, amounts to a stab-in-the-back for British, American, Chinese, and Indian troops defending his country against the Japanese.

American troops have landed in the Solomons.‡

Thursday, August 13. 10 pm. Room is rather quiet. The radio is turned off, and most chaps are over in the concert/dance hall—where I would be, drinking if not dancing, were it not for being too tired: only half an hour ago finished work with Wilson. Also, there is a blonde WAAF I don't want to meet now, but with whom I have a date tomorrow night.

---

  * Bournville is a model village on the southwest side of Birmingham founded by the Cadbury family for its employees and best known for its association with the chocolate industry.

  † Mahatma Gandhi and Jawaharlal Nehru as senior members of the Indian Congress Party, worked tirelessly for Indian independence. On August 8, 1942, the Congress Party passed the so-called "Quit India" resolution. The entire Congress working committee, which drafted the resolution, was arrested and imprisoned, including Gandhi and Nehru.

  ‡ U.S. Marines landed on Guadalcanal in the Solomon Islands on August 7, 1942. The military campaign lasted until early February 1943 and ended in an American victory.

Her name is Pat and I met her on the bus back from Coventry where I saw a good film (George Raft in "Broadway") and downed a few beers in the Smithfield. Locals talking war and politics.

Two new flight mechanics (Airframe) posted here just came off an MSFU [Merchant Ship Fighter Unit]. What this consists of is a single Hawker Hurricane carried by the ship and catapulted off it when German aircraft are about. Whatever the outcome of any encounter, the Hurricane, of course, cannot return to the ship. If land is near enough, its pilot sets course accordingly. Otherwise, he bales out near enough, hopefully to be picked up by the ship (or any other, assuming a convoy). Assigned to each ship are a fitter, rigger, radio-man, and armourer. Other than daily inspections, they have nothing to do—and nothing at all, of course, after the Hurricane is catapulted aloft for it never comes back. But at least they have the knowledge or feeling that theirs is a useful duty. Also, they get sea travel to distant lands. For some time, Wilson and I have contemplated trying to get on this MSFU program. One of the new arrivals here has been to Gibraltar, to Canada (with an 18-day stay at Halifax), and to Russia. This last trip provided action, when Junkers 88s and Heinkels attacked the convoy. The Hurricane took off and did so well that its pilot was subsequently awarded a Distinguished Flying Cross. But, relates the newcomer, this didn't save the ship which was hit and sunk. He and others of the crew were picked up and landed at Murmansk [Russian port city near Barents Sea], where "there were three cinemas. I went to one, couldn't understand any of the talking. Anyway, it all seemed propaganda. We lived for three weeks on black bread and soup—it was spring, the snow just melting." On the return voyage from Murmansk, his ship was for the most part shielded by thick fog. Both these fellows want to get back on the MSFU. Wouldn't mind a crack at this myself.

Tuesday, August 18. 9 pm. At seven last night in a pub off Piccadilly, Manchester, I beamed at Bill Twiss because a hunch of mine had proven correct. Churchill is in Moscow for a meeting with Stalin. Doubtless their main topic was the [opening of the] Second Front, which surely can't be far off now.

Manchester still has lots of pretty girls. And most of the city's bomb ruins are cleared away. The Twisses made me really at home, fed me good Lancashire cooking. I met exuberant, ginger, Ethel Twiss. And Saturday night, recaptured memories at the noisy George and Dragon, the Piccadilly Bar, and the Britannia. Had the shock of my life as I saw May, of whom I was so fond two years ago—until learning that she was married. Now we were again together. Billy was with her sister. May said she would tell me the whole story next night at the Brit. But Bill and I arrived late. No sign of May.

We left for the Oxford Hotel, which was crammed with brightly-clad "good time girls," prostitutes, and genuine war-workers, Tommies, RAF types, drawling Americans. (Pubs and movies crowded. Does anyone go to church in Manchester these Sundays?)

All in all, a lively weekend. And though seeing May again stirred some of that old feeling, it wasn't as strong as in those tense and strange summer days of 1940.

Friday, August 21. The big Dieppe raid* fills today's newspapers. Most people thought at first it was the Second Front. But evidently a dress rehearsal. A costly one, by all accounts, with heavy losses, especially among the Canadians.

Our little outfit has grown—into a Wing, we do night-flying, have more men and aircraft. Arranging shifts gives our C.O. Da Costa a headache. Well, next week he will marry a Canadian WAAF, and on that day, the Army will have to do without our cooperation in AA practice for our entire staff will make it a holiday.

Tuesday, August 25. Yesterday morning at a little village church three miles from here, Army and RAF officers, WAAFs, and a dozen flying and non-flying members of No. 285 Squadron attended Fl. Lt Tony Da Costa's wedding. Afterwards, outside the church, an officer fired two Verey pistol cartridges into the cloudy sky. Upon this prearranged signal, four Beaufighters thundered low in repeated dives, saluting the newly-weds and exciting elderly villagers. As Tony and his Canadian bride scampered for their car, we threw rice at them. When they had left, the rest of us went into Birmingham with the Australian Pilot Officer Milne, who had been given five pounds by Da Costa to buy us beer. We all had a hectic afternoon and night, during which certain odd incidents happened. But more on this anon.

Thursday, August 27. My birthday. Twenty-four. Worked like hell most of the day in blazing heat.

Country mourns tragic death of the Duke of Kent, killed with fifteen others when the Sunderland flying boat, aboard which he was a

---

* On August 19, 1942, the Allies launched a major raid on the French coastal port of Dieppe. The assault was designed to test the Allies' ability to launch amphibious assaults against "Fortress Europe." The raid was a disaster with more than 900 Canadian soldiers killed, and thousands more wounded and taken prisoner. The seriously wounded were taken to local hospitals. The other captured Canadians were sent on cattle cars to POW camps in Mülhausen, Molsdorf, Eichstät and Lamsdorf. Despite the disaster on the beach, the raid provided valuable lessons for subsequent Allied amphibious assaults on Africa, Italy, and Normandy.

passenger, crashed in Scotland [August 25, 1942]. Germans making headway in Stalingrad.

Sunday, August 30. 8:30 pm. My left arm swollen and painful, resulting from this afternoon's inoculation. I also received a medical, and my paybook is now stamped "Fit, O.S." meaning I'm okay for overseas service.

Saw "Saboteur" in Birmingham last night with Bill Twiss. Film has the, by now, familiar Hitchcock ingredients, but they still make for suspenseful entertainment.

Sunday night. Hope there is no night-flying scheduled for my arm is still sore.

Good to read that the Russians have checked [Field Marshal Fedor] von Bock at Stalingrad.

But the RAF lost thirty bombers in Friday night's raid on Nuremberg. Damn! We have to wait until 8 to see if there is any flying....

Tuesday, September 1. Here at Honiley, a big security drive is under way. It seems a lot of careless talk has crept into letters home from many of the personnel here. At a special gathering of the lot of us yesterday afternoon in the concert hall, this camp's CO read extracts from some. The names of the writers were not disclosed, but they were in the audience no doubt, and can expect disciplinary action. The loose talk concerned bombing (exaggerated accounts for the most part) and arrivals or departures of individuals and aircraft. CO warns that if this continues, the names of the offenders will be read out. He has also arranged for compulsory attendance at showings of the film "Next of Kin." At a follow-up lecture this evening, a security officer revealed that when a Focke Wulf was recently forced down intact and promptly locked away for secret inspection, 386 letters from people at that airfield disclosed the fact to civilians.

Note by LFG (March 1992 on completing this copy)

I probably continued to keep a diary of sorts but if so, it has long been lost. It would have covered the latter part of 1942 into 1943, during which months I remained at Honiley. Bill Twiss was posted overseas—to India, I later learned. My friendship with Arthur Wilson continued until, in April 1943, I was posted overseas. That month found me in Blackpool—blustery, the wind blowing surf and spray across the seafront promenade, soaking the tramcars. Received overseas kit at Blackpool, eventually we were herded aboard a slow-moving train to Glasgow, then onto a ship, Boissevain,* *a Dutch vessel with Javanese crew. A convoy*

---

* The Dutch liner MS *Boissevain*, under the control of the Dutch government in exile, was converted into a troop transport ship before sailing on a multitude of convoys to Australia, New Zealand, and North Africa.

formed and after a day or two, we were out in the North Atlantic—not bound west, as I had tremulously hoped, for Canada, but south—for the Mediterranean and North Africa.

Celebrated Easter 1943 afloat (actually Palm Sunday). Our convoy was perhaps attacked while passing through the Mediterranean—there was certainly some gunfire from some of the escort ships. But arrived safely off Oran. At an American camp, we were introduced to peanut butter and bartering with GIs just back from the Tunisian battlefront. I (improperly) swapped my RAF issue jack-knife for a pair of captured German binoculars. By train then via the French Foreign Legion base at Sidi Bel Abbes (where we drank and sang with Russian legionnaires) over the Little Atlas [mountains] to Fez (French Morocco) and by truck to the airfield at Ras el Ma.* Here we set up a staging post for aircraft headed to the battle zones. But not long afterward, we left the Moroccan interior—Fez, Meknes—for a coastal location, Rabat-Salé,† close to the Moroccan capital and not far from Casablanca. (My surviving diary picks up at April 1944.)

1944

Sunday, April 9, 1944. Easter Sunday. Sale-Rabat, Morocco

I recall last Easter spent in a crowded cattle-truck clanking through gullies, across plains, over mountains, past mud huts from which little Moroccan kids emerged yelling and giving the V-sign. We had left Oran, our port of disembarkation, and the weather was wet and cold.

Since the present 24-hour shift routine began, I've had more time to read and write. Nearly finished "Kings Row" [Henry Bellamann] and Graham Greene's "Brighton Rock." In the past three days over twenty [B-24] Liberators have flown in from Newfoundland or the Azores. Managed to get some American magazines—Collier's, Saturday Evening Post, and Time out of them.

We were recently entertained by a British concert party featuring Leslie Henson and Hermione Baddeley, with some leggy chorus girls. The show was a rousing success and, for once, nobody booed our commanding officer.

---

* The airfield served as a support facility for the port, allowing Allied aircraft to be assembled and prepared for combat duty, then flown from the airstrip as replacements during the North African Campaign.

† The walled city of Salé, located in northwestern Morocco, is situated on the right bank of the Bou Regreg River, opposite Rabat.

Wednesday, April 12. Exactly a year ago, I boarded the train at Blackpool and twenty-four hours later the ex–Dutch vessel Boissevain in the Clyde. Disgusted with its past policies and leadership, I shan't attend a meeting tonight for forming a new Welfare Committee. We need a new Welfare Office. I hear we are getting a new CO.

Under the watchful eyes of an S.P., an army sergeant, and orderly sergeant, half a dozen unshaven and dull-eyed German prisoners filed into the dining hall this evening as I was finishing late supper. They received the same dishes as did our chaps, ate them hungrily, and spoke very little. They are en route for England and POW camps.

Friday, April 14. Reading J.B. Priestley's "Daylight on Saturday," relaxed against the wall of a Nissen hut, and stripped to the waist, the sunshine being warm though tempered by an Atlantic breeze. The only arriving aircraft to disrupt the lazy afternoon were three Liberators. Little else to be heard other than the sound of bat meeting ball as a few of the lads played cricket.

In Rabat yesterday, I finished up at the Café Coq d'Or, a rather low dive converted into sort of a club for British and American troops. Drums, accordion, and saxophone provided—music?

Monday, April 17. Can't believe all the stories about the shooting affair in Rabat's Medina (native quarter) last night. It seems the British airman had refused to obey French police who ordered him out of the area. Some say he pulled a gun first. Anyway, the police shot him in the leg and/or stomach, not fatally.

Much laughter in Servicing Flight yesterday over the two documents which the parents of Walter Hughes, who is in my refueling party, received from the York city government and sent out to him. They are addressed to him, the first asking why he has failed to carry out his fire-watching duties, the other, an ultimatum ordering him to report for such duties forthwith or risk prosecution under the National Defence Law.* Wally Hughes has been out here thirteen months, in the RAF two years. Such Bureaucracy!

No stopping the Red Army, apparently. Its troops are now battering their way into Sevastapol's [Crimean port] outskirts.

Thursday, April 20. Having little better to do, Vic Ball and I, with deadpan humour, discussed the startling phenomena suggested by current

---

* Parliament passed the Emergency Powers (Defence) Act in 1939 in response to the German-Soviet Non-Aggression Pact of August 23, 1939. Passed one day later, August 24, the Emergency Powers Act's purpose was to prosecute the war effectively by letting the government use emergency powers. The British government declared war on Germany 10 days later.

and recent popular song-hits. Surgical progress, we agreed, has reached such a point that it is possible or so we have heard, for the heart to be removed from a living human [and] cleaned and replaced without serious consequences. But now we hear of hearts being left behind in servicemen's canteens, like umbrellas forgotten in buses and handbags in railway station waiting rooms. According to today's crooners, hearts can also convey information as in "My Heart Tells Me." Not long ago, hearts were handed to others with strict instructions to handle them carefully—"It's not a book you're holding." In the palmy days of peace, we heard (and sang) of an explosive type of hearts that go "pop!" And hearts that went "boom!" What is the origin, I wonder, of the traditional relationship between the body's principal organic pump and the emotion "love?" Incidentally, would these heart-songs retain their appeal if the more practical term "pump" were used? Could even Sinatra do anything romantic with a song beginning "My Pump Tells Me?" Would American bobbysoxers [teenage female Sinatra fans] howl instead of swoon if he sang "Be Careful. It's My Pump" or "Your Pump and Mine?"

We're only asking…

Monday morning, April 24. Feel better now after a long sleep since 10:30 last night. God, how I needed it. Previous day, my party started in on the Sale run, sucking 100 octane petrol out of the railway tankers that had come into Sale Station, four miles away, bringing it here to the airfield and pumping into aircraft. The CTO (chief technical officer) wanted us to set up a reserve supply in the two storage tanks on this camp, but I pointed out that there were aircraft to refuel, including thirsty Liberators, and it was either those or the storage tanks.

But the fellows worked so damned hard that we had all the aircraft on the field filled by 10 Saturday night, so from then on runs were made from Sale to the storage tanks. By the light of flash lamps, we connected up about 60 feet of hosepipe. Draping one end over my shoulder, I began to climb up the storage tank, the weight of the hosepipe trailing behind and below me and the fierce wind both doing their damndest to pull me off the iron ladder. But I made the top, opened the filler cap, and pushed in the nozzle of the hosepipe. Down below, torches glimmered in the darkness as the other end of the pipe was cemented to the bowser [petrol fuel trailer], which then started pumping. And from then on, through the night, my five bomber/bowsers plied back and forth sometimes hitting 45 mph with a full load, scaring an occasional nocturnal Arabic wanderer, roaring past the ancient walled town of Sale, headlights picking out bent trees, sleeping native outcasts, a man about here, a lonely white farmhouse there.

As the night grew on, bloodshot eyes smarting through strain, sleeplessness and gritty sand due to previous day's high wind, the noise became monotonous, eventually I had all the railway tankers empty. We had brought up 25 loads. It was half past 5 in the morning. We lay on our beds by 6. It was dangerous to fall asleep for we were due on again that morning, so I routed the fellows out again at 8 am, and we worked through until 12:30 yesterday. The CTO phoned me, was surprised to hear we'd worked all night, congratulated me, and sounded well pleased: he ought to be.

Reason for all this is that the Casablanca pipeline normally feeding us with 100-octane is running 80-octane fuel to Port Lyautey [75 miles northeast of Casablanca]. And until this job is completed, we have to fill our aircraft and accumulate a reserve from railway tank-cars shunted up from Casa [Casablanca]. I go on again at 12:30 this afternoon.

Some silly censorship—a letter I sent to England, telling of my leave in Casablanca, arrived with the city's name cut out. Yet other letters naming Casablanca have gotten through, and we are allowed to send picture postcards of Casablanca, Algiers, and Oran.

Our new CO appears more popular than his predecessor, Fleming, whose farewell message (printed on Daily Routine Orders) was a masterpiece of illiteracy, bad grammar, clumsy phrasing, and lack of tact.

Wednesday, April 26. Days back home lately, according to meteorological reports in the Dover area, have been fine and warm. The battlefronts are in the main, subdued, except for Sevastapol and far away in the Pacific. Allied landings on Dutch New Guinea. Joint communique issued by the RAF and the USAAF [U.S. Army Air Forces] headquarters two days ago, says the Luftwaffe's fighter force is almost exhausted. There has been no let-up in the sky war.

Yesterday we were still drawing our fuel from tankers at Sale railway station. I went down there the other afternoon upon hearing that the fellows' attention was being distracted from work by the dubious charms of two unwashed eighteen-year-old girls. By the time of my arrival, the girls had left for Port Lyautey, presumably to work on Yank sailors.

Juvenile delinquency apparently a problem back home, too, but I cannot agree with the Chairman of East London's juvenile court who reportedly complained that "children go to the pictures several times a week and see what they imagine is the high life of America when actually it is a libel on that country. They also suffer from the effects of listening to wild raucous jitterbugging noise called music. Jitterbugging is only a sex-exciter for negroes…."

Public smack in the eye for Barrett was the announcement on orders that he had ceased to be welfare officer, his replacement is Flying Officer Allen. The paragraph states in conclusion that "Officers are reminded that it is their duty to interest themselves in the welfare of their men ... it is only too obvious that in the past this duty has been sadly neglected." This official reproof delivered by the new commanding officer of course is aimed as well as at our former CO Fleming.

Saturday, April 29. Something of a threat was posed to Allied unity by last week's allegations of anti-semitism, and even hints of torture, among Polish troops in Edinburgh.* And the Greek navy mutinied on account of its dissatisfaction with the Greek government and King George.† Both situations seem to be well in hand at the moment.

Announcement of the increase in service allowances was received more or less favourably, but married men with no children have a reasonable gripe against being left out in the cold. Well—in accord with the government's stated desire to foster large families, and because many childless husbands would give anything to start families right now, I suggest in all seriousness that the government set up military insemination centres overseas to which men can go and yield their sperm, which can then be flown home in suitable storage and the childless wives appropriately impregnated. In other words, babies by proxy. I suggested this to several of my married colleagues, who at once shouted me down, arguing that if they couldn't give their wives babies in the "usual fashion," they wouldn't do so at all. . .

I'm only trying to help. . . .

A copy of the American serviceman's paper <u>Stars and Stripes</u> came my way and I like this story from it. Seems an American sergeant was having wife and girlfriend trouble at the same time. He dreamed up an ingenious idea—wrote a letter to his wife asking for a divorce, another to the girlfriend breaking the affair, and deliberately put the letters into the wrong envelopes. This (he hoped) would square him with both ladies, they would assume he had committed an error, each thinking she was reading a letter intended for the other. Certainly, the wife would

---

* Jewish soldiers serving with Polish forces in exile numbered about 850. A majority of them, perhaps as many as 600, had complained they had been subjected to rabid anti–Semitism by fellow soldiers, particularly their superior officers. As many as 50 were under arrest, and awaiting or undergoing, courts-martial for desertion. These and possibly many more had requested transfer to the British military, causing a crisis between the Polish government-in-exile and the British government. That issue was then being debated in the House of Commons.

† Sailors on five ships of the Royal Hellenic Navy instigated a naval mutiny over the composition of the Greek government-in-exile. The "King George" mentioned here is George II of Greece.

feel satisfied that hubby wished to renounce the other woman. Unfortunately, the censor opened both letters and decided to perform a good deed by correcting the "mistake." Result: the poor sergeant lost both wife and sweetheart!

Tuesday, May 2. There's an atmosphere of expectancy here, as evidently, elsewhere in the world. The big invasion can't be far off, surely. From home comes a letter telling of the large numbers of U.S. troops, male and female, thronging Cardiff streets. The old man thinks the U.S. serviceman's uniform is "sloppy," that of the women's is "smart," and that American soldiers drive too fast. "They take no notice of our traffic lights."

Wednesday, May 10. Spent last weekend in Casablanca. Showered a lavish supply of chocolates and chewing gum on the ravishing Renette, who, however, while giving me frequent affectionate smiles and glances, withholds anything stronger. She tells me in her appealing broken English (my broken French is not nearly so appealing) that she remains faithful to her fiancé who, she believes, is somewhere in Italy and from whom she hasn't heard in five months. Peter (Martin's) affair with Charlotte progresses favorably. All four of us dined together before leaving Casablanca. Peter and I also dined with the Cormiers. Cormier is an architect who has designed a number of the administrative buildings in French North Africa. His work also includes a big factory near Paris, since destroyed by the RAF, and Cormier is happy about this, being a true French patriot. After dinner, Pete played piano while I sang (?) and Madame Cormier performed quite commendably upon a saw [violin].

Cormier's latest design is for a memorial to the defenders of Stalingrad, and he hopes the Russians, to whom he will submit it via the Soviet ambassador in Algiers, will consider it favorably.

Tuesday, May 16. Sundays' newspapers—I saw one or two yesterday aboard a plane just in from England—devotes much space to the "vision of the crucifixion" supposed to have been seen a week or so again in Ipswich by hundreds.* The vision lasted fifteen minutes and appeared during an air raid alert. Some people even claimed to see the nails in the feet and hands of the figure on the cross.

Every war produces its visions, but, until now, this conflict has been singularly barren. Assuming God is on our side, as many believe, a

---

* On May 8, 1944, the Rev. Harold Godfrey Green, vicar of St. Nicholas Church and chaplain to British forces, reported that he had verified the story of hundreds of Ipswich residents who insisted they saw a vision of Jesus on a cross in the sky during an April 27 air raid alert.

"vision" during the desperate days of Dunkirk would have been in order. None occurred as far as I know.

Friday night, having heard of some Jewish religious festival* to be held in a cemetery some miles from here, I walked to the scene and found myself in a strange throng, people in and out of tents, many carrying candles. Guitar-type musical instruments played. Children danced in and around tombstones. Couples prayed or made love. Some groups waved their candles over graves, wailed at great length, then threw their candles into a great stove. Beer was sold in some tents and at high prices. A good-looking Jewess from Casablanca told me the festival was held annually, and those in attendance included visitors from as far away as Fez and Meknes. I took her back to the friends with whom she was staying—in the Mellah† district within the old walled city of Sale, and where her chaperoning friends permitted us no more than fifteen minutes alone together. When I walked back the three miles to camp, the cemetery I passed was still full of life, lights, and celebration despite the near midnight hour.

Monday, May 22. My diary entries are few and far between. There isn't much to write about these days, and little work—only a few incoming Wellingtons each morning, and at sundown an occasional B-24 Liberator. All I found to write of in a recent letter home was that some of the chaps out here include pictures of Princess Elizabeth, a favorite pinup along with the expected likenesses of [Hollywood actresses] Betty Grable, Rita Hayworth, etc.

Almost two hours playing gin-rummy last night. Also, with Jack Mariden and "Bishop" Brine, arguing about religion, discussing the utility-or-futility of Christianity in our time.

Wednesday, May 24. Heard yesterday that in Italy the Allies are only 30 miles from the Anzio [Italian port city south of Rome] beachhead. And still no "Second Front," although, as the old man says in a letter, "We are all on tip-toe."

The Russian front seems quiet. And a Sunday Pictorial columnist complains against American soldiers pointing rifles at British soldiers, in Britain, and demanding proof of identity.

---

* Lag B'Omer is celebrated on the 33rd day of the Omer, a light-hearted Jewish holiday that marks a break in the mourning customs associated with the counting of the seven-week period from Passover to Shavuot. Jews traditionally celebrate the holiday with outings, bonfires, weddings, and other community ceremonies. In the Moroccan Jewish community, celebrations often bring Jewish community members and visitors together to visit the grave of a tzadik, or righteous one, where they pitch tents, light candles, and pray for health and prosperity.

† Urban Moroccan Jews lived in neighborhoods called "mellahs."

I hear that our new CO, deciding that the basement "club" Coq d'Or in Rabat was a potential source of ailments ranging from sore throat to venereal disease, has ordered the place put out of bounds.

Our food rations have been changed from American to British. Early results are not satisfactory, but nobody expected improvement.

Monday, May 29. Went into Rabat with Pete Martin to see "Mrs. Miniver" but found the Renaissance Cinema closed. So we went to the Royale, which was showing an Errol Flynn film. The Arabs in the audience loved it, cheering each of the many daring deeds Flynn performed. The French viewers were less impressed—and Pete and I were quite bored.

No aircraft in today. Rumours of postings in the air. The monotony is more oppressive than the early summer heat. The radio sets in both the Malcolm Club* and the Corporal's Club are unserviceable. Managed to hear from someone that the Allies are only fifteen miles from Rome.

I could use a letter or two from somewhere to relieve this horrible boredom—which, perhaps naturally enough, is mingled with sexual yearnings.

Sunday, June 4. Just heard that the Eighth Army has crossed the Tiber.

Two Yorks came in at 6 last evening and I sent two bowsers [petrol trucks] across to Transport Flight to help refuel for they were to go off again as soon as possible. Passengers emerged to stretch their legs. And the most conspicuous of a distinguished looking array of British and French civilians and brass was—supreme leader of the Free French, General Charles de Gaulle. By now, I suppose, he is in London, either to patch up differences with Churchill or rally his people, via radio, in preparation for the Second Front. Or both.

Last night the sergeants threw a party in their mess. I was among the guests, who included not only corporal but our commanding officer, W [Wing]/Commander Sutton, and the British consul in Rabat. Sutton gave a drunken speech in the course of which he said, "I've been dining with General de Gaulle and that always makes me sick." This caused a roar of laughter, in which I didn't join.

Much drinking, sandwich consumption, darts tournaments, displays of amateur comedic and ventriloquial talent. Jerry Levy, a West End band pianist before the war, played some nice hot piano, when he wasn't, over his protests, pressured to render, "Salome," "Roll Me Over," "Bless 'Em All," and other obscenely-worded favourites. Half-drunk

---

* Malcolm Clubs were named for Scottish Wing Commander Hugh Malcolm, an RAF pilot shot down on December 4, 1942, over Tunisia. These were welfare clubs for RAF personnel and provided books, newspapers, radio broadcasts, and refreshment.

Leonard (second from right) and refueling crew beside petrol bowser (fuel truck), 1945.

myself, I asked a BOAC [British Overseas Airways Corporation] officer if the sole woman employee of the company on this station is as loose-moraled as gossip implies. To my horror, he said she was his secretary and suggested, with a wink, that I direct my question at her. Incidentally, the way BOAC personnel lord it about this camp, apparently preparing for post-war business, is becoming quite a joke.

A bunch of drunken aircraftsmen tried to gatecrash the party, gave trouble, [and] were locked in the guardhouse overnight. This morning a sobered and probably liverish CO sentenced them to ten days detention. One culprit refused CO's punishment and demanded a court-martial. Some hopes, he has!!

Tuesday afternoon, June 6. All this morning there was but one topic on the camp. From the minute half a dozen men heard Algiers radio quoting German announcements that the invasion had begun, the news buzzed from mouth-to-mouth. "Have you heard?" "I got it from Taff," "Chiefly told me." "In Normandy, they say": "False alarm maybe," "Second Front? Christ, at last!"

Over on the flight dispersal, men emerged from Liberators they had been working on, agog with excitement, and struggled to restrain themselves in order to give coherent reports of the news bulletins they had heard on the Lib's [Liberators'] radios. "Airborne troops ... 4,000 ships... Le Havre... Dieppe... Cherbourg ... 11,000 frontline planes." The morning wore on; a Halifax and two Wellingtons came in from England. Said the Halifax skipper in response to my queries: "Last night when we were being briefed, we were told to take no notice of concentrations of shipping because it would only be the invasion." Turning to his crew, he added, "What did we see, blokes?" "F____ all," they grinned. From one of the "kites" [airplanes], I procured yesterday's newspapers, all about the capture of Rome <u>Daily Herald</u> had one-inch-thick banner headline: "Two railway ammunition truck explosions, great raids on Invasion coast." King is to broadcast tonight and Haakon VII ... of Norway ... and de Gaulle ... destroyers are shelling shore batteries ... three beach-heads.... Churchill gave the "gen" [information] in House of Commons.... I heard Eisenhower say it's started....

Men who normally take little heed of war's progress now developed interest [saying] "Germany'll pack in inside three months ... bloody good show eh.... We'll be home by Christmas... Jerries are back 30 miles. North of Rome ... bloody good show...."

It was a cool morning, fresh and moist after last night's fierce thunderstorms. At 12:30, I handed over to Len Butler "We're doing well ... pushed 'em back ten miles," he said.

There were the inevitable instances of Drake-like unconcern. When Pete Martin told Underwood that the Second

Leonard Guttridge's entry from the original diary dated June 6, 1944, says it all in just five words: "Second front? Christ, at last!"

Front had started, he gazed at Pete with seemingly no attempt to grasp the impact of the tidings, then turned to big Bill Thomas and said, "...and there's 45 M.U. [Maintenance Unit]. We'll have to scratch up a team to play them." Business, or cricket, as usual!

But to most, the news brought a feeling of mild excitement and relief. I found myself trying to mentally picture the scene in the English Channel this morning. I'd love to have witnessed it, and I wish that at least I was in England right now. So D-Day has arrived—almost exactly four years since our country was the only one still on its feet and listening to Churchill declare [June 4, 1940, in the House of Commons] that "we shall fight on the beaches, we shall fight on the landing-grounds, in the fields, in the streets, and in the hills. We shall never surrender."

Tonight, there is an ENSA show* in the camp. The lads will enjoy it and are now in the mood for anything. Second Fronts don't take place every day!

A copy of Look magazine arrived for me from America. My brain still slightly dizzy following its absorption of today's great news I was confronted by four well-illustrated pages all about Frank Sinatra getting his first screen kiss [in "Step Lively"].

Wednesday, June 7. Touch and go on the beachheads this morning but now I hear that the situation has improved. A battle is raging for Caen,† eleven miles inland. Here in my billet lies a Union Jack‡ with headlines "Allies in France." Also, today's local Rabat paper, Maroc Matin, headlined "LA LIBERATION de la France a Commence."

On a sour note—while most of my colleagues are more or less pleased and excited by the news of these events, I still hear such stupid remarks as "I bet there are more British than bloody Americans" and "We'll go in first to make it safe for the bastard Yanks." I heard those very words today and they typify an ugly if not dangerous attitude.

Tonight, the Malcolm Club is crowded, much beer consumed and much singing to the accompaniment of a heavily thumped piano. I was somewhat dismayed to note a revived popularity of songs that had died a merciful death in 1940, for instance, "We're gonna hang out the washing on the Siegfried Line" and "Somewhere in France." The pianist reached

---

* Keeping up morale among British armed forces personnel was considered essential. Entertainments National Service Association (ENSA) was organized in 1939 to send groups of entertainers to factories and military camps.

† The Battle for Caen, a two-month battle, June 6–August 6, 1944, was a protracted struggle where British and Canadian forces tried to drive out German forces holding Caen, located 11 miles south of the Normandy coast.

‡ The *Union Jack: The Newspaper for the British Fighting Forces* was the British equivalent of the U.S. military's *Stars and Stripes*.

Wellington medium bomber with ground crew. Salé, Morocco, 1944.

even farther back in time to the last war, and thumped out "Tipperary" and "Pack Up Your Troubles in Your Old Kit-Bag." Then everyone became boozily patriotic and sang "Land of Hope and Glory."

And so to bed.

Thursday, June 8. pm. Crews of two Warwicks and ten Wellingtons that came in through the rain from England this morning brought the first English newspapers we had seen since the Invasion began. The <u>Daily Express</u> headline: TEN MILES INLAND.

Leon, the young French boy who does our laundry, told us this afternoon of the days before the Allies invaded North Africa, of what he called French-Nazi conferences in the "Galleries Lafayette" [upscale department store in Paris] every week. This vicinity was "defendu"—off-limits to Jews—And for being near the place one day, Leon, who is Jewish, was hauled before the local police chief, who hit him twice because he could not, or would not, write his name other than in Hebrew. Under Vichy rule, all the cinemas and restaurants in Rabat were banned to Jews. Leon used to retaliate by furtively defacing the portraits of Marshal Petain* plastered throughout the city.

---

* Marshall Phillipe Pétain, the "lion of Verdun" in World War I, headed the Vichy government after France's surrender to the Germans in June 1940. Vichy, in central France, was the headquarters of Pétain's Vichy collaboration with the Germans from 1940 to 1942. In 1942, the Nazis took over full control of the Vichy government. After the war, Pétain was tried and convicted of treason.

Sunday, June 11. It appears that the Allies are trying to isolate the Cherbourg Peninsula [Cotentin Peninsula into the English Channel]. But most news seems confined to accounts of individual acts of heroism and eye-witness reports of military action. There is a lack of overall survey, doubtless due to military censorship, so we don't know fully how things are going.

A letter from home tells of a remarkable 15-hour thunderstorm, the worst in Cardiff's memory which followed a Whitsun* heat-wave.

Tuesday, June 13. Churchill and a bunch of big shots have crossed the Channel to France where Montgomery† has already set up headquarters. No doubt about it, Churchill thrives on this sort of thing.

Second Front or no Second Front, hundreds of race-goers crowded the trains for Ascot on Saturday.

In Italy, [Field Marshal Albert] Kesselring's 14th Army is on the run, far north of Rome. The Preston Sturgis film "Miracle of Morgan's Creek" is being criticized in London for its alleged bad taste. Everyone here enjoyed it, though, myself included. Sinatra's first film "Higher and Higher" caused no great sensation. In my opinion the much-publicized Voice is hardly better, though no worse, than many of today's dance band crooners.

Tuesday, June 20. Cold, windy and cloudy all day. Three Wellingtons arrived this morning, from one of which I procured yesterday's newspaper. [Home Secretary] Herbert Morrison reassured the nation about these pilotless bombers.‡ Nothing supernatural about them, and their use might be little more than a measure of desperation on Germany's part, or even indicate a shortage of human pilots in the Luftwaffe. The News Chronicle reports that they are variously designated "bumble bombs," "whirlies," "D-planes," "robot bombers," "one-way aircraft," "buzz bomb," "flying bomb," "power bomb," or simply "secret weapon."

A Union Jack, which just arrived, says that the pilotless plane is jet-propelled and not radio-controlled.

On the Normandie battlefront, the Americans are eight miles

---

* Whitsun (also Whitsunday or Whit Sunday in Britain and Ireland) is a holiday celebrated on the seventh Sunday after Easter by Catholics, Anglicans, and Methodists, as the Christian festival of Pentecost.

† Field Marshal Bernard "Monty" Montgomery commanded British forces in North Africa and the Italian and Normandy invasions.

‡ The V-1, also known to the Allies as the "buzz bomb," or "doodlebug," was a pulse-jet powered cruise missile. On June 13, 1944, the first V-1 fell in London. It landed on Grove Road, destroying the railway bridge, nearby housing, and killing six. By the end of the war, 6,725 were launched at Britain. Of these, 2,340 hit London, causing 5,475 deaths, with 16,000 injured.

from Cherbourg—Americans who a few weeks ago were being criticized by some members of Parliament for "rowdyism," "moral laxity," and "drunkenness." Locally there has been a noticeable decline in anti–American rhetoric, probably not only because of U.S. military performance in Europe, but also the generous offer made by Casablanca's American Red Cross to provide us Britishers with more shows like the amusing seven-man entertainment the whole camp enjoyed two nights ago.

Talking of American shows, Marlene Dietrich (complete with superlative legs) was at Casablanca's Vox Theatre the night before Pete Martin and I began a pleasant two-day visit. We dined with the Cormiers, also with the Countess de Portalaisse and her charming 16-year-old daughter, both of whom speak excellent English. When discussion touched on the coolness shown Charles de Gaulle by Washington (and, to a lesser extent, London), it was generally agreed that this is related to de Gaulle's suspicion of American postwar plans. Apparently, it is no secret that American big business has its eye on such bases as Dakar [Senegal], Martinique [Caribbean], and Indo-Chinese ports [in Southeast Asia]. In Casablanca, we saw the Sultan of Morocco flash by in his shiny limousine, followed by more cars and with an American motorcycle cop escort. We looked in at the Candiottis where I feasted my eyes on Renette's charms. All in all, a pleasant break.

Friday, June 23. Disturbing article by Rex North* in last week's Sunday Pictorial, who estimates that 60 percent of allied casualties in Normandy are due to French snipers. North tells of young French girls screaming abuse at British soldiers and clinging to German prisoners of war; he cites other instances of a pro–Nazi sentiment among many French. He offers no explanation or solution, but says he is simply reporting what he saw. Well, I can understand a certain feeling of resentment among a populace which after years of more or less uneventful German occupation, finds itself disrupted, bombed, and shelled by invading British and Americans. Still, by contrast, the liberating armies in Italy were greeted with flowers. Perhaps, I hope, North's account exaggerates. But even here, in Morocco, I have sensed among its colonial population a sort of complacent disregard for the war. This is mostly evident among the smartly dressed young, who saunter serenely along the palm-studded boulevards and seem to studiously ignore we uniformed foreigners.

---

* Rex North was war correspondent for the *Sunday Pictorial*, the newspaper which eventually became the *Sunday Mirror*.

Sunday, June 25. Last night I felt quite blue, that old mixture of boredom and frustration. Even with the amenities, proximity to a town, running water, electric light, brick housing—denied many men on active service—it is still not possible to totally eliminate monotony and cheerlessness. What may have brought on this mood was news that both Glenn Miller and Artie Shaw have arrived in England and I wish that I were on the scene.

The Leary Constantine case* is a test of democratic justice. Are we to sacrifice our traditional sense of fair play because of the Americans among us who oppose racial mixing? Incidentally, Peter Martin tells me he once asked for a room at the same Russell Square hotel and was told there were no vacancies. At the time, he was in ordinary RAAF [Royal Australian Air Force] "other ranks" uniform. He believes that's why he was refused a room, for an officer who requested one some minutes later succeeded in getting one. This sort of thing is what we are fighting for?

Wednesday, June 28. Last night it was feared that RAF personnel might have to be called out in support of South African troops, white, who were standing by to quell a mutiny among West African blacks employed on aerodrome reconstruction here. The trouble apparently stems from an incident in a Rabat Medina (native quarter) brothel the other night when a bunch of blacks held off American military police and South African soldiers. The blacks were punished, it seems, and now rebel against whatever were the penalties. These black soldiers are encamped just outside our camp gates.

Our CO, drunk as usual, issued melodramatic orders to Pete Martin on duty in charge of fire picket, whose principal function usually is collecting francs at the camp movies. Pete forthwith began rounding up NCOs and men to act as special guards. While Pete was dashing hither and yon, the CO changed his mind, called a weary Pete to say there was no need for special guards. When Pete protested that he had already organized them, he was told—"disorganize 'em." Our CO is popular enough with the lads—and his constant insobriety hasn't prevented his promotion to Group Captain.

Saturday, July 1. Last night, the camp theatre was about half-full—the

---

* Learie Constantine, a black Trinidadian professional cricketer, who lived in England, traveled to London to play in a match. Although he had a reservation to stay at London's Imperial Hotel, the desk clerk informed him that he could stay only one night because white American military personnel, also guests at the hotel, had complained about his presence. The outraged Constantine claimed the hotel was in breach of contract. No statute then existed outlawing racial discrimination. Nevertheless, a judge ruled that, even though Constantine suffered no pecuniary damage, the violation of the right justified a remedy. He was awarded the small sum of five guineas in damages.

CO in the middle of the front row, naturally—on his right, a LAC with crutches and a single leg. He'd had his left leg amputated—three attempts were made to stem the gangrene, following a bullet wound inflicted by a beserk Frenchman in Rabat's Medina during the unrest a few months ago. We were all entertained by an Italian POW orchestra—a real musical treat, drums, piano, valve trombone, trumpets, guitars, accordians, two violins. Light selections mostly, interspersed with Italian folk tunes, sung with gusto and charm. The musicians were apparently in the charge of a British army corporal whose bumbling onstage manner was in sharp contrast with the easy confidence they displayed and who capped his idiotic introduction: "These are Eyetalians, so don't expect too much" with, announcing a selection. Now one of 'em is going to sing an English number,"My and is Frozen!" These former enemies played for us "You'll Never Know Just How Much I Love You." And after excerpts from the "Barber of Seville," "Ave Maria" and "O Sole Mio," they served up "Bless 'em All" no doubt at the insistence of the ENSA people sponsoring the show. And they finished with a spirited rendition of "God Save the King"—not indicating, of course, which monarch they may have had in mind.

Sunday evening, July 2. After a long spell with nothing coming out of England (owing either to prolonged bad weather or Second Front operations) I've just heard that a shower of Sterlings and Halifaxes will arrive tomorrow. And my back is sore after prolonged exposure—half an hour—to strong midday sun yesterday. Dangerously stupid of me, but I didn't notice the swift passage of time, being absorbed in a gin rummy school.

Deanna Durbin's latest film on camp tonight.

By all accounts, we now control 150 miles of French coastline while on the Eastern front the Germans are falling back in disorder under the hammer blows of Stalin's summer offensive.

I try hard not to think of how lonesome I might be when Pete Martin leaves. He has heard of his posting to Heliopolis.

Thursday, July 6. Pete goes tomorrow, weather permitting. He has been my best friend out here. The sort of person who really fits in with me, like Ted Mansell, Bill Twiss, and, of course, Arthur Wilson, is hard to find and Pete wasn't one of that type. Often his dour Scot's temperament irritated me, but we grew tolerant of each other's faults and cultivated mutual interests. If my passion is music, his is golf—and we are deprived of both. And we each like good reading. I'll miss him—but, as M. Cormier would say, "C'est la guerre!"

The only other occupant of this room, after Pete's departure, will be

Ken Hamilton, whose characteristic bitterness (partly, I believe, resulting from long spells of pre-war unemployment and the destruction of his home in Plymouth during an air raid) has replaced whatever interest in life he may once have had. But most times he is amicable enough, and fortunately well-read so is far from being a bore.

Enjoy "Going My Way" the other night at the camp cinema, not only because of Bing Crosby's surprisingly good performance but Barry Fitzgerald's portrayal of a loveable if cranky Catholic priest. But that's enough of singers playing ministers and the like, thank you. I don't want to see Frank Sinatra as a bishop or Dinah Shore as a Mother Superior.

Friday, July 7. Pete goes definitely tomorrow morning. Wish I was going with him.

"Voting?" "Load of balls." This the general reaction of the men when Flight Sgt. Hodkinson told them they could register by filling in little cards. "If you don't fill in these bloody things," he then said, "you won't be able to vote when the general election comes around, and you won't be able to kick out the bloody government that landed you in this mess."

I tried to impress the importance of voting upon the least politically-conscious of my refueling party. And with affected airs of concentration, and much coarse blasphemy, they signed the cards— (2040's) I'd handed out.

I've yet to hear Churchill's response to the widespread criticism of his government for its refusal to publish flying bomb casualty figures. But I've heard that over 2,000 flying bombs have got through.

Today I received an income tax notification that I paid 6 pounds too much and the local accounts officer must refund. Well!

Monday, July 10. Very warm, with a dazzling sun, and not much work. Twenty aircraft came in yesterday.

Saturday, July 22. Sniffing and sneezing from a cold I caught at the Temara* rest camp where I spent a week on leave. This rest camp for RAF personnel consists of a converted casino, where dances are held each Sunday, and some chalets. Tourists and French colonials frolicked here before the war. Now the pleasant bay echoes to the laughter and obscene banter of airmen as they lounge on the beach, horseplay in the surf, fish, or simply stare in fascination at the crustacean life in rock pools. Views along the shore and out across the Atlantic are simply glorious, and added interest in the sky is provided by the pair of United

---

* Temara is a coastal city in Morocco. It is located in the region of Rabat-Salé-Kénitra, directly south of Rabat.

States Navy blimps* that move to and fro on their coastal patrol between Port Lyautey and Casablanca. The food here is excellent—basically the same as we get back at camp, but the difference is in the cooking.

I hitch-hiked into Casablanca a couple of times, once with a blonde Viennese refugee, now serving in the French army who, in excellent English, gave me an eyewitness account of the Socialist revolt in Austria ten years ago. Had Dollfuss† been more amenable to the socialists, Hitler's Anschluss‡ might never have succeeded.

At Casablanca on the 14 July, Bastille Day, I visited some sort of fete in Port Lyautey. Some of the booths had bands, one a lively little outfit playing congas and rumbas, led by a former Parisian music-teacher. Also met a pretty English-speaking French girl named Huguette, who invited me to dine with her and her mother, which I did. The father had died as a POW in Germany and Huguette has a sister who, having refused to work for the Nazis, is believed to be in a concentration camp.

Also dined and wined with the Cormiers who greeted me as usual with embraces and kisses and were sorry to hear of Pete Martin's departure. We toasted his good fortune, as we did that of General de Gaulle, Roosevelt, Churchill, the Second Front, King George VI and the rest of the royal family, by which time I was more than somewhat tipsy.

This may prove the last leave I'll spend in North Africa. I shall miss Casablanca and those of its people whose hospitality and charm have so enlivened my service out here.

Sunday, July 23. Whole day seethed with rumours, many spun from radio reports. Just what _is_ happening in Germany? There is talk of generals under arrest, and rioting in some cities. Locally here, another rumour, that the Transport Command Avro York, that landed here this morning and soon took off again, was carrying the King. I hear that he was accompanied by Anthony Eden and that their destination is Naples or Rome, or both.

I have a cold, will not attend the camp movies tonight, thus won't hear the nightly news broadcast there. Ken Hamilton will probably bring back the gen [what was reported].

Among the rumours—Himmler is chief of all Germany's armed forces; Rundstedt is imprisoned; Kesselring§ is sacked; German navy

---

* The Goodyear K-Type airship was the main maritime patrol airship for the US Navy during World War II. The non-rigid airships—or blimps—were about 250 feet long.

† Engelbert Dollfuss was an Austrian politician who served as Chancellor of Austria between 1932 and 1934. In early 1933, he dissolved the Austrian parliament and assumed dictatorial powers. He was assassinated on July 25, 1934.

‡ The German annexation of Austria on March 12, 1938.

§ Heinrich Himmler, a founding member of the Nazi Party, and later Commander in Chief of Home Forces (1944–1945). Karl Rudolf Gerd von Rundstedt was a German field marshal. Albert Kesselring held the rank of general field marshal.

has mutinied. There's even a report that Hitler is in hospital—but my favourite is that a German submarine had put into a British harbour, its commander, a 17-year-old boy, and crew singing "God Save the King"!

Last Sunday night at the Temara rest camp, we were dancing on the Casino terrace when our attention was caught by a deep red glow in the night sky along the coast towards Rabat. Next day, I learned that a cork factory had blazed all day and most of the night. American sailors from Port Lyautey and our RAF personnel were called in to help the French firemen who, according to eye-witnesses, seemed not to know their job. But sabotage was behind the fire. And other Fifth Column news locally is of a police raid on a Rabat church where eight French civilians and a priest were celebrating mass for the assassinated French—quisling Herriot.*

Saturday, July 29. Blame the heat, the monotony, the frustrations of life these days, but anyway, I made overtures to the swarthy little Algerian maiden who works at the Hotel Balima's baths and that night slept with her. This lapse should cause me to be less emphatic in my criticism of those married men who seek solace in Rabat's and Casablanca's brothels. Also, I felt somewhat guilty upon returning to camp and finding no fewer than seven letters from Helen.

Well, perhaps this unnatural life won't last too much longer. The Russians are only 140 miles from Germany. On the Western Front, though, [Field Marshal Erwin] Rommel's forces still stubbornly resist a breakthrough by the British and Americans probing and jabbing at his defences.

Now that the King has visited his troops in both Normandy and Italy, I suggest he make the journey to Burma where sweating Tommies consider themselves (or so I hear) a "forgotten army."

Flying bombs [V-1s] still causing damage and fatalities in Britain, southern England mostly, and, of course, London.

Nothing else to do, it seemed, out on the hot dusty airfield yesterday than indulge in a discussion, mostly with Mitchell, who is one of my refuelers and a 40-year-old Christian, on the mystery of creation. He claimed that the evolution theory didn't justify disbelief in God because it offered no solution to the question "who created Life"? Mitchell's solution: God did. But who created God? I suggested there may be no

---

* The author may be referring here to French admiral and political figure Jean Louis Darlan, who was fatally shot by an anti–Vichy assassin in Algiers on December 24, 1942. Edouard Hérriot served as Mayor of Lyon from 1905 until his death, except for a brief period from 1940 to 1945, when he was exiled to Germany for opposing the Vichy regime. "Quisling" refers to a traitor who collaborates with the enemy. Prime Minister Vidkun Quisling headed Norway during the Nazi occupation.

need for a Creator. He, Mitchell, believed in life everlasting, without end? Then why not believe it always was, without beginning. This theological chit-chat was interrupted by the arrival of two Liberators needing petrol.

Thursday, August 3. Because I like a Hitchcock movie, I missed seeing King George VI last night. His Avro York drew up onto a guarded tarmac while I was inside the camp theatre, reading Dickens' "Mystery of Edwin Drood" and waiting for "Lifeboat" to start. The film was a good one, although its portrayal of the Nazi U-boat captain as super-efficient and the "democratic" characters a bunch of quarrelsome nitwits left me feeling a bit uneasy.

While I watched the movie, Sir Alan Brooke and our CO (sober for once fortunately!) entered the Malcolm Club along with His Majesty [George VI]. The surprised NCOs and airmen slowly rose to their feet, the French girls behind the counter staring open-mouthed. Jack Marsden stood quite near the King who, Jack tells me, said "goodnight" directly to him on his way out. According to this morning's news on the radio, the King is now safely back home.

Churchill, in the House of Commons yesterday, revealed that 80,000 houses have been destroyed or damaged and over 4,000 people killed by flying bombs. He also expressed the belief that the time between the end of the European War and that of the war with Japan will be much less than he had earlier thought.

Sunday, August 6. American troops, after racing across the Brest peninsula [northwest France] and cutting it neatly to isolate thousands of Germans, are actually fighting at Brest [port city] itself.

Long awaited letters from home arrived yesterday. The old man puts in three afternoons a week tending wounded soldiers at the hospital. He says he could tell me quite a bit about the battlefields, but the censor would disapprove. The folks hadn't heard from me for so long (the fault of a mail hold-up in England) they thought I was on my way home.

Wednesday, August 9. Eight Wellingtons, a Warwick, a Halifax are the first aircraft to fly out in daytime, which suggests that they have nothing now to fear from the Luftwaffe. Hitherto, aircraft would leave England after midnight.

From what I hear, British railway stations are chaotic, due mainly to the government's secretiveness concerning extra trains, etc. Soldiers on leave and war-workers seeking much needed holidays are quite baffled by misleading time-tables at Torquay, Blackpool, Weston-Super-Mare, and other resorts. Thousands are sleeping on the beaches.

Friday, August 11. Last night I received fourteen letters from Helen. She writes to me almost daily. This batch had accumulated somewhere en route. One letter contained a lock of her hair.

Had a strange dream the other night. I was in some large hall amid a crowd expecting Winston Churchill. He appeared suddenly but instead of a characteristic burst of oratory, all he said was, "Does anybody here believe in God?"

Wednesday, August 16. Half an hour before I checked out yesterday afternoon, someone told me the Allies have landed along the South Coast of France.* In Rabat, I visited the Coq d'Or Hotel and announced the news to all present—none of them were yet aware of it. A Frenchman and his girlfriend were so delighted, they insisted I accompany then to Sale's beach, which I did. We were rowed across the Bou Regreg River and found the beach aswarm with sun-bathers. My French companion introduced me to a plump young lady with a moustache, who he told me was his sister. Her central ambition, or so it appeared, was to sing, "You Are My Sunshine" in the loudest possible voice. Others on the beach joined in—they were obviously doing this in my honor so I reciprocated with a spirited if tuneless rendition of "Sur La Pont, d'Avignon."

Back of Sale beach, some Jewish fete was under way, and I investigated this, too, sampling a little wine. And then returned to camp.

Sunday, August 20. Allied troops are only six miles from Paris. And the whole of [Field Marshal Günther] von Kluge's armies are reported to be crumbling in northern France. Advances also reported on the Mediterranean front. At last night's noisy and boozy party in the Corporal's Club, who should show up but our revered commanding officer, himself drunk and oddly resembling the burly Hollywood actor Albert Dekker. He sang, frightfully, "The Mountains of Mourne."

Not long ago I wrote the Melody Maker inviting letters from fellow jazz-lovers. So far, three have arrived, all from girls, one of them collects photos of bandleaders. "I've got Glenn Miller, Harry James (autographed), Tommy Dorsey, and Geraldo." In another letter, the writer states that she works on a farm, her father's, and that "we have 2 cows, 3 horses and a few pigs... We grow swedes [rutabagas], oats and turnips."

Wednesday, August 23. NCO i/c fire picket—fire instruction consisted solely of looking for a fire hydrant that leaked badly. Remainder of the duties include collecting francs for the camp cinema and attending the colour-hoisting and colour-lowering parades. This latter ritual

---

* From August 15 to September 14, 1944, in Operation Dragoon, American and French troops landed along the French Riviera and then pushed north through France.

I can never take seriously—six men, stolid and motionless, before a few square yards of coloured cloth going up a pole in the morning and descending in the evening.

No news yet of whether or not the Allies are in Paris. The Sunday Pictorial had a foolishly premature headline: ALL FRANCE RISES: PETAIN IN FLIGHT.

Two breezy letters reached me from a girl named Win and another named Wyn, both who seem to know their jazz and wrote in response to my Melody Maker appeal (which I have yet to see).

An ENSA concert last night, pianist Ruth Early playing Bach, Beethoven, Mendelssohn, and Brahms. The music was accompanied by the chirping of countless crickets.

Evening: the Arab newsboy "Joe" has come around selling La Vigie Marocaine whose 2½ inch thick headline shrieks PARIS EST LIBERE. French Resistance fighters freed the city, it seems, and Petain, Laval, and other Vichy rats have fled, apparently heading for the German border. Some of our fellows in Rabat this afternoon were thumped on the back by well-wishers, kissed by girls. And here I am, stuck in camp on fire picket!

Friday, August 25. Night. The celebrating was premature. Streetfighting continued in the French capital and only now, with Allied troops supporting the Maquis,* is it being cleaned of German soldiers.

News from the Balkans is confusing—that part of the globe always was a devil's cauldron.

Scattered communiques remind us of that all but forgotten campaign in Burma.

And—a Liberator bomber crashed upon a school near Preston, England, exploded, set whole blocks ablaze. The death toll includes 20 soldiers, a dozen civilian adults—and 34 children all under age five.

Much of the above news was received via courtesy of London newspapers carried in the Italy-bound Mosquitoes and India-bound Beaufighters that flew in this afternoon.

Saturday, September 2. This war is certainly in high gear. American forces have swept across France at such a lick, they are now—according to even the Germans—only fourteen miles from the enemy frontier. Their feat rather overshadows the struggle of the British and Canadian troops engaged along the banks of the Seine.

The Nazi edifice is tottering. Romania calls it quits, Bucharest

---

* The Maquis were rural guerrilla bands of French Resistance fighters called maquisards.

welcoming the Red Army. Bulgaria pleads for peace. Hungary dithers. And meanwhile, the flying bombs keep striking London and southern England—showing little regard for the presence of such newly-arrived notables as Bing Crosby and Fred Astaire.

I celebrated my birthday last week with the Benoliel family at Meknes.* The two-days celebration for the liberation of Paris had ended, the town was its usual dusty self. I returned by train, paid 130 francs for a first-class ticket, found the train crowded, was forced to spend the journey in a drafty gloomy corridor.

Sunday, September 3. Fifth anniversary of the war's outbreak. Most fellows here think it will all be over long before Christmas. Certainly, the advance continues in Western Europe, also on the Russian front. What a grand sight it must be and how I'd love to be on the scene. Instead, I'm caught up in a spate of heavy work due to an increase in the flow of aircraft from England.

There is a report that Hitler will make some important announcement tomorrow. What will he say? What can he say?

How I recall that Sunday of five years ago. We managed to get out of camp in the afternoon, Will Price and myself, in his Morris Minor. The country roads were wet from the previous night's thunderstorms. We drove through Cheltenham and over the Birdlip. A strange quiet prevailed. Occasionally we were overtaken and passed by a fast-moving car heading west and laden with baggage seeking safety, it appeared, but from what? Months would elapse before the bombs began to fall. Of course, no one could know that then.

Tuesday, September 5. I hear tonight that American units are across the German border. Belgium is liberated, Antwerp and Brussels in Allied hands.

Rain all day here. The other night in Rabat saw "Jane Eyre" in which Orson Welles gives a thoroughly hammy performance—which I enjoyed immensely.

The flying bomb campaign against England is evidently over. It lasted eighty days and proved a triumph for British defence forces. More than 4000 people were killed, but the figure could have been much higher. Some eight thousand were launched. One day, ninety-seven out of 103 were intercepted and drowned. Nice to hear that in ten days' time there will be a partial lifting of Britain's blackout.

Some bad news—increased bitterness between Poland and Russia,

---

* Meknes is a city in northern Morocco about 95 miles east of Rabat. Its rich imperial history is illustrated by the Bab Mansour, a huge gate made up of arches and decorated with colorful mosaic tiles.

specifically over the Warsaw battle.* Military victories all over Europe conceal a hundred different political and ethnic problems that will have to be solved if a future European war is to be prevented.

A Beaufighter landed here today. Out stepped Field Marshal [Harold] Alexander, who stepped into a waiting car and was whisked away from the busy tarmac.

Saturday, September 9. I heard yesterday that the Allies have launched an all-out attack in the Balkans, one object being to link up with Tito's force whose right flank is already joining with the Red Army on the Yugoslav border. But there is little or no news from the Western Front. There arrived for me today four literary gems, chiefly D.H. Lawrence's "Women in Love," Voltaire's "Candide," and Anatole France's "Thais." I ordered them two months ago from a Canadian publisher.

Tuesday, September 12. Just received a breezy letter from Wyn Caster, telling me that the RAF Squadronaires backed Fred Astaire's tapping and Bing Crosby's warbling at a star-studded opening of London's Stage Door Canteen a week ago. I'd have given a month's pay to have been there.

Yesterday a York slewed off the runway, its port wheel burst, and collapsed on one wing. Its passengers, all VIPs, emerged shaken but unhurt. This morning a Mosquito crashed on take-off and erupted in flame. Crew were lucky, got out safely.

Sunday, September 17. Five more (sea-mail) letters responding to my Melody Maker appeal for jazz correspondents. I can't carry on correspondence with them all, but I shall answer the lot. So far, I've received letters from eighteen persons, some written in adolescent scrawl extolling the virtues of such as Harry James and Benny Goodman. Others are more mature, including a self-professed blues singer—"I have made ten recordings, privately" and a Win Roberts of Bolton, evidently a cheerful and intelligent girl with above-average letter writing style. All are enthusiasts of good jazz.

And little wonder the wall newspaper at the Malcolm Club has a piece this week saying "Bowser King Guttridge's fan mail is so large these days he is thinking of running an extra truck to carry it in from the post office."

---

* The Warsaw Uprising took place in the summer of 1944, led by the Polish resistance Home Army. The revolt lasted 63 days and was to coincide with the retreat of the German forces from Poland pursued by the advancing Soviet forces. The Red Army temporarily halted as it approached the city's eastern suburbs, enabling the Germans to regroup, defeat the Polish resistance, and destroy the city in retaliation. Only then did the Russians enter the remains of the Polish capital.

Vic Ball has just looked in to ask if I'll join him for a drink across at the club. We are going into Casablanca tomorrow for a few hours, and I'll introduce Vic to the Cormiers.

Friday, September 22. Everybody talking about demobilization, and how the government is expected to enact it. Other gossip running like this—"We're getting a pay raise when the Germans pack in." "Yeh, if you've done over three years' service." "Right and those going out to fight the Japs will get the highest increase." "What about those who have fought them up to now? It's a poor show the way they've been treated. Look at their pay compared with that of the Yanks." And so on.

Hope to God the rumour I heard this afternoon—that the airborne division at Arnhem had surrendered—isn't true. Certainly, there has been little or no news from that bloody battleground.

Friday, September 29. Persistent rumour that aircraft from England bound for Italy or the Far East will soon be taking the direct route across France instead of the present roundabout journey over the Bay of Biscay, around Portugal and Spain. What will happen to us? Staging posts have already been set up in Southern France.

The airborne troops of Arnhem have added to history a brilliant story of courage against fearful odds, but there is no denying that the heavy losses amount to a terrible blow for the Allies.* Sure to be questions in Parliament about it.

Some "back-home" news: the Lord Chamberlain [George Villiers] has banned the play "Jasmine Ermine" after its first-night London audience booed it. Play is about the attempts of a mother, her daughter (husband is soldier overseas), and an adolescent girl to seduce an American officer... I've also heard that the BBC has banned Glenn Miller's SHAEF [Supreme Headquarters Allied Expeditionary Force] concert broadcasts from its Home Service. Stated reason: the music is unacceptable to British listeners.

Viscount Cranborne [Robert Gascoyne-Cecil] in the House of Lords: "There is steadily growing evidence that the German general staff are already making preparations to win the next war."

Thursday, October 5. Returned from a 48-hour pass this morning. Intended to learn to swim at Tamara Bay, but nipped into Casablanca. Saw disappointing film, "Cross of Lorraine," whose cast included Jean Pierre Aumont, Peter Lorre and, surprisingly, Gene Kelly.

---

* The Battle of Arnhem kicked off "Operation Market Garden." It was fought in and around the Dutch towns of Arnhem, Oosterbeek, Wolfheze, and Driel September 17–26, 1944, and resulted in an Allied defeat. The 1977 film *A Bridge Too Far* dramatized the events.

Irritated and bored by a capricious Charlotte, no longer impressed by Renette's smile, I've decided to break off the acquaintance.

Met up with an affable American of Polish descent who told me that as he was about to leave home, his father, Warsaw-born, said, "If you reach Poland, son, just grab a handful of soil—and bring it home to me." And in the Bar Montmartre, I talked with a handsome young Austrian who spoke perfect English, and an Italian with, obviously, a passionate love for, and much knowledge of, music. Best of all, I also met and rather fell for a French girl, Josine, who is, however, married, and her husband was with her. He, and perhaps she, too, is Jewish, and they had fled Occupied France, pursued by the Gestapo, who fired at them as they began the crossing of the Pyrenees. The husband appears worn and frail. She seems in better physical shape and has a most attractive smile.

Back at camp, a letter awaited me from Pete Martin, now in Heliopolis [Egypt] and clearly in his element, golfing with Egyptian professionals. He deplores the reaction (or rather, lack of it) on the part of fellow airmen to the government's social security plans. Reflects Pete: "The greatest enemies of a good social system in Britain are the very people who would most benefit from it."

Funny thing, Pete sounds more friendly in his letters than I took him to be here. Absence making the heart grow fonder?

Am reading D.H. Lawrence's "Women in Love," which doesn't move me as much as did his "Sons and Lovers"—and neither book strikes me as favorably as did another of my recent acquisitions, Forster's "A Passage to India".

Monday, October 9. Sadly, surprising news that Wendell Willkie has died. He quite endeared himself to the British on the visit he made as FDR's emissary.

Although a route across France and via Marseilles has been established, Bostons, Liberators, and other aircraft still come in from the USA, via the Azores. But I'm snatching a day off tomorrow and will visit new friends in Casablanca.

I read of growing resentment back home against alleged pampering of Italian former POWs, now called "co-operators." Railway compartments are reserved for them while British soldiers stand in corridors.

A letter in Picture Post* says: "Very important feature seems to be overlooked in the plans for postwar housing, namely, the provision of air-raid shelters. There is no 'harm in being prepared.'"

Friday, October 13. A two-days' headache got so bad last night, accom-

---

* *Picture Post* was an illustrated newspaper published in Britain from 1938 to 1957.

panied by severe vomiting fit, that this morning I reported sick. Temperature, pulse were normal. Urine sample showed negative. Yellow jaundice was briefly suspected. An aging medical orderly knowingly diagnosed excessive intake of anti-malaria pills—until I told him I hadn't taken any in six weeks. Well, I feel better now and plan on a Casablanca visit tomorrow.

The Americans' ultimatum to Aachen* expired yesterday and they [U.S. forces] are now systematically destroying the town. Ugly business but, I suppose necessary. Since writing the above, have just seen a headline that Aachen is in flames under attack from 300 bombers and 200 heavy artillery.

Tuesday October 17. Another city virtually destroyed—Duisberg [western Germany], by 10,000 tons of bombs in two raids. Is all this militarily necessary? Some said to me yesterday that we should emulate the old martyrs who lost their lives rather than stoop to evil. We are stooping to evil to save ours. Perhaps he has got something there, but I wonder whether we can isolate any particular element of war, e.g., air bombing, from war itself, which is intrinsically evil.

A Vickers Wellington from here, and Catalinas from Port Lyautey were out over the Atlantic yesterday searching for a Boston believed to have ditched. No news yet.

I was almost in trouble Sunday by my failure to book in at the guardhouse the previous night. I'd arrived ten hours late, having tried to hitch from Casablanca and found myself stuck eight miles out of that city when darkness fell. I put up for the night with a lonely bunch of Britishers and Italians of a Pioneer's outfit near the American Camp Duclair. The station warrant officer gave me, as expected, a chewing-up and took me to our assistant adjutant Flying Officer Messenger, who according to rumor, is getting light in the head. Judging by his burblings to me, the rumor is well grounded. Of course, it was all my fault, but I found it difficult to leave the side of Josine.

Monday, October 23. Listening to an AFN [Armed Forces Network] radio program of dance music tonight, I was struck by the inclusion of several twelve- or fifteen-year-old hits, e.g., "Stars Fell on Alabama," "I Just Couldn't Take It Baby" and "Sweet and Lovely." The popularity of these nostalgic melodies is reported to be growing on both sides of the Atlantic.

Saturday night in town I enjoyed "The Maltese Falcon" (Humphrey

---

* The Battle of Aachen, October 2–21, 1944, was one of the largest urban battles fought by U.S. forces in World War II, and the first city in Germany to fall to the Allies.

Bogart, superb), then to the Garrison Club dance, organized by the South Africans with the assistance of some countess or other. Atmosphere was pleasant, the girls—mostly hand-picked from schools, convents, seminaries, etc.—charming, cultured, but not very good dancers.

"Battle of Britain" shown in the camp last night revived memories of those hectic days and nights of late 1940, of gunfire, siren, and bomb....

Friday, October 27. Over at the Malcolm Club this afternoon, I read on the wall newspaper of an eye-witness account of the Jack Benny incident at an RAF station in Iraq. Apparently, the first two rows at the concert Benny gave had filled with officers and their ladies. Benny opened proceedings by praising the RAF, then saying his show was primarily for the enlisted men. "So would you folks mind leaving your seats in front and going to the rear." A terrific storm of cheers erupted from the men and NCOs, only to die away lamely for nobody in the front rows had moved. Benny broke an embarrassed silence by saying he could easily move the whole show to the Americans' camp where the enlisted men could and would occupy the front rows, as was the American tradition. More cheers broke out. Benny silenced them with a gesture. Then one blue-clad figure arose from the front. Others followed, made their way to the back rows. Enlisted men filed to the front. The show proceeded and was a rousing success.

Also, on wall newspaper results of a recent camp poll showing that half the NCOs and other ranks had failed to fill in their "vote by proxy" forms for the national election.

Tuesday, October 31. There were morning and afternoon showings today of a film warning of the dangers of venereal disease. It included shots of sore-encrusted penises, swollen groins, and the festering tongue of a victim with a syphilitic throat. At the performance I attended, an officer fainted and someone tells me two men, after watching these scenes, staggered outside and were physically sick. The movie was American (I recognized character-actor Samuel S. Hinds as the lecturing officer). Such scare tactics, I suppose, are more effective than mere appeals to moral sensibility or even plain common sense.

There's a Beethoven record recital in the church tonight. Think I'll go.

Thursday, November 2. Nine Liberators flew in this afternoon from the Azores. One had giant figures "1000" doped all over its fuselage signifying that it was the one-thousandth bomber to roll off the assembly line, and on the giant fins were scrawled hundreds of names, male and female, also addresses, of the defence plant workers who had helped build the aircraft. While my fellows were refueling, others were seen peering closely at the names, some copying them onto scraps of paper. I estimate about a dozen RAF men will be acquiring American pen-pals from today's visitation—all female no doubt.

Last night saw "The Phantom of the Opera," latest film version. Good music, good colour, but Claude Rains' always interesting face was masked most of the time—he being the Phantom—and losing interest in consequence, I found myself wondering how the disfigured old boy got a well-tuned grand piano down those stone steps into the sewers.

Three nights ago, an American USO concert party gave a show for us, and it featured a lovely blonde named Helen Young who caressed the microphone as she sang "Embraceable You" and many of the lads, myself included, all but slid off our wooden benches when she crooned the line "Come to mama, come to mama, do." Much the same, I suppose as American teenaged bobbysoxers are reported to do when sung to by Frank Sinatra. They are said to squeal and swoon en masse.

Last night at the Garrison Club down town, I talked with a Russian lady of aristocratic origin—"The Revolution was no good for us but good for the people," said she and a pretty French girl who lived three years in New York and has a flying license. I promised to go riding—horseback riding, that is—with her next week. A rash promise, for I've never ridden a horse in my life.

Churchill thinks the war with Germany won't be over until next spring or early summer and that the war with Japan will go on a further eighteen months.

Tuesday, November 7. Lord Moyne assassinated in Cairo.* Not having seen any newspapers, I have no idea what this means, other than that somebody didn't like Lord Moyne or the system he represents.

Polling in the USA. It seems widely believed that if Roosevelt wins, he won't serve a full four-year term but will resign when the war ends—if it ends during that term.

Certainly, I can't imagine any meeting of wartime or postwar significance attended by Churchill, Stalin—and Thomas Dewey.

Spent this past weekend in Casablanca, part of the time with Josine, and later, accompanied by Vic Ball, at the Cormiers'. Vic is intelligent and witty, at the moment one of my best friends. He has been overseas

---

* Walter Edward Guinness, 1st Baron Moyne, was an Anglo-Irish politician and businessman, leader of the House of Lords, Secretary of State for the Colonies, and Resident Minister in Cairo. Perceived by militant Zionists as being against the establishment of a Jewish state, members of Lehi, a Jewish terrorist group. was responsible for his assassination.

four years, in Palestine, Cairo, Algiers, Malta, followed the Eighth Army across Libya, and arrived in Morocco from Biskra, Algeria.

Wednesday, November 8. Jack Marsden last night attended a meeting of the Sale camp newspaper editorial board, presided over by the padre, who told of how a few weeks ago he went down to Marrakesh to conduct burial services for five RAF men killed in the crash of their Dakota. The British consul was most inhospitable, made the padre feel unwanted. The padre officiated, however, and some time later visited the graves, found them quite neglected without even headstones, wood crosses, or other markers.

Latest news says that Budapest has fallen to the Russians.*

Saturday, November 11. Wish that this was this war's Armistice Day. Celebrations locally—ours, that is—include a military parade and rugby and soccer games. Only a Mosquito and a Liberator came in today, which was fortunate because I only had one tanker manned. Two men were playing football, another two on the parade. Len Butler and I knew better than to protest when these men were chosen for we have more than once been told, in effect, that such functions have priority over the fuel needs of aircraft heading east for the warfronts. But this camp (or "garrison" as it is officially designated in DROs [Daily Routine Orders]) is doing some good for currently a fund is being held here for the benefit of bombed out London pensioners. Everybody contributed.

Yesterday's Daily Express came out here today aboard a Mosquito. V-2† was headlined. Goebbels is making fantastic claims for this latest vengeance weapon. First snow has fallen on both east and west fronts. East front relatively quiet, second front alive with the roar of 1300 bombers walloping the enemy in the Metz [northeast France] area, supporting Patton's new drive. Some American and Canadian deserters formed a Chicago-style gang in Rome and killed a café owner. Eisenhower says "the future can be nothing but gleaming."

Herbert Morrison has decided to permit restoration of street lighting in London, but confusion reigns over just where and how much. Vera Lynn,‡ popular songstress, says "malicious and unfunny impersonators"

---

* Budapest actually surrendered to the Russians on February 13, 1945.

† The V-2, the second of Hitler's "Vengeance Weapons," was a ballistic missile and the first rocket to achieve sub-orbital spaceflight. More than 1,400 were launched at Britain, with more than 500 missiles striking London.

‡ Vera Margaret Lynn was an English singer, songwriter, and entertainer whose musical recordings and performances were wartime favorites. Known as Britain's "Forces' Sweetheart," she remained one of the nation's symbols of resilience and hope. With songs such as "We'll Meet Again" and "The White Cliffs of Dover," she was a potent morale-builder. Lynn died in 2020 at age 103.

are trying to "discomfit me." A member of the 6th Gurkha Rifles [British Indian Army] has been awarded the VC [Victoria Cross] for charging a Japanese troop concentration, killing three Japs, "dispersing" fire to others, and capturing two light guns.

Following a gunfight outside the Crown Hotel in a Hampshire village, in which two American MPs and the hotel licensee's wife were killed, two Negro soldiers will be court-martialed for murder. A 27-year-old WAAF was found strangled in a Suffolk ditch and Scotland Yard is investigating. Thus the Daily Express, London, 10 November 1944.

Last night the corporals held a dance in Rabat at the Paradise Restaurant. Tom Bradley introduced me to a nice girl with whom I danced most of the night. Took her home at about 1 am—a hell of a long walk—received no goodnight kiss but a promise of a future meeting. Walked briskly back through empty shadowed street—at least they seemed empty, but are apt to contain Arab "aggressors" according to the girl, Paulette, who had asked me before we parted if I was afraid. "Oh, no." I replied with false vigour, "not at all...."

Wednesday, November 15. I'm thinking of taking up a course with the London School of Journalism, seeking confirmation of my belief that I can write. Right now, though, I have to collect my rations at the Corporal's Club. Then I'll be at the Malcolm Club to hear a lecture on Arab customs, delivered by a British Consular official who has been in Morocco twenty-five years.

Corporal Guttridge off duty in his billet with pinups for company, 1945.

Jack Marsden, making corny wisecracks, is busy attaching fresh pinups to the wall. Vic Ball used to claim that far from titillating him, pin-ups were a bore. "The models have exhausted the number of possible physical poses," he would say, "and now it has become monotonous repetition." But Marsden, refusing to believe that no nudes is good news, presses on plastering the wall with them. Up goes a picture of Shirley Temple. She is clothed, but, in my opinion, too young, only sixteen, for pin-up service, and I say as much. Marsden yells back that if she were here, he'd find her old enough to cuddle.

Josine and her frail but good-natured husband Rene have returned to Casablanca where I will visit them next week. Josine really is nice and my not-so-secret feelings toward her are warmer than just friendly.

Friday, November 17. That lecture on Arab customs proved quite interesting but I had the impression that the lecturer—a former missionary—was not without the prejudices a member of one religion harbours for other religions. Several times he raised a laugh describing superstitious beliefs and practices of the Islam faith, but it [Islam] certainly has not the monopoly on these!

Saturday November 18. Prevailing topic among groups of men standing around idly because of the pouring rain is home leave. There wasn't very much detail in the statement Churchill made yesterday about a proposal that 6000 men in selected theatres of war—North Africa included—be allowed to go home for four weeks' furlough. Churchill says many could be home for Christmas. There's a catch in it, was the cynical response of some of my colleagues here. Any seemingly generous gesture on the government's part these days is apt to be greeted with—"What's the catch?"

Saw "Gaslight" two nights ago—the Hollywood version. Charles Boyer quite good, Ingrid Bergman splendid, Joseph Cotton miscast. All in all, not as good as the earlier British version with Anton Walbrook and Diana Wynyard.

Friday, November 24. Casablanca's Bar Celtic is notoriously "red," its proprietor a Spanish communist, most customers Spanish, all leftist. Josine, Rene Espouteille, and I have dined and wined there often. Yesterday they introduced me to Leon Capazza, a middle-aged gaunt communist zealot who spent 15 months in a Vichy jail and is proud of it. He told me that arms are being smuggled into Spain from Morocco for use against Franco. He also told me that Franco and his buddies plotted the revolution against the Spanish government back in 1936 in

Casablanca's Hotel Anfa—site of the Allied leaders "Unconditional Surrender" conference.*

Wednesday, November 29. Visited the Cormiers in Casablanca night before last and introduced Derek Roberts to them.

Surprised to read in the Sunday Graphic that the Belgian political crisis has grown violent. These "resistance" movements seem determined to exploit the present turmoil in order to create a people's government. Also heard that an RAF munitions dump at Burton-on-Trent blew up killing over 200.†

Thursday, November 30. That explosion is the worst wartime disaster not caused by enemy action. Shook the Midlands.

"Not to be construed as a mutiny," says the Canadian government about recent troop protests against [Canadian Prime Minister] Mackenzie King's new compulsory overseas service plan.

Last month an 18-year-old London striptease dancer met an American soldier in a Hammersmith café. Some nights later, they hailed a taxi, had the driver take them out of town, where they shot him to death—well, the GI did—and robbed him, afterward dumping his body in a ditch. That, anyway, is the prosecution's case at the trial opening December 6—the first time an American soldier has faced a capital charge in a British civil court.‡

Arduous day, twenty aircraft came in.

Sunday, December 3. From Frances today, I received a Christmas gift, Howard Spring's latest novel "Heaven Lies about Us."

Monday, December 4. After France, Brussels now Greece, whose guerrillas have refused to yield their arms. RAF planes have dropped leaflets warning partisans the British will support the "legally constituted"

---

* The Casablanca Conference or Anfa Conference was held at the Anfa Hotel (January 14–24, 1943). There, President Roosevelt and Prime Minister Churchill planned the Allied European strategy for the war's next phase. Negotiations resulted in the "Casablanca Declaration" and the conference's most important intention: the unconditional surrender of the Axis powers.

† The RAF Fauld explosion occurred on November 27, 1944, at the RAF Fauld underground munitions storage depot in Staffordshire. With an estimated 4,000 tons of exploding ordnance, it was one of the largest non-nuclear explosions in history. The 100-foot-deep explosion crater, known as the "Hanbury Crater," is still visible just south of Fauld, east of Hanbury, Staffordshire.

‡ The murder became known as the "cleft chin murder" because the murder victim, a taxi driver, had a cleft chin. The culprits were Karl Hultén, a Swedish-born deserter from the U.S. Army, and Elizabeth Jones, an 18-year-old waitress. They were both found guilty and sentenced to be hanged. Hultén was executed at Pentonville Prison on March 8, 1945. Jones was reprieved and released in May 1954.

government. There must be many British soldiers who sympathize with those brave anti-fascist bands.*

Wednesday, December 6. Greek crisis worsening. British troops, instead of enjoying a well-earned break after clearing out the real enemy, now have the task of trying to subdue recalcitrant Resistance fighters.

American Forts [B-17 Flying Fortresses] bombed Belgrade [Yugoslavia] by mistake, killed more than a thousand—also their bombs struck a German hospital ship. At home the Home Guard stands down, with thanks from the King. And Princess Elizabeth has launched the world's most powerful battleship [HMS *Vanguard*]. Nice to be getting a few English newspapers again. I'll see they go up on the Malcolm Club wall tomorrow for all to see.

Friday, December 8. 10:30 pm. A strong wind is sweeping sheets of fine rain across the camps. Somewhere in the thick low cloud above a Liberator probably BOAC, has been flying for the past hour, unable to safely land. Rockets have soared into the night sky, bursting and scattering balls of light over the landing field. But conditions are still too bad. Now all is quiet but for the hiss of rain, and I imagine the plane has flown off, perhaps to Casablanca.

Saturday, December 9. Sad to hear that British soldiers are fighting Greek partisans.

Sunday, December 10. Twenty-one aircraft came in today, eight of them Liberators from Canada via the Azores.

Churchill, defending the government's policy on Greece, says, "When countries are liberated, it does not follow that those who receive weapons should use them to achieve their own ends by violence and murder."

Yesterday afternoon, the rain having ceased, Jack Marsden and I hiked to the Sale side of the Bou Regreg across which scores of boats plied back and forth. Sale's buildings shone in the sunlight. And on the Rabat side of the river, the sun glinted off the walled Medina atop the steep cliff. We climbed into a boat and bid the grinning Arab boatman to relax while we took turns at the oars. For almost an hour, we dawdled on the river where it broadens to meet the blue Atlantic.

---

* By late 1943, individual Greek resistance groups began fighting among themselves. In September 1943, civil war broke out within the resistance. On December 3, 1944, after the Germans had retreated, Athens police, with British forces, opened fire on a pro–National Liberation Front rally in the central square, killing 28 demonstrators and injuring dozens. This caused outrage in Britain, and even troops stationed far afield weighed in, as we see here among RAF personnel in Morocco.

Wednesday, December 13. I have a day off. Weather sunny but cool. Malcolm Club's Quiet Room walls plastered with write-ups (locally composed and from Fleet Street) on the Greek crisis. This station's padre, who gave the once-over to all contributions for the wall newspaper, is away in Jerusalem. Now, it seems Corporal Whitaker has the say-so upon stuff handed in so the results can be imagined. He is a communist ex-journalist. The Quiet Room should be renamed the Red Room. Whittaker has himself written and put up an article full of leftist venom directed at reactionary Greeks, Georgios Papandreou, international bankers, King George II of Greece,

In tropical garb and pith helmet, Corporal Guttridge mixes with locals at his new overseas duty assignment near Rabat, Morocco, 1944.

and the British government. I've seen no officers reading the wall newspaper for the Malcolm Club is off-limits to them (except officers on duty or the padre), and I rather think the Officers' Mess is blissfully unaware of the increasing socialistic trend of thought in this camp. Maybe it's as well.

"The most hateful order I have had to give was to use my Air Force against Greek nationals"—Air Commodore [Geoffrey] Tuttle, AOC [Air Officer Commanding] Greece.

Thursday, December 14. Forty NCOs and men and one officer, attended last night's discussion group. Subject: Greece. Whittaker did most of the talking, giving his (i.e., communist) interpretation of Churchill's motives for the military intervention. He says the purpose is to safeguard British financial interests from a leftwing takeover. One LAC

Sim caused a mild sensation by stating that fascism was preferable to communism, and today the Malcolm Club wall sports an appeal to the camp's anti–Reds, urging that they unite in defence of "our precious heritage."

Whittaker, who runs the printing of the camp's monthly magazine at the Echo de Maroc's printing presses in Rabat, told me that French police looked in there apparently in search of those who print the illegal communist news Egalise out here. Whittaker at that time had a copy in his pocket, given to him by me; it was one of half a dozen that the communist Leon Cappaza pressed upon me when I was last in Casablanca.

A welcome and expensive present from Helen, a self-winding shock-proof waterproof watch, just what I needed. Perhaps I'm misnaming the strong feeling of gratitude when I say I must love the girl.

Met Leon Capazza again yesterday in Casablanca. He told me wearily that he was wasting his time in Casablanca, doing clerical work. He wants action—laments the communists' lack of arms. Capazza told me that a year ago it was simple to buy arms from the Americans. But not anymore.

Wednesday, December 20. These pre–Christmas days, when the mere utterance of the words "peace and goodwill" is a mockery, are black and stormy. Disunity and friction threaten even those so-called United Nations. At home, British workers clamor against the government, British soldiers are fighting and dying in a probably unnecessary battle in Greece, while Washington shifts uncomfortably from one foot to another, and Russia looks on in grim and foreboding silence. And meanwhile, Rundstedt has launched a violent counter-attack in the Ardennes.* Not the happiest of Christmases.

Thursday morning, December 21. I'm Orderly Corporal today—which is okay with me for it removes the possibility that I'll be on duty Christmas Day.

Thoroughly enjoyed "Hail the Conquering Hero" the other night. A Preston Sturgess masterpiece. Eddie Bracken and William Demarest superb.

Saturday, December 23. A Liberator came in at three this morning, its crew in a hurry to make their delivery and get home for Christmas. So

---

* From December 16, 1944, to January 25, 1945, the Germans launched one final major offensive against the Allies in the Ardennes (Belgium and Luxembourg). This offensive, known as the Battle of the Bulge, eventually stalled, and clear weather allowed allied air power to destroy enemy ground forces. The offensive's final collapse assured final German defeat less than four months later.

after refueling, it took off promptly. NCO i/c [in charge] duty crew was Len Butler. I may be on sometime over Christmas, but for the day itself, just a skeleton crew will service any aircraft requiring it, and I'll have to sort out a "stand-by" refueling crew.

Incoming Christmas cards and letters from jazz-loving correspondents wish me lots of the righteous stuff over the holiday. I doubt whether I'll hear anything as remotely like the "righteous stuff" as even Glenn Miller's "In the Mood."

Still, it's Christmas—with no peace, and precious little goodwill. The Germans are 30 miles into Belgium.

A dance at the Malcolm Club starts things rolling here tonight. I hope to meet Paulette again. And it's weeks since I lost track of Josine and Rene. I think they're somewhere in Rabat where yesterday I saw French shoppers buying cheap toys in dimly lit shops and Arabs in rags or colorful robes and colorfully costumed Sultans Black Guard. Outside the Collisee Theatre, a couple of Arab kids fought furiously, egged on by their elders, while French passersby glanced contemptuously at them or ignored them entirely. The Collisee billboards displayed Jean Arthur in "The Westerner."

Monday, December 25. Christmas Day. I expect to see Paulette tomorrow night. We resumed our friendship at the Malcolm Club dance Saturday night. I'll take her to a repeat of the camp's pantomime. Should also see her at the Garrison Club hop Wednesday night. So I'm feeling pretty good, all things considered. Yesterday there was little work, but due to a piece of unforgiveable incompetence on the part of a senior NCO, I had to supervise the draining of a Mosquito long-range fuel tank at half-past 5. So by the time I'd had dinner, it was too late to attend church for carol-singing.

Last night at the

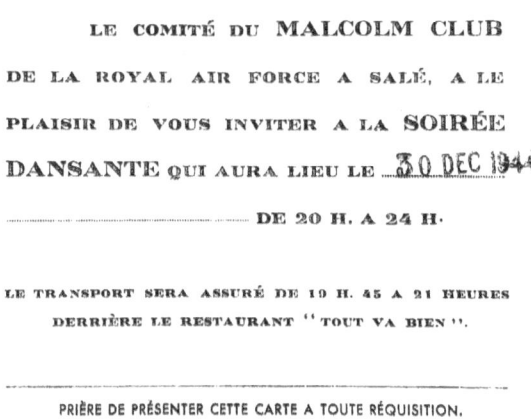

Saturday night dances at the Salé airbase Malcolm Club were a welcome diversion from long hours of duty punctuated by many other hours of boredom.

invitation of some of the lads, I visited the airmen's canteen, which was all bright and decorated, named for the occasion the "Pig and Whistle." Before the booze and noise affected my senses, I learned that the previous night our padre tried to get our CO Group Captain Sutton to leave the P and W so the place could be locked up. Sutton was quite drunk and kept resisting the padre's efforts, at one point turning to the lads and shouting, "Do you wanna go to bed?" All hands waved NO! The padre persisted—"Yes, they do, sir, so come along." The CO thereupon told him, "Go to hell. Who's the bloody boss of this camp, you or me? Now, bugger off."

No one seemed to recall the padre's reaction to that. As for me, I finished up in the airmens' canteen singing hoarsely, the room filled with spilled beer and smelling of the stuff, also of cigar smoke and male bodies. Men danced, pranced, yelled, and screamed, sang solo and communally. Some, I regret to say, lost tempers and fought.

Afterwards I was in the Corporals' Club where the atmosphere was cleaner and quieter.

Then in somebody's billet. Beds were overturned, more fights. Someone got me to sing a solo. Nobody listened. They were all singing solos. Next, I was in Mac's billet where, of all things, a fierce discussion on Christianity broke out. I talked myself hoarse, beer has that effect on me.

I rolled into bed long after 3 a.m.

And at half past seven, Flight Sergeant Hodgkinson and Sergeant Gullis and Allport banged their way into the billets of all Servicing Flight personnel, doling out a mug of hot tea and a cigar to each man. After breakfast, I slept most of the morning while others braved heavy rain to watch a football match. Joe, the black kid who brings us French morning newspapers, entered, seeking as usual to buy cigarettes, chewing gum, or playing cards. Jack Marsden sold him a surplus mosquito net for a hundred francs. So he could get it past the Goum* guards, who frisk native labourers at the camp gates, Joe half-stripped and wound the net around his torso. Reclothed he looked a fatter than usual Joe.

Dinner in the Malcolm Club—cream of tomato soup, boiled and roast potatoes, pork, chicken, bread sauce, Christmas pudding, nuts, tangerines, beer, sweets, mince-pies. Three long rows of tables stretched the length of the Malcolm Club's decorated interior. Grinning French girls served from behind the counter while red-faced officers and senior

---

* The Moroccan Goumiers were indigenous Moroccan soldiers who served in auxiliary units attached to the French Army of Africa. The term Goum designated a company of Goumiers.

NCOs waited upon us in traditional fashion. The CO wandered about chatting good-naturedly with everybody, the padre keeping a paternal eye upon him. Someone thumped a piano and a fat flight lieutenant with a fat cigar sang "Mountains of Mourne" and "Besame Mucho." Nobody asked him to and I suspect he did it to get out of the serving. The CO gave a little speech and was roundly cheered. Some kid on the camp is 21 today so Flying Officer Messenger, assistant adjutant, brought him onstage and we all roared "Twenty-one Today," accompanied by the tinkling of a piano, cracking of nutshells, chomping of jaws on hunks of chicken. Even the usually anxious-visaged CTO managed a smile as he dashed up and down and dodged around with plates of food.

I slept it off afterwards, then read the Union Jack Christmas issue, just in, which reports the German attack held, and clobbered by our aircraft, the weather having improved.

This is my second Christmas away from home.

Wednesday, December 27. Another Christmas come and gone. And with what fury it departed. All day yesterday and until half an hour ago, about 1 p.m. rain, has poured in wild torrents, lashed by a bitterly cold wind. The storm was so severe it was feared Rabat folk invited here for the pantomime wouldn't venture into it. But quite a crowd arrived. Paulette was here and although her knowledge of English is limited, she evidently enjoyed the show—the slapstick humor, the music, the colorful costumes were easy to appreciate. Baxendate (a theatrical producer before the war) told me today he had worked the cast and technicians damned hard. Everyone gave of his best, including Peter Norris, whose startling contralto voice made him a perfect Cinderella. At the show's end, "she" presented "her" bridal bouquet to the Comtesse de Preux, Rabat's leading organizer for British troops. The countess (Comtesse), an active old lady, reminded me of Dame May Whitty in "Mrs. Miniver." She is, of course, English.

The CO made a speech, and with a bus running up outside to take civilians home and the rain still pouring, the whole affair ended successfully.

Of Christmas night, I remember quite little because most of the time I was quite drunk. I vaguely recall helping to carry Charlie Giddings (and his bed!) out of the billet and across to the RAOC's [Royal Army Ordnance Corps] mess hut where the Army were celebrating. And—who else but Winston Churchill would travel thousands of miles at Christmastime to settle a Balkan civil war?*

---

* Churchill arrived in Athens on Christmas determined to influence negotiations between the Greek government and the EAM. The goal was to create a provisional government and avoid the outbreak of civil war.

German thrusts in the Ardennes, continue and are reported to have isolated American units.

Friday, December 29. Last night I dined with Josine and Rene, both of whom I met by accident on Wednesday just before the Garrison Club dance.

Weather here remains very cold.

Heard some story today about bandleader Glenn Miller missing somewhere on the Western Front.*

A stock of English books has arrived in Rabat, and I bought a volume of Montaigne, Arnold Bennett's "Literary Taste," [Literary Taste: How to Form It] and a collection of translated French short stories, Everyman edition.

Sunday, December 31. 11:30 pm. Half-an-hour left of 1944 and I have a sore throat—too much talking and singing, not to mention drinking over in the Corporals' Club. No Auld Lang Syne for me—I am off to bed with Montaigne's essays. These days, or nights, I contend that getting into bed with a good book is the next best thing to getting into bed with a bad woman.

1944 has gone by remarkably fast, seems to me....

Whoops! Within the past ten minutes Fl/Sgt. Hodgkinson and Sgt. Allport and Gullis, all of whom came around with tea and cigarettes on Christmas morning, have staggered in here with whiskey and port and we—Jack Marsden and I—had to partake of same. I'll hand it to Hodgkinson, he is—well, a damn good type.

Many men died this past twelve months. Most of them loved life as I do. It all seems so senseless.

Midnight and quiet now. Well almost. Jack Marsden turns a page. Distant voices are singing Auld Lang Syne. It is nineteen hundred and forty-five.

1945

Tuesday, January 2. Bad way to begin the new year. Yesterday I smashed my mirror <u>and</u> lost a thousand francs. The money equals about five English pounds and I haven't a clue where I lost it. Carelessly and no doubt drunkenly, I slapped the note down somewhere and also no doubt some unscrupulous character picked it up.

---

* On December 15, 1944, while flying to Paris, the aircraft Miller was aboard, a UC-64A Norseman, disappeared in bad weather over the English Channel.

Last night I saw—for the second time—"Double Indemnity," a first-rate film based on a story by James M. Cain, who wrote "The Postman Always Rings Twice." Superb acting by Barbara Stanwyck, Fred Mac-Murray, and Edward G. Robinson. Direction—Billy Wilder, first-class, and never a line of dialogue wasted.

Americans yielding ground on the Western Front [during the Battle of the Bulge]. We seem to have been caught napping by the German offensive, according to critics back home—where Christmas in some parts, was the coldest in 50 years.

From Win Roberts, Bolton, comes a letter saying, "We are a target area for these doodle-what's-its" [V-1 buzz bombs]. And of some rare earthquake tremors in the north of England on December 30—"the bed was really rocking ... the joint was jumping."

Much nonsense aired by the ignorant here of the Allied command changes. Apparently, Montgomery's command has been extended to embrace American forces. Reports of American resentment have provoked loud anti–American sentiments and I have made myself rather unpopular by vehemently denouncing such unreasoned criticism of the American military. There are some fools around here who seem more at war with the Americans than with the Germans.

Weather here in French Morocco continues cold, ice coating some aircraft wing surfaces, and the grass is dusted with frost.

Friday, January 12. pm. All last night and today, continuing even now, torrential rain and strong cold wind with frequent outbursts of thunder and lightning. These storms come surging in from the Atlantic. I have just returned from a rain-soaked journey, floundering in blackness through pools of mud and water, buffeted by gale force gusts, all for a mug of tea and two fried egg sandwiches consumed at the Malcolm Club.

I have decided to take advantage of the government's emergency training scheme for teachers as soon as I am demobbed [demobilized]. Teaching is a profession that appeals to me. Teaching in England, however, will mean cancellation of my proposed trip to America.

I am trying to plod through Meredith's "The Ordeal of Richard Feverel:" But his florid style makes for difficult reading. I am one-third of the way through the book and I still can't give a damn what fate has in store for Feverel. Maybe the fault is mine. Other reading these days include, whenever possible, World Press Review, Life magazine, Picture Posts, the Times, New Statesman, and Nation. I am in the fortunate position—we all are here—chronic grumbles to the contrary, of being on a station where discipline is relatively light and there isn't much work at the moment.

Sunday, January 14. I have a fever tonight—last night at the Garrison Club dance, I felt tired, and Paulette had frequent, if unwelcome, glimpses of my medically considered over-large tonsils as I yawned repeatedly. I struggled gamely around the dance floor—a conga line came in useful, for I was propelled along without any great strain on my ever-diminishing store of energy.

Wednesday, January 17. Another rainy, wind-swept day, with much thunder and lightning. And all western Europe, from England to Italy, is suffering great snowstorms. Amid these icy conditions, the Allied troops are steadily forcing back the Germans. To the east, Warsaw is liberated, Cracow soon to be as the Russians keep up their pressure.

A truce signed in the Greek civil war. Reading Alexander Woolcott* the other day, I liked this on Chaplin: "Charlie has brought to a sore and anxious world a gift of healing laughter and quickening, cleansing, inexplicable tears ... a gift comparable to the sweet melodies Franz Schubert left behind him... Primarily Charlie is innocent courage, gallantry—the unquenchable in mankind—taking on flesh and walking this earth to give us heart. His like has not passed this way before. And we shall not see his like again." What a superlative epitaph! For epitaph it is. The Charlie Chaplin of former years, the pathetic little man beloved of the world, is indeed dead.† Bearing his name is the white-haired trembling fellow clutching the sides of the Criminal Court dock screaming, "You're trying to make a monster out of me." Not the man Woolcott wrote about in 1931.

Monday, January 22. The Red Army's massive assault is going ahead full speed. It's back to the wall now for Germany, and not even Goebbels can keep the truth from the unhappy Germans.

I attended a party the other night with Paulette, Hugette, and the rest of the Rabat "sorority." Great fun and some Basie on the radio, numbers like "One O'Clock Jump" and "Rock-a-Bye Basie."

In an old (last November) English newspaper, I read of more than one hundred teenaged English girls who invaded a U.S. Army camp in Staffordshire to get at their American boyfriends who were confined to barracks. MPs and civil police, who tried to keep them out, were stoned.

And these kids are among tomorrow's adult citizens? Scary!!

---

* American author, critic, and actor known for his acerbic wit.

† Chaplin's popularity declined in the 1940s after he was accused of communist sympathies, involvement in a paternity suit, and marriages to much younger women. Under investigation by the FBI, Chaplin fled the United States and settled in Switzerland. He died in 1977.

Thursday, January 25. Took a countess home last night. Well, I think she is a countess. She must be for her husband is a count. I had intended having a quiet night, had booked a seat at the Colisee, and killed time drinking at the Garrison Club. She was on the other side of the counter, serving beer. A talkative officer nearby abruptly left, and no longer having to suffer his puerile chatter, I sucked at my pipe in silence. She suddenly fixed her blue eyes on me and asked if I were going dancing at the Garrison on Saturday and Paradise Club on Monday. I said possibly. We were soon on good terms despite her halting English and my near-stationary French. Nine-o'clock—movie time—came and went. I blinked when she asked me to take her home, which I did. Unfortunately (or fortunately?) her husband was there, speaking quite fluent English and vaguely resembling a Hollywood impression of, well, a French count. Which he is, and, moreover, holds some office in the local Rabat administration.

Sunday, January 28. "His Majesty the King has been graciously pleased to approve the following awards to personnel in the Mediterranean Group of RAF Transport Command...." Thus begins the official announcement that some of us here, including yours truly, are Mentioned in Dispatches.* I'd be a liar if I denied that the news gave me a thrill of pride, and I wouldn't be human if I didn't feel one. Young Derek Roberts told me that, quite frankly, he considered that I had earned it, as had Len Butler. Well, it's true we have run the Refueling Party efficiently for well over a year. No aircraft have been delayed on our account. But does doing one's job well warrant a special award? I'm not so sure.

Anyway, right now I'm most conscious of stomach distress, the result no doubt, of some of the poisonous trash we get at times from the cookhouse.

Monday, January 29. I've just received a letter from Arthur Wilson's mother in reply to one I addressed to Arthur some months ago. Wils and the rest of the crew were reported missing after their bomber had gone on ops [operations] over Hamburg last July. Since then, the air-gunner and the bomb-aimer were found dead in Germany where they are now buried. There is still no news of the remainder of the crew. Mrs. Wilson writes, "We must hope and pray."

What can I say? Arthur Wilson was probably the best friend I ever had. In my life. I have made few real friends although many good

---

* To be mentioned in dispatches indicates that a member of the armed forces has been named in an official report forwarded to the high command. In that report is a description of the member's gallant or meritorious action.

acquaintances. The few were men like Bill Twiss, Ted Mansell, Johnny "Legs" King, Vic Ball, and Arthur Wilson. There's nothing I feel like saying right now.

Tuesday, January 30. One-time Paris orchestral conductor, now private, Hubert d'Auriol, French Army, gave another gramophone recital tonight at which just eighteen men were present.

But I wish d'Auriol wasn't so damned heavy-handed on the machine. The scratching of the needle on the record's surface at each beginning was a bit of a distraction. Selections included Beethoven (Fifth Symphony) and Liszt—and a saxophone work by Debussy, sort of a novelty to me for saxophone means Coleman Hawkins, [Leon "Chu"] Berry, Benny Carter.

Letter from home says the old man is busy at hospitals and getting firsthand accounts of the fighting. Cardiff, incidentally, is buried under two feet of snow—Britain is suffering the coldest winter for 50 years.

Thursday, February 1. Wish to God I could see a British newspaper. We get our news piecemeal. Hitler is said to have made a speech warning the democracies against the "Bolshevik tide" sweeping Europe. Adolf is reading from one of his old scripts, it seems. Well, his Germany is now very much Europe's battleground. Since this war started, millions have been made refugees in France, Belgium, Holland, Russia, Italy, Scandinavia, and the Balkans. Fascism's counterpart in the Far East has turned millions more into refugees. Hitler used to tell his followers they were the master race, supermen. Now he has made of his Germans the continent's last refugees.

Last night, at the apartment of the Comtesse de la Forest, we wined and listened to the radio—among other things. But the evening was rather marred by my constant expectation of the count's return.

Sunday, February 4. Current rumors: F.D. Roosevelt passed through Casablanca en route to some important conference. German aircraft landed at Casa yesterday with "important" Germans on board. Current facts: 2500 tons of bombs rained on Berlin last night. Allied forces are penetrating deeper into the Reich from the west, while from the East the Russians are closing in on Frankfurt.

Yesterday Charlie Giddings received a letter from Jock Marshall, written while Jock was en route home following temporary imprisonment by the ELAS* in Greece. Giddings says the ELAS ill-treated hostages, forced many to strip and march bare-footed in the snow. They fed

---

* The Greek People's Liberation Army was the military arm of the left-wing National Liberation Front during the Greek Resistance.

us when they felt like it, and when they did, it was bread and cold water. Churchill's policy seems right after all. Reports like this one give food for thought for our irresponsible left-wingers who never cease to criticize the Prime Minister.

Tuesday, February 6. Last night's film (the last for some time because the Yanks have taken away the projector we borrowed from them), was a joyous Hollywood satire called "Doughgirls." With a title like that, I feared the worst. But Jack Carson, Jane Wyman, Eve Arden, and Charlie Ruggles kept the fun going until the movie spluttered out to a rather lame finish.

Thursday, February 8. Wonder who were the occupants of the Avro York that crashed on the shores of the Black Sea? Thank God, Churchill wasn't among them. Britain without Churchill now would be like a ship without a rudder. An inquiry hereabouts is probing the mystery of LAC Lees, who was found on a Rabat sidewalk with shattered legs and pelvis. Story is that he made himself a nuisance in somebody's apartment and was thrown out of the window.

Affectionate letter from Win Roberts—"I get my inspiration from a rather good-looking corporal who looks as if he might be nice to know"—arrived yesterday. But none from Cardiff, mail service still interrupted by a phenomenally heavy snowstorm.

General MacArthur has entered Manila. War Minister announces that when the war ends, Britain's demob program will cost over 200 million pounds.

Friday, February 16. Spent the past three days in Casablanca. Dined twice with the Cormiers, also ogled the pretty girls, French mostly, serving at the Union Jack Club. M. Cormier told me he places beauty above ability to cook as a necessary qualification in a prospective bride. But first he would insist upon intelligence—the sort of judgment that perhaps we might expect from Voltaire or Demosthenes, whose busts adorn Cormier's bureau.

The Crimea Declaration* hit the headline during my stay in Casablanca and Frenchmen at café tables discussed the statements and decisions of "Le Grande Trois [Churchill, Roosevelt, Stalin]." Personally, I rather suspect that unnecessary appeasement of Stalin is taking place by a worried Churchill and an uneasy Roosevelt. Perhaps I'm wrong. But

---

* The "Declaration of Liberated Europe," introduced at the Yalta Conference of February 4–11, 1945, promised that Europeans could "create democratic institutions of their own choice." It also pledged "the earliest possible establishment through free elections governments responsive to the will of the people."

decisions made in favor of carving up Poland, without any representation of that country consulted, has a Munich taint....

Some newspapers just in. One carried the story of an Irishwoman charged with conveying letters and food to German prisoners. She and one "Heinz" exchanged love letters concealed in the snowballs they threw to each other.

In Casablanca last week, I saw Hollywood's version of Richard Llewellyn's "None But the Lonely Heart." Cary Grant is badly miscast as Ernie Mott, June Duprez mournfully lovely, Ethel Barrymore first-rate. Frances St. John Smith sent me a gift of Noel Coward's "Middle East Diary." Coward roamed the line from Gibraltar to Habbaniyah, [Iraq] singing in camps and hospitals, also wining and dining with commanders and diplomats and ladies. The book is sprinkled with first names—Dicky's, Georges, Pennys, Erics, Connie's and Tonys. Coward comes through unashamedly nostalgic for the green fields and class distinction of dear old England, he derides American politicians, and manages to insult wounded American soldiers, something which I hear has got him in hot water on both sides of the Atlantic.

Saturday, February 24. Two letters from Helen today, one beginning, "God, how I love you." But still no news from home.

Wednesday, February 28. The powers-that-be have inaugurated something called a "Moral Leadership Course." It is conducted in Rome, which means a nice trip to that city for those lucky enough to be selected—like Ross, for instance, whose affected air of piety, since his return from Rome, is somewhat offset by his continued boasting, "Moral Leadership" notwithstanding, of the affair he enjoys in Rabat with the wife of a soldier in the French army. He says he learned, while in Rome, that the Darwinian Theory of Evolution is no longer supported by today's scientists—a remark, which persuades me that by failing to wrangle myself onto this Roman junket, I am not missing much of any value. Ross, because he had to, entered several places of worship, "When you've been in one church in Rome, you've been in the lot," he says. But adds, recalling the frescoes and murals and mosaics and with eyes reverently lowered, "What our Lord must have gone through!"

What Ross went through was three weeks of Moral Leadership training at government expense. He now avows soberly that he has given up cursing as a result. And when he advised me, if I go on the course, to take plenty of cigarettes because "you can sell them to the Wops for a terrific price," I believed that he probably had given up that vice because, after all, he could have said "Sell them to the f-ing Wops." Couldn't he?

Thursday, March 1. The hell with Ross and Moral Leadership. Last night I was most absorbed in "Thousands Cheer," a sparkling musical with Gene Kelly, Eleanor Powell, Judy Garland, Lucille Ball, Mickey Rooney and bands led by Kay Kyser, Bob Crosby, and Benny Carter. And our new projector equipment gave us sharp visual clarity and good sound. We even saw a newsreel showing the Luftwaffe's surprise New Year's Day attack that destroyed many of our planes on the ground.

Just finished reading Thomas Hardy's "Life's Little Ironies" and have found it more disturbing than entertaining. Had a sad letter from Arthur Wilson's mother. She has received word from the Air Ministry that there were two bombers shot down over Hamburg that night, and out of both crews, eleven bodies were found—three of Arthur's crew identified, five of the other crew and three unidentified. Three are still missing. I still cling to the hope that Arthur may be safe.

Saturday, March 3. Am duty crew NCO this evening. Three Libs and a few Mosquitoes came in, the latter from Canada by a circuitous route touching the USA, Brazil, the Ascension Islands, West Africa and from here they go on to Algiers, then across the Mediterranean, across France to England. The reason they don't fly directly across the Atlantic has something to do with prevailing winds, I believe.

Frances St. John Smith, informed of my MID [Mentioned in Dispatches], writes "We are very proud of you." She also paints a pretty picture of "pussy-willows and catkins decorating our hall and dining room ... tiny yellow flowers of jasmine like little stars ... woods nearby have a purple and yellow carpet of crocuses." And in reference to my gift of silk stockings "It is very sweet of you... You are a perfect peach."

Saw "Home in Indiana" a technicolored treat for the eyes ... lovely apple blossoms and June Haver and sleek brown horses and June Haver and deep green turf and June Haver....

Thursday, March 8. "COLOGNE: MILE TO THE RHINE" the headline in a Daily Express I found aboard the Beaufighter that came in yesterday en route for the Far East. By now, the Americans will be in control of Cologne, a much-battered city and I feel some sympathy for its dazed surviving citizens. In the "Cleft-chin" murder case, I hear that the girl [Elizabeth Jones] is sentenced to life imprisonment, the American soldier [Karl Hulten] to hang.

Friday, March 9. Churchill on German soil... I am reminded of a tale by Thomas Hardy in which—it's his "Life's Little Ironies"—Napoleon Bonaparte himself makes a secret national landing on the south coast of England and proceeds to plan landing sites for his armies. If Hitler ever arrives in England, it will be in chains.

Two nights ago, at George Cross's invitation, I dined with officials of Radio Maroc and their wives. The radio station—Morocco's most powerful—is available for any RAF personnel who wish to air their talents. Already pre-war West End pianist Jerry Levy, young Pete Norris with his astonishing contralto voice, and Wing Commander Coppinger have broadcast on these "half-hours." But talent seems limited, Cross tells me he has not found any more potential broadcasters.

We dined in a back-room at the Paradise.

Monday, March 12. All day, at intervals, pain surges through my stomach. Food poisoning? Breakfast—fried egg usually—is often the day's best meal. The freshness of the meat at dinner is always open to question. And potatoes, when we get them, are usually unpeeled, their skins black. And the food is slapped messily on one's plate by listless Arab boys who make no effort to separate the meat from the potatoes, the potatoes from the carrots.

Win Roberts tells me that most letters from overseas have been opened by the censor—mine included.

I'm pleased by the government's promise that men who have served eighteen months overseas will not be sent to the Far East war.

Saturday, March 17. In the camp hospital. Thought I'd be discharged today but the doctor keeps feeding me M and B tablets [bacterial medication] every four hours and imagining there must still be something gastronomically wrong with me when I'm sure there isn't.

I had reported sick Wednesday, suspecting a mild case of dysentery. The MO [medical officer] thought it might be something more serious, and evidently decided to starve me. Fortunately, on Thursday, when a surprisingly large number of medical orderlies were running hither and thither without colliding (I could only deduce because of long practice) I managed, by a stroke of brilliant strategy, the nature of which must remain a secret until the war's end, to secure a meal, thus rescuing myself from death by malnutrition.

My sleep was delayed that night thanks to a studious but talkative young orderly whom I had never seen before, and fortunately have not seen since, who sat at my bedside and discussed at great length the possible causes of blood in the feces.

The hospital ward library is small. I made several attempts to read [Laurence] Sterne's "Sentimental Journey," but damned if I could make much headway. Later I had more luck, but still can't recommend Sterne as sick-bed companion. But I was absorbed in a collection of Professor J.B.S. Haldane's biological essays and have finished Harold Laski's "Introduction to Politics." This my own book.

No peace during the daylight hours, not only because of the frantically dashing orderlies, but a sour-faced Frenchman is often on the scene with a busy hammer, a step ladder, and an Arab assistant he frequently cuffs.

The Frenchman steps from the ladder, his serf carries it farther along the wall, and the whole pantomime begins again. All this is towards the installation of electric wall lights. Of course, I've heard some good radio, from Count Basie to Schubert and Mozart. And some not so good. There is one BBC program principally aimed at sick-bed sufferers. It opens with a chorus shrieking "We Wish You Well Again," and when the program ended, I felt measurably worse than at its start.

A relay from the New Theatre, Cardiff, stirred nostalgia. Those folk laughing, I told myself, are going out into Queen Street shortly. I wondered if they included any of the seventy Germans who escaped from a Bridgend POW camp.*

Later, the news was that all but three of the POWs are rounded up. And war news—repeatedly, of General Patton's tanks, until they haunted me as much as they must haunt Rundstedt. This ward became the Remagen† bridgehead. And the RAF's Mosquitoes over Berlin for the twenty-fourth consecutive night. Then the BBC waited until I had developed a slight headache, and sprung upon me an "expert" describing the RAF's new 10-ton bomb. I heard the war interpreted by Rear Admiral this and Lieut. Colonel that and Air Marshal the other—as well as innumerable lesser armchair strategists. Derek Roberts came in with peace rumours (not true, I told him having heard the news twenty times over), brought an orange, and wishes for a speedy recovery, which I could hardly reconcile with the size of the book he had brought for me, Taylor Caldwell's "Dynasty of Death," fully 780 pages long.

Sunday, March 18. Still in hospital. Feel generally okay but weak. Am allowed out of bed, sat outside in the sun this morning. General Patton's tanks still gang up on my senses, however, and Mosquitoes were back over Berlin.

Yesterday, being payday, brawls occurred downtown in Rabat, one fellow was brought in here after having been kicked in the face by a Frenchman. Bandages muffled his groans, which was fortunate for me because the orderlies have placed him in the next bed.

---

* POW Camp 198 called "Island Farm" was located near Bridgend, Wales. On March 10, 1945, 70 German POWs escaped from this camp. All POWs were eventually recaptured.

† American forces captured the Ludendorff (railroad) Bridge across the Rhine River on March 7, 1945. It was one of the last remaining bridges across the Rhine.

Found ideal sick-bed reading, and should have known: Damon Runyon.

I hear some mail has arrived. Wish Marsden would bring mine over, if any. Ron Urwin dropped in last night and says there is absolutely no work. I believe the war's end is only weeks away, thanks largely to those tanks of General George Patton.

6:45 pm. Of all the coincidences. In the Forces Request program, sandwiched between Artie Shaw's "Blues" and the Inkspot's "Pork Chops and Gravy," was a request, duly complied with, for Turner Layton singing, "It's My Mother's Birthday Today." And it is, though I don't know how old she is—probably near 60.

Thursday, March 22. Since a York came in yesterday and its crew told of people back home listening expectantly to their radios, rumours are flying. One that we can discount is that Britain has declared war on the Republic of Ireland. Those of Germany's imminent collapse are more plausible. Work here at this staging post has slackened significantly. Only an occasional Mosquito, Liberator, or DC-3 comes in, bringing mail or top brass.

A nice photo of Win Roberts arrived.

Friday, March 23. The Air Office Commanding paid this base a visit yesterday—and of all times for such an incident to occur. A 45-Group warrant officer died on the steps of the disreputable Tour Hassan Hotel last night. Some say he was attacked, but he may have accidentally fallen. Anyway, the place is now off-limits.

Ludwigshafen [on the Rhine River] has fallen, the German Seventh Army is fleeing in broken remnants. Mainz is in ruins and the roads heading east are choked with enemy transport which is heavily bombed day and night. Mosquitos visit Berlin nightly. (Incidentally, the smaller variety are active around here, but our MO assures me they are non-malarial).

Judging from the occasional British newspapers we see, quite an epidemic of child abuse has broken out back home.

I'm reading [W. Somerset] Maugham's "The Razor's Edge." Helen sent it to me with "A Tree Grows in Brooklyn" [by Betty Smith].

I hear Len Butler is posted to Sardinia. He has been off refueling for some time, his place along with me being filled by newly promoted Corporal Urwin. But the men have little work to do these days. Airfield dispersal over at Servicing is empty, football matches are organized daily. I was roped in to play, though it's ten years since my last game. At this match, 20-minute, 7 a-side affairs—I traversed at least four miles, kicked the ball perhaps three times.

Attended a gramophone recital tonight—Mozart. It included his Violin Concerto No. 7, wonderfully played by [Yehudi] Menuhin, but I became awfully conscious of the hardness of my chair. Pity no cushions were available.

Monday, March 26. By all accounts, the ground offensive in Europe is going well. I wonder where der Fuehrer will make his last stand—if any?

For no apparent reason, the orderly officer grinned directly at me when, at dinner, I said "no" to his routine "Any complaints?" And he said, "There'll be beer in your mess tonight—American beer."

Our water supply is found to be contaminated; we are under orders to boil it before drinking. Perhaps this explains my stomach trouble of last week. Downtown in Rabat, the non–French community are thanking Allah, who has answered their prayers for rain.

Pete Martin writes to tell me he is sending a brocade dressing gown. "I think Helen will like it." I hope so, for I haven't bought her anything in exchange for all the things, especially the watch, she has sent me. Pete goes on to say that he played golf with two lesbians on Cairo's golf course and slept with a girl in Alexandria "who must have been reading "Rennie McAndrew."*

"This is not our choice," says the Wall Newspaper after announcing an end to any further discussion of present-day religion. The ban was imposed by our new RC [Roman Catholic] padre who takes a dim view of recent disparaging references to the Pope.

Wednesday, March 28. Patton's army is racing across Germany, hell-bent for the Austrian and Czech frontiers. Montgomery is far eastward of the Rhine. Nazi resistance everywhere is crumbling. The Russians have entered Danzig. The sweet smell of victory is in the air.

But I am almost too sleepy to appreciate it because barking dogs about this camp kept me awake half the night.

Parcel of South Wales Echo arrived from home yesterday reporting on the phenomenal snowfall of January 25—2½ feet of snow fell within three hours, heaviest since 1895 and it paralyzed the city more than any of the Blitz ever did. The newspaper praised postmen and others who struggled through drifts to do their job, thanked the American army that helped out with bulldozers, but fiercely criticized the city councilmen who evidently proved unable to adequately cope. But all this was back in January. Now dear old Cardiff is basking in an unusually warm spring.

---

* Rennie McAndrew was an author on topics of intimate relationships.

Sunday, April 1. Easter Sunday. And I'm Orderly Corporal today. Was on Duty Crew yesterday when three Liberators came in. Good Friday we had our worst meal of the week—sickly liquid cheese over hard toast, followed by tasteless apple slices and watery custard. Still, the news from the European battlefronts continues favorable. Hitler's armies are in full retreat.

"The greatest Welshman that unconquerable race has produced since the days of the Tudors"—Churchill on David Lloyd George,* who died the other day [March 26, 1945].

Wednesday, April 4. Back in England, the "Cleft-Chin" murder case has prompted an outburst from George Bernard Shaw deploring British justice.

Yesterday at George Cross's invitation, I was at the Radio Maroc studios in Rabat where rehearsals were held for Sunday's broadcast. In an adjoining studio could be seen a Moroccan native reading the news. As for our show, the only pianist George could find is far from adequate—out of the 500 or more men on our camp, he is apparently the only tolerable piano player.

Tom Bradley, back from a course at Naples, tells of a pitiful sight of half-starved kids hanging around military camps begging food.

The inside story of our RC padre's censorship goes like this: some Spanish Catholics "saw" a vision of the Virgin Mary who told them the godless Russians would be stopped in Germany, and they thereupon praised fascism. This item, having appeared in the leftist Tribune back home, accompanied by derisive comment, was not surprisingly tacked up on the Malcolm Club wall by our local "red," Corporal Jock Whittaker. The padre made him take it down.

Monday, April 9. I approached the cinema people and asked them to switch this week's program around to show "It Happened One Night" the first half of the week and the Judy Garland film (I forget the name) the second half. I've read so often about "It Happened" since it scooped so many Oscars years ago, and I've never yet seen it. Now it has been reissued, but over the scheduled three days of its showing here, I shall be either in Casablanca or Marrakesh on leave. The cinema people told me with regret that it was too late for rescheduling, that I should have asked them sooner. Oh, well, I'll catch up with it someday perhaps.

Thundery today.

Saturday night at the Garrison Club in Rabat, I was introduced to Denise Thibaud, whose father is governor-general of Chad Territory.

---

* Prime Minister of the United Kingdom from 1916 to 1922.

Denise speaks good English, is rather freckled, very pretty, and wore a white satin blouse with Scots tartan skirt. After the dance I met Paulette, and we greeted each other with a warm embrace.

Saw in an old Time magazine article that at the opening of Paris's Stage Door Canteen, the appearance onstage of Noel Coward was greeted with boos from Brooklyn soldiers.

Thursday, April 19. Last week's events are but a memory, part pleasant, part horrid. My leave began without hitch. I'd packed khaki drill slacks and sleeveless shirt in my blue side bag, a camera and films generously loaned me by Derek Roberts. After a relaxing two days with the Cormiers in Casablanca, I paid 170 francs for a seat on the daily CTM [Compagnie de Transports au Maroc] autobus and at 7:30 am on Friday April 13 ("I'm not superstitious," I told myself) set out for Marrakesh. The vehicle was overcrowded—they usually are, I believe—I was tightly sandwiched between a snoring and pimply-faced youth and a plump old Arab woman who alternately belched and coughed throughout the whole trip.

I settled down as best I could, read a little of "Airborne Invasion," an account of the Crete campaign, until two seats ahead a young French girl decided to shade herself from the sun's glare by wedging the single sheet Petite Marocain up against the window. And I saw its photo, that so familiar face and the headline above it, MORT DU PRESIDENT ROOSEVELT. And felt shocked. The news stayed on my mind as the bus sped across rolling country through native towns I had previously noted from a map—Khemesset, Sidi Rahal, [Souk] El Arba des Skour, Ben Guerir. Hardly towns, for the most part a café and a cluster of weed huts.

But the skyline was soon dominated by the snowcapped Atlas Mountains, and before long we were into Morocco's oldest city—whose French quarter, however, with its wide tree-lined streets and sun-drenched white-walled restaurants, is probably Morocco's newest.

Few people were about. After alighting from the bus, I spotted and spoke to an American soldier who philosophized on Roosevelt's death. "We all have to go the same way. The Lord called him at his time." He directed me to the American Red Cross, an impressive building half-cloaked by palms. From here I thumbed a ride to the USAAF [U.S. Army Air Forces] base, where I sought the RAF corporal who, I'd previously ascertained, was the only Englishman on the base. Found him—newly promoted to sergeant—he has an ideal job, as liaison to the French Wellington squadron, B4 Escadrille. Unofficially, he is host to any British personnel coming to Marrakesh, sort of local ambassador and even, given his linguistic talents, sort of a peacemaker at times of friction between American and the local citizenry.

He is, I should think, what Americans and French alike would consider an example of perfect casting—tall, good-looking, and wearing khaki shorts, has a hearty laugh and an Oxford accent and smokes a pipe. We became good friends over drinks in the French pilots' mess hall where he introduced me to several genial French airmen, including several just back from operations over Germany. The French air minister arrived that very afternoon, and I watched as he was greeted on the airfield by a dazzling and pompous parade complete with brassy French martial music and French colonial troops clad in red baggy trousers, blue jackets, white turbans, sunlight flashing from their bayonets.

Everywhere, on the base and in the town, flags flew at half-mast. And of course, social events are cancelled.

Aircraft lined up on the field included Wellingtons, Dakotas, a few Flying Fortresses, and an assortment of American fighters. Behind all this, looking both mighty and unreal, the eternal Atlas Mountains.

Sergeant Ken Staley whisked me off to an American transient camp and found me a bed in an otherwise unoccupied tent. After visiting a PX [post exchange] where he helped me procure chocolates, cigars, and a new toothbrush, Staley ushered me on board a truck and off we went into Marrakesh. My intention to savor the city's historic and scenic attractions was rather thwarted by Staley's affable chatter, most of it concerned with local episodes of intrigue—his own latest mistress is a 36-year-old brunette (her husband is in a German POW camp), whose handsome but surly 17-year-old son and delightful 11-year-old daughter were present when I met her.

Saturday, my sergeant escorted me on a tour of Marrakesh—saw the tombs of saints and sultans, their wives, concubines, favorite slaves, visited the Museum of Native Art, passed the Garden of Crimes,* strolled across the thronged marketplace with its noisy and colorful entertainment, featuring snake-charmers, storytellers, jugglers, musicians. I had intended a return visit to the marketplace, but that Saturday night, my indulgence in holiday gaiety, already somewhat tempered by the news of Roosevelt's death, was well and truly clobbered by a more personal misfortune.

---

* Most likely, LFG is referring to a site in Marrakesh where a serial killer in the early 1900s perpetrated his crimes. Hadj Mohammed Mesfewi was a shoemaker and trader. After luring women to his shop, he drugged and murdered them, burying many of his victims in a garden behind his dwelling. He later confessed that he killed them for their money. Mesfewi was convicted and walled up alive in the Marrakesh marketplace bazaar.

Leaving Ken with his doxie [mistress], I had caught a truck back to the transient camp. En route to my tent, I looked in on a signals hut and my rather boozy chat with the friendly Americans therein touched on names as diverse as Somerset Maugham and Eddie Condon, Thomas Hardy, and Frank Sinatra. It was after 1 am when I finally got to bed, the only sounds outside my tent were those of bullfrogs, crickets, and a lone American guard crunching past. And it was well after 3 am when I awoke yelling and the two Arab thieves rummaging around my bed, fled from the tent. I leaped after them, cursed as my bare feet met the stony ground, hobbled, and staggered to a halt. The solitary guard rushed up. We roamed around the widely dispersed tents—to no avail. I had lost shoes, PX rations, toiletries—and Derek's camera.

A Jeep full of MPs scoured the camp. My shoes and toilet articles, dropped by the fleeing scoundrels were recovered.

I finally returned to my bed shaken and miserable, clutching my belt and hoping for the thieves' return so that I could hit them, catch them.

Next morning the MPs could offer little help, they were to attend a parade of tribute to the dead American Commander-in-Chief. I watched it in gloomy silence, my thoughts at times on the war, how Roosevelt's death might affect its course, but repeatedly returning to the lost camera. How could I explain to Derek?

I searched out Ken Staley, who could supply only sympathy—but also took me to dinner, followed by a party where I drank a lot and a gramophone played Bing Crosby, Benny Goodman, and Xavier Cugat.

Back to camp where I slept in that damned tent for the last time. At 8 next morning, I boarded an American truck for Casablanca.

I still felt miserable and anxious. And gazing mournfully at the distant Atlas Mountains, they were a study in blue shadows and pink-tinted mists with fleeting glimpses of their white peaks. I wondered when next I should visit Marrakesh, and hoped it would be under happier circumstances. I stayed the night at the Cormiers, dined and wined excellently with them, and on Tuesday, April 17, returned to Rabat.

The exuberance of Derek's greeting vanished when I finally convinced him—he could not at first believe it—that his camera was stolen. But generously he insisted that I should not worry and repeatedly assured me that he knew I was not to blame.

I'm now busy as hell reorganizing the Refueling Party into a central Refueling Flight for the whole station. Also seeking out good voices for a choir George Cross and I hope to broadcast from Radio Maroc on May 6.

Saturday April 21. My KD (khaki drill) slacks are at the tailor's, and it's far too hot for dancing in battle-dress so I've given the Garrison Club hop a miss tonight. Instead, was one of a dozen practicing our songs in the old sergeants' mess. Only a few days before we rehearse at Radio Maroc studios. And we have to compete for use of the camp's only piano with a play-reading group led by Ellis, Whittaker, and Daniels, our inveterate communists. And George Cross gets little cooperation from our so-called "welfare officer"—Flying Officer Warner, who has been overheard to say that Corporal Cross has no right to embark on local cultural projects without his permission.

Latest news is that Russian troops are fighting in the outskirts of Berlin. Yesterday, Hitler's birthday, Nuremberg fell. Other news tells of Allied units reaching some of the atrocity camps and disclosing to the world that the horrible stories we have heard of these places are by no means propaganda.

Sunday, April 29. Massive critical battle* raging in Europe, but here a peaceful Sunday. Birds singing, a soft breeze rustling the pin-ups on each wall, a single aircraft droning far overhead in a cloudless blue sky.

I managed to lay hands on a couple of three-day-old English newspapers, read more of the horror stories from the now uncovered hell-holes of Belsen and Buchenwald. A third camp, Dachau, is within reach.† Most of Berlin is in Russian hands.

And not to be forgotten, on the Far Eastern Front, our men are advancing on Rangoon [Burma].

A York, a Liberator, several DC-3s came in last night diverted from Gibraltar by bad weather. Our new centralized refueling system successfully stood the test.

I have an article on jazz in the current wall newspaper at the Malcolm Club.

Monday, April 30. Mussolini has been seized and hanged in northern Italy. It is said an old Italian woman fired five bullets—"one for each of my sons"—into the body which dangled upside down. With Il Duce were executed fifteen others, including his mistress.

Wednesday, May 2. Last night it was but a rumor. This morning we have heard it officially announced over the radio. Adolf Hitler is dead.‡ With German resistance crumbling on every front, the dictator's death is an irrelevancy. But assuredly, he was the man who caused millions to

---

* The Battle of Berlin, April 16–May 2, 1945, resulted in the German surrender of the capital to the Red Army.

† Bergen-Belsen was in northern Germany, Buchenwald in central Germany, and Dachau was near Munich.

‡ Hitler died by suicide on April 30, 1945 in the Chancellery bunker in Berlin, along with Eva Braun, his longtime mistress,

tremble and awoke the gods of war. Should Hitler's grave be honored with a headstone, its words might well be those he himself so often deceptively uttered—"<u>This</u> is positively my last territorial claim in Europe."

With the war's end imminent, to be followed inevitably by talk of demobilization, the question one asks oneself is—"What do you intend to do in the peace?" I have no job to return to. My postwar life is a complete mystery to me—except that I hope to <u>write</u>, for pleasure or profit.

Friday, May 4. I am Orderly Corporal today. It's rumored that when victory is proclaimed from London, we will all be confined to camp for three days. If it's true, it's certainly a silly ruling. Of course, the men would celebrate by getting drunk and rowdy, but they get drunk almost every night anyway, most of them.

I hear that back-home preparations are already afoot for floodlighting, bonfires, church-bell ringing, and other manifestations of celebrating.

Last evening in Rabat, crowds gathered to hear different speakers, and the oratory was followed by dancing in the streets. I dined with the Espourteilles, then spent considerable energy dancing in the town square with the girl friends of Tom Bradley (promoted sergeant and just posted), Carter (away on a course), and Jim Hart (posted).*

Did I say dancing? We were all part of a solid mass of humanity slowly rotating about a group of heavily perspiring musicians. Fireworks sputtered in the damp night sky. All this was in celebration of the fall of Berlin [May 2, 1945].

9:45 pm. Just had two beers and a cigar at the Corporals' Club. Everyone in a good mood because of the news. True there are pockets of resistance in Czechoslovakia, Norway, Austria. But the military might—of what four years ago was the world's most formidable power—is shattered. This is no hand-shaking conclusion to the contest, no honouring a beaten foe; no sympathetic the best man won, you led us quite a dance but we beat you fair and square; no gladiatorial nonsense, no chivalry. We have triumphed over evil of the worst type. We must never forget that. With few exceptions, this generation of Germans proved their bestiality by following Der Fuehrer and are deserving of no mercy, no compassion.

Sunday, May 6. 11 am. Is this V-E Day? Last night at the Garrison Club dance I heard that the only German resistance left is that of a garrison in Norway. Rumor has it that Churchill will broadcast at 12 noon,

---

* 1993 note from LFG: "I vaguely remember Bradley, cannot recall the others."

and tonight, the King. Now, this may turn out a little awkward for our camp choir is scheduled to broadcast over Radio Maroc at 8:20. Well, I hope that whoever is listening to us will derive some comfort from the last lines of the second verse of our Welsh selection (not sung in Welsh, of course) of "All Through the Night": "Tho sad fate our lives may sever, parting will not last forever, There's a hope that leaves me never, All Through the Night."

> "Tho' sad fate our lives may sever, parting will not last forever,
> There's a hope that leaves me never,
> All Through the Night."

Monday May 7. 3:40 pm. The war in Europe is ended.

Outside my billet, men's cheerful voices mingle with the song of birds. Even they sound happy. I haven't heard the radio, but I'm told that Derek Roberts stalked into his billet and, with an admirable display of self-restraint, announced the complete and unconditional surrender of the German army. As I write this, sirens echo from Rabat, sounding the final "all-clear."

And guns are going off, and the scorching air seems to tremble.

Churchill is broadcasting at 5, I hear.

Most men will go into town tonight. Think I'll stay in camp. With luck I'll be free tomorrow (last night, after our choral broadcast in Rabat, I got quite tipsy).

Now the voices outside have died. Only the birds are now heard. A feeling of quiet relief seems to have taken over. Relaxed on my cot, clad in shorts and a sleeveless shirt, I am conscious of no great inner emotions, just sleepiness—and a steady reassuring thrill of satisfaction. Shortly, though, I'll go over to the Malcolm club and mingle with the lads.

10 pm. There is news of heavy fighting continuing in Prague where Nazi diehards refuse to acknowledge the Unconditional Surrender.

But tomorrow is V-E-Day. The French here are already celebrating. They've been at it for a week.

Goebbels killed his family, then himself.* The Russians found their bodies.

Peace will probably get off to a shaky start. Judging by the news from San Francisco† of proceedings stalled by the Russia-Poland squab-

---

* Joseph Goebbels, Minister of Propaganda, and his wife Magda killed their six children (ranging in ages from 4 to 12) with cyanide capsules and then killed themselves on May 1, 1945.

† The United Nations Conference on International Organization met in San Francisco from April 25 to June 26, 1945, where delegates drafted the UN Charter designed to secure international peace.

ble, the United Nations are not exactly united. And I couldn't help noticing (indeed no one can) that on the big "V" erected in the centre of Rabat and composed of national flags, the Union Jack and the French Tricolor are level with each other, then comes the Hammer and Sickle, and the Belgian flag, with the Polish flag and the Stars and Stripes at the bottom. Perhaps I'm reading too much into this, but I rather suspect the positioning of the flags has some significance.

Last night's broadcast went off rather well, except that "My Darling Clementine" went flat halfway through. Because of Victory bulletins the recital was cut short, we hadn't sung much beyond "Clementine," "John Brown's Body" (the program wrongly identifying Brown as a Confederate hero of the American Civil War) and "Marching Through Georgia," causing several of our number to complain that "there were too many bloody American songs."

Afterwards Radio Maroc's director-general invited us into an adjoining studio where drinks were poured and we toasted victory.

Win Roberts, in a letter I received from her yesterday, says, "You must have been a journalist or a vacuum-cleaner salesman, you've always got something to say."

Well, I'm not saying much on this historic night, going to bed instead and will read either H.G. Well's "Tono-Bungay" or an anthology of verse. Earlier tonight at the Corporal's Club, I sipped a Muscatel and listened to the Andre Kostelanetz orchestra playing "To a Wild Rose," and Benny Goodman's "Wang Wang Blues," the two best, if well-worn, records over there.

Tuesday, May 8. V-E Day. The impact of this great and glorious day leaves us here on this camp not greatly moved, for our life continues much as before. But, of course, today is special. This afternoon most people are heading into Rabat. A few aircraft may come in so a skeleton staff is necessary. I hope to be in town tonight. Derek has gone into Casablanca, will celebrate with the Cormiers. Wish I were with them. Or home in Britain with my folk. Wonder how they feel now after six long years of blackout and bombs and food rationing. The German foe is destroyed. "—much was to happen after—murder and flaming folly and madness in earth and sea and sky; but all men knew in their hearts that the—Prussian thrust had failed and Christendom was delivered once more...."*

5:30 pm. The cinema was packed this afternoon to hear Churchill. For once his speech was shorn of dazzling oratory, the verbal ostentation

---

* Gilbert K. Chesterton, *The Crimes of England* (New York: John Lane Company, 1916), 173.

that characterizes his broadcasts and that, for all their brilliance, are apt to irritate and tire. This time simplicity—but how impressive!—was the keynote. There is still Japan to contend with, he reminded us after briefly glancing back over the past six years. But today he bade the people celebrate, and he ended on a glorious note, which fittingly climaxed this most historic broadcast: "Advance Britannia! God Save the King!"

It was impressive all right, the message we had waited so long to hear and announced by the man most worthy of announcing it.

Thursday, May 10. 8 pm. Yesterday's <u>Daily Herald</u> arrived here—historic issue, with memorable photos of London's vast crowds celebrating, and of a happy and proud Churchill surrounded by delirious multitudes. From the balcony of floodlit Buckingham Palace, where he stood in company with the royal family, he addressed the thousands, telling them, "This is your victory." But it is also his. If Churchill, Prime Minister, needed a people behind him united in purpose and inspired with a spirit of self-sacrifice, they and no less needed an indomitable leader, a man of courage and integrity and, yes, of stubbornness. For if Churchill's obstinacy often emphasized his mistakes, it also made for profitable decisions, ably acted upon, decisions a less resolute leader would hesitate to form, let alone follow through.

Last night, I was quite drunk by 9 o'clock. I remember little of what happened thereafter. I have fleeting impressions of a long cavalcade of Spanish warriors flanked by torch-carrying French infantrymen and of the pink and white Rabat Municipal Building, floodlit. Of a French colonial band, the rattling and shrieking of its drums and horns. At the Renaissance, I believe it was, I danced fast waltzes to the point of exhaustion with a girl named Marguerite and later met, then missed in the crowd, a smiling Paulette. I weathered a stomach upset following eggs and bacon and cognac with vermouth at the Garrison Club. Jack Marsden accidentally knocked a glass-ladened tray from the hands of a hapless garcon. There were rumbas at the Comedy and the Lambeth Walk at the Victory Bar. And finally, a hell-for-leather ride back to camp at 5 am, a quick breakfast, then into bed until noon.

Tonight, I aim to catch up on my sleep. Tomorrow afternoon, the CO is to address us in the camp cinema. Tomorrow night, a Victory Dance at the Garrison Club.

Contrary to recent reports, neither Hitler's nor Goebbels's body has been found. (Incidentally, I'm still angry over reports that de Valera expressed condolences upon hearing of Hitler's death.) Goering is reported to be arrested. Kesselring, von Rundstedt, are captured. Von

Bock a suicide.* Fighting continues in Czechoslovakia, the Germans hoping to surrender to the Americans instead of to the Russians.

Sunday May 13. When Group Captain Nichols, our new CO, told us of his intention to take the salute at a Thanksgiving parade with the Sultan of Morocco in attendance, we all knew that laid on at such short notice the affair was sure to be a balls-up. So it proved. Added to the confusion of hastily mounted drill rehearsal, no one could decide on what the proper dress should be. Some of us only have battledress, not all have regular blue, some have only khaki drill, and that appeared to be the sort of sartorial common denominator. So this morning we paraded in shorts, shirts, khaki drill stockings, and caps. The weather turned unexpectedly cold, our bare knees became goose-pimpled, and we were not comforted by the spectacle of the CO and his adjutant warmly clad in service blue. A French band, enlisted for the occasion, appeared unfamiliar until British march tempo, which threw most of us embarrassingly out of step.

After the march past, came the service, our hymn-singing, ruined by the piano-player's inability to keep proper time. The Sultan of Morocco did not show up but he sent the Crown Vizier, and our padre, having decided to wear clerical robes, it was difficult in the gloom of the hangar to tell the two apart. The service, like the parade, was outdoors, and when hurried and mumbled prayers followed the unmelodious singing, an evidently disgusted Almighty blew with His winds and scattered the mimeographed hymn sheets.

Eventually, we were dismissed and each element went its separate way, the brass and guests to dine in the Officer' Mess, the NCOs and men to eat in their messes, a meal publicly designated as special. And so it was, inasmuch as it was edible.

Tuesday, May 15. Goering confessed to his captors that it was he who ordered the bombing of Coventry. Why do we continue to mollycoddle this fat beast? Himmler is still at large.

No reply yet from Stalin regarding the arrest of the Polish democrats. An ugly situation this, partly hidden behind the victory news, and the postwar going on in Europe.

Arab riots in our next-door country, Algeria, quelled by French aircraft, I've heard. Also have heard of Americans murdered in Casablanca. Arab discontent seems to be spreading, but so far, all quiet in Rabat.

---

* Fedor von Bock sustained serious injuries in an Allied air raid on Hamburg on May 3, 1945, and died the following day.

At their base near Rabat, Guttridge and his comrades pass in review on a cold Sunday in May 1945 to honor victory in Europe. "Our bare knees became goose-pimpled, and we were not comforted by the spectacle of the CO and his adjutant warmly clad in service blue."

Nat Gubbins, caustic humorist of the <u>Daily Express</u>, writes of a peace hangover. "Perhaps it is the sight of the British people at peace which caused this depression. They looked so splendid in war. The narrowest, meanest face looked noble under a steel helmet, when they were gray and lined with fatigue and grimed with the all-night-long battles of London. The same faces under funny paper hats, with mouths wide open singing foolish songs, looked narrow and mean again, and unbearably pathetic. Their finest hour was over." Waxing ever more gloomily, Gubbins foresees "comradeship ... disappear overnight, and Englishmen, with no foreign foe to hate, hating each other. I hear interminable arguments about who won the war and who made the greatest sacrifice, those who made none at all putting in the biggest claims. I see the black marketeers of the war becoming controllers of cartels."

And so on, ad very nauseam. But perhaps the cynically pessimistic Gubbins is really warning us that if we sink back into the apathy and blindness of the 1930's. our fate will ultimately be another bloody war.

Last night I saw "Laura," a film in the "Double Indemnity" tradition and a first-class mystery. The more I think of the plot, the weaker it seems, but the performances of Dana Andrews, Gene Tierney, Vincent Price and especially Clifton Webb were superb. Newsreel included some grim shots of the Iwo Jima battle* with a shocking glimpse of Jap soldiers caught in a flame-thrower attack.

De Valera reported to have expressed sympathy on the death of Hitler—what a character!

My left thumb, poisoned from unknown cause (insect bite perhaps?), throbbed and kept me awake all last night.

Attended a concert at the Royale Theatre in Rabat and enjoyed most of all one Lili Boniche† and his Oriental Orchestra—just piano, small tom-tom, tambourine, and a handsome Arab who sang quite effectively and played first violin, then guitar.

Sunday, May 20. I can think of better ways of spending a warm Sunday morning than waiting uneasily for part of my thumbnail to be sliced away and a poisonous growth to be lanced. Still don't know for sure what caused this. And for the past 24 hours, I have had severe pains between my shoulder blades.

But overshadowing these unpleasantries comes news in a letter from Manchester that Arthur Wilson was indeed killed over Germany in July of last year. He is buried as "unknown" five miles west of Duisberg. This grievous news outweighed in emotional impact the description my other letters contained of V-E celebrations at home, the flags, the bonfires, speeches, floodlit buildings, and street-dancing. Wilson was a friend whom I shall never forget.

Saturday, May 26. The Europe War has been over for nearly three weeks now, and the first political crisis since V-E day has erupted in Britain. Churchill's socialist cabinet colleagues, Herbert Morrison and Ernest Bevin, opposed his call for a continued coalition government, and in the resultant row, Churchill resigned—but within hours, was back in the saddle, the King having asked him to form a new government that will run things until the election, perhaps in July.

Last night, a Ministry of Labour [MOL] representative, one of fifteen touring overseas bases to give "resettlement lectures," told us that there will be plenty of jobs after the war, that a kind of bureaucracy is being set up to aid demobilized servicemen in finding employment. During a question period, one of our fellows expressed concern that jobs might be already filled by enemy prisoners of war. The weak response was that most German captives were building or repairing sewers, "fitting work for the likes of them."

---

* The Battle of Iwo Jima lasted from February 19 to March 26, 1945. The most iconic photograph of World War II was of the large American flag being raised on Iwo Jima's Mount Suribachi on February 23.

† Algerian born French singer of Andalusian-Arab music.

The government has issued little blue books entitled "Release and Resettlement."* Our CO proudly announced that he had received five, and was quickly reminded by the MOL lecturer that there were eight hundred men on this station so he'd better get cracking and secure hundreds more.

Tuesday, May 29. Saw "Arsenic and Old Lace" last night—fitfully funny, some unexpected (and not entirely welcome) over-acting by Cary Grant, not enough offered by those comedic stalwarts Jack Carson, James Gleason, and Edward Everett Horton. And seeing Grant cavort with her in the graveyard sequence, I decided that Priscilla Lane is the girl I'd "Most Like to Chase Around the Tombstones."

Saturday, June 2. A film of the atrocity camps was shown here last night. Among the memorable images: Mavis Tate, Member of Parliament, snuffing hastily at a phial of smelling salts; the slowly waving arms of a partly hidden victim still alive but dying amid a vast heap of already dead; dazed human skeletons staggering blindly into each other; other scenes beyond description, drawing gasps of horror from the 600 or so men in the audience. It should be made compulsory for everyone in Britain to see this film. Even now there are fools who deny it all as "propaganda."

"In civilized countries wounded men are not treated like peepshows," says William (Lord Haw Haw) Joyce from the stretcher upon which he lay, to British soldiers curious to see what a traitor looked like.

Wednesday, June 6. Some eighty men leaving here Sunday, including my roommate Jack Marsden. Most of the postings are for Cairo en route for somewhere else, no doubt, trouble-spots like Habbaniyah, Iraq.

This big postings surge has missed me. I shouldn't care if I'm posted, as long as I had time to say goodbye to friends in Rabat and Casablanca.

Odd and frightening experience last night when about half past 1, I saw in the shadows a thick-set Arab slowly approaching the building. When I yelled at him, he didn't flee but turned to come at me, his appearance that of a very large man, long arms swinging slowly at his sides. I backed away, shouted, and Norman came out. We chased the figure, others joined us, we spotted him, just once more. He crouched like a statue. Then shot off into the darkness. Later we rode around with the camp patrol but found nothing.

---

* The blue booklet is titled "Release and Resettlement: An Explanation of Your Position and Rights." At the end of World War II, as part of the demobilization program, this informational booklet was issued to the 5 million men and women serving with the British armed forces.

I was in the Squadron Leader (Admin)'s office this morning with George Cross, trying to arrange a second recital over Radio Maroc. We hoped to get recordings from ENSA but, to our surprise, were advised to steer clear of that organization. "They're difficult to get on with ... non-cooperative." We next called on the padre, who told us the same thing, and added that he'd experienced difficulty bringing seventy classical records from Gibraltar. He was ordered to have them censored first! How to censor gramophone records? The chief censor at Gibraltar, equally baffled, at last said, "Oh, well, I'll just look at the labels. We haven't got a gramophone here, anyway."

The CTO, in quite friendly fashion, has told me to warn the men of the Refueling Party against chalking "Vote Labour" on the sides of our bowsers and other equipment. Friendly, yes, but my guess is that FL/Lieutenant. Baines's vote will be cast for the Conservative Party.

Friday, June 15. Friday night. Wednesday afternoon. Derek Roberts and I climbed the stairs to the Cormiers' apartment in Casablanca and rang the bell. The door was opened by a pajama clad and white-faced M. Cormier. And we knew, even before he uttered the words, "Madame est morte."

She was so cheerful, fun-loving, music-loving. She was devoted to her husband and bravely patriotic. And so kind to us. We learned she had died the day following V-E Day when Casablanca's lighted streets were thronged with Victory celebrants. Later that evening, Cormier sobbed in our presence and there was little we could do to console him. He recovered later to talk with pride and enthusiasm about his plans for the design of a Stalingrad Memorial. Cormier is a veteran architect, and we learned that the Soviet ambassador in Algiers, Russian architectural societies, even Stalin himself, have expressed interest in his proposal and designs.

Tuesday, June 19. I spent yesterday afternoon sea and sunbathing at Tamara Bay, the warm little curved stretch of sand where airmen from the RAF bases at Rabat and Gibraltar find rest and relaxation. Truly pleasant to do little more than stretch on the sand or perch about the rocks and contemplate the Atlantic surf.

Wednesday, June 20. Signs of my approaching demobilization: The little blue books entitled "Release and Resettlement" have arrived, designed by the government to guide us through the transition from service life to that of a civilian. And my arm is painfully swollen following yesterday's TAB and ATT inoculations.*

---

* TAB vaccine provides protection against typhoid and paratyphoid A and B infection. The vaccine can induce severe localized and sometimes systemic reactions with fever and malaise. ATT, most likely, refers to tetanus.

Friday, June 29. Nothing much happening around here. No voting literature has yet arrived. An occasional newspaper reaching here tells of Churchill's triumphant tour through the Midlands—it bodes ill for socialist chances. I think Churchill will win this election—after six years of his leadership, the people, by and large, feel safe with him. Moreover, the Tory machine is making headway—thanks to Harold Laski*— at portraying British socialists as altogether too dangerous.

A Daily Mast came my way and it is a bit disturbing to see how the Far East War has been relegated to the back pages.

Much repatriation taking place all over the world now. From this airfield yesterday, a DC-3 took off for France, laden with women and children, bound after God knows how many years of absence, for their homeland.

Wednesday, July 4. Tomorrow is polling day back home. I've read all the campaign speeches accessible out here, and nothing seems more obvious than the Tories' inability to offer the electorate anything other than Churchill's war-winning prestige. And though multitudes cheered him as he toured throughout England and Scotland, it doesn't follow that they will all vote for his party. If he passed where I happened to be, I'd cheer him as loudly as anybody. And then still vote Socialist. My ballot paper, envelope, and pamphlets arrived two days ago. It is a straight fight in my (Cardiff) constituency: Sir Arthur Evans, Colonel (ret.), Tory to the backbone, versus Labour Party candidate James Callaghan, ex Royal Navy Volunteer Reserve lieutenant.

I placed an X alongside Callahan's name, thus recording my first vote, and sent the thing off.

This election has been clean enough, although each side sought to paint the other as dirty. For instance, the Tory Daily Express expressed disgust at the heckling of legless air ace Douglas Bader.† And there were the inevitable accounts of besmirched Churchill posters, slashed tires, and other nefarious tampering with candidates' cars.

---

* Harold Laski, an English political theorist and economist, served as chairman of the British Labour Party from 1945 to 1946.

† Sir Douglas Bader (1910–1982) was an RAF flying ace during World War II, credited with 22 aerial victories, four shared victories, six probables, one shared probable, and 11 enemy aircraft damaged. Having joined the RAF in 1928, Bader lost both legs in a crash. After recovering from his injuries, he retook flight training, passed all check flights, and requested reinstatement to flying status. Despite proving himself a capable pilot, he was medically retired. With the outbreak of the war, Bader returned to the RAF as a pilot and scored his first victories over Dunkirk during the Battle of France in 1940. He then took part in the Battle of Britain. In August 1941, Bader was captured after bailing out over German-occupied France. Despite his disability, Bader made a number of escape attempts and was eventually sent to the prisoner of war camp at Colditz Castle, where he remained until April 1945 when the camp was liberated by the U.S. Army.

I visited our station adjutant, F/O [Flight Officer] Messenger, yesterday and asked for a "Guide to Careers" booklet (acting on advice given by the "Release and Resettlement" booklet). Messenger was his usual sleepy self and could only promise that shortly the camp would have an Education Officer who would see to that sort of thing. Typical apathy nowadays among this camp's officers.

Meanwhile, morale is steadily dropping. In the dining hall, the other day, airmen, dissatisfied with the poor quality of our food, staged a little riot, subdued only when the Orderly Officer, the Medical Officer and the Commanding Officer himself were brought on the scene. I was talking of this afterwards with Flight Lieutenant Baines, our rather nervous CTO. He told me he was aware of the food situation and somewhat irrelevantly offered to lend me a book on careers in engineering.

The Yanks put on a USO show for us the night before last, only a small company, they worked damned hard, raised more laughs than some of our ENSA people would. Poor ENSA! Buffeted, kicked at from all sides, this hapless organization can never be improved until more and better artistes give their services to entertain overseas troops. But it is a purely voluntary affair, and most entertainers no doubt prefer to stay in Britain than make uncomfortable and hazardous journeys to staging posts like ours and still more remote camps and bases in Far East jungles. Understandable, I suppose.

Friday, July 6. 11:30 pm. Long vigil as commander of the guard. I have all night before me and "The Brothers Karamazov" to help me get through it.

Scattered all over the world, Britishers are voting. Ballot papers are being filled out upon empty petrol drums in the desert, in Berlin bunkers, and dropped by parachute for our chaps in Burmese jungles. This is the most fateful election in British history, no question about it. Some last-minute scare tactics (mostly by the Tories) will probably have little influence.

Eight German POWs in Scotland* are on trial for the murder of a fellow prisoner.

Tuesday, July 10. Our CO erroneously convinced that the men have little to do, has ordered that all vehicles—recently painted brown—must now be repainted green.

---

* Cultybraggan Camp lies close to the village of Comrie, in west Perthshire, Scotland. Designated POW camp No 21, it was built in 1941 to house those considered to be the most fanatical Nazis.

Saw a Daily Herald—for the record, dated July 2, 1945—with a wonderfully misprinted sentence ["Mr. Churchill] appears to regret that the Lamour* ministers are not still with him."

Especially if they were wearing sarongs?!

Saturday, July 14. This week dragged miserably. For this has become a miserable camp. Our CO is a social-climbing snob—but he received a setback some nights ago when, drunk, he was kicked out of the Chanticleer restaurant. I hear he is soon to be posted. But meanwhile, he still runs the show, and instead of launching EVT [Educational and Vocational Training] projects, he has had the entire camp, painting railings, fences, equipment, and vehicles—all a sickly green. All this, to "keep the men busy," take their minds off demobilization problems, no doubt. And while we thus daily waste time and tons of paint, overhead fly Forts [Flying Fortresses] and Dakotas [DC-3s] taking Yanks from the Middle East and Mediterranean theatres home. Rightly or wrongly, the fellows here assume that it is the Yanks who are getting things done, getting their men home, while our demob scheme lags far behind.†

Friday, July 20. At the rest camp, Tamara Bay, I am enjoying another welcome week. The sun beats down daily, soon scorching the exposed flesh. The ocean is calm and dazzling, except when it breaks in thunderous surf against the rocks that flank the bay. Thanks to donors back home, reading fare at this rest camp (the site of a pre-war French casino, I believe) consists mostly of old volumes of Punch [British weekly humor and satire magazine], some dating from the early 1920s. I've read so many, I'm verily Punch-drunk!! Came across a single, May 12, 1926, "General Strike" issue, a rarity I intend to keep. My roommates are not of choice quality, but tolerable. One is a Rabat-Sale telephone operator who boasts of listening in on private conversations—he had plenty to say about BOAC's agent Mrs. Smith, who has a somewhat notorious reputation, is believed to sleep with BOAC pilots at the [Hotel] Balima in Rabat. According to my eavesdropping roommate, she chuckled on the phone to a boyfriend, "It's all the better, isn't it, when our ETAs coincide."

The sun has burned my face, especially my nose, which is so red

---

* Referring to Hollywood actress Dorothy Lamour.

† LFG's note: "In truth, the Americans had their own demobilization problems as I learned in detail while researching for *Mutiny*. Mutinies, in fact, broke out as the morale of the GIs collapsed in the Pacific and Europe." As cited in Leonard F. Guttridge, *Mutiny: A History of Naval Insurrection*. Naval Institute Press, Annapolis, MD, 1992, 232–234.

that one wag, upon observing it, was overheard to remark "Give generously for your poppy this year."*

Hope it will lose some of its redness by tomorrow night, I'm going into Rabat to attend a dance at the Garrison Club.

Tuesday, July 24. I am back at camp and into oven-like heat. Yesterday's temperature failed to drop below 88° F, rose to 119° F. So was it even at Tamara Bay on Sunday night—that as soon as Al Mears and I arrived back from the clifftop restaurant where we had danced fast waltzes to a French concertina band (and watched a colorful sunset over the Atlantic)—we stripped naked, plunged into the warm sea, and floated on buoyant waves beneath a hard bright moon.

That morning, Jock Cunningham and I had struggled with an octopus—quite a hair-raising experience, even though the creature was not very large. Ankle deep in a seawater pool some yards from the thrashing waves, Jock had been fishing, our gaze fixed on the bait, and a fish that refused to bite. I chilled inwardly as I sensed rather than saw tentacles slithering from a hole in the pool's bed and approaching our bare feet. I yelled, splashed backwards. But Jock nimbly flicked the bait—a winkle-off the hook and replaced it with a fish and attempted to lure the octopus out.

He bit. "Got him!" yelled Jock. "Got the bastard!" He lifted the rod, the octopus on the line extending tentacles to grasp it. The creature's weight caused Jock to drop the rod, and the octopus made to escape. As I groped for a jackknife in Jock's pocket, he retrieved the rod, swung it at the octopus and snapped the damn thing—the rod—in two. Using both knife and half a fishing rod, Jock attacked the octopus who eventually lost the battle, and there it lay, a slimy ruin, to be shortly collected, for meat, no doubt, by a passing knot of smiling Arabs. Jock wasn't smiling. That broken fishing rod wasn't his. He'd borrowed it from the rest camp's commanding officer.

Thursday, July 26. Throughout the afternoon, Terry Haile and his colleagues, who keep this camp informed of news from home and receive precious little thanks for doing so, strode repeatedly from the Listening Room across to the Malcolm Club, on whose walls they pinned election bulletins as fast as the BBC announced them. Early reports of Labour victories raised hopes among those like myself who wish for a change in

---

* Since World War I, the artificial poppy has been worn to commemorate those who died for their country. In the UK, Remembrance Poppies are still sold by The Royal British Legion (RBL), a charity providing financial, social, political, and emotional support to those who have served or who are currently serving in the British Armed Forces and their dependents.

government. And it quickly appeared that a landslide victory was in the making. Tory strongmen went down in defeat one after another.

By 4 pm, the camp buzzed with excitement. The delay to Air Chief Marshal "Bomber" Harris's* Lancaster (engine trouble) out on our airfield took second place to the big news from home.

Odd situations arise. The Potsdam conference† will be resumed shortly and Attlee, not Churchill, will be Britain's chief representative. Will Churchill go back with him? I doubt it. Churchill's power and prestige are inevitably diminished. It would be humiliating for him to attend merely as a bystander, in second place, in the company of Attlee, Truman, and Stalin.

Saturday, July 28. Ernest Bevin will be Foreign Secretary in the new cabinet. Attlee has returned to Potsdam this time as British Prime Minister, and without Winston Churchill.

I wonder what the rest of the world thinks of Britain's swing to socialism?

Last night I was guard commander. A scar-faced SIB [Special Investigations Branch] corporal who did, indeed, physically resemble Cramer,‡ the commandant of the Belsen concentration camp, brought into the guardhouse three scared-looking RAF types from Gibraltar, who had been caught selling NAAFI cigarettes to an Arab kid. This lad, aged about 14, was himself also brought in but didn't look particularly scared—one reason I suppose, why the SIB corporal began punching him and calling him a "thieving bastard." I had no seniority to order a stop to it, but told the corporal bluntly that I would report his conduct—which I did in writing for the Station Warrant officer's attention. I can't stand bullying in any form. We've been fighting a war against this sort of thing. And I feel even a bit guilty, instead of (or as well as) reporting this thug I should have set about him myself. But at least I did something and in proper disciplinary fashion.

Wednesday, August 1. The Home Leave scheme is now under way. Men will leave here at the rate of about nine per week. Of course, this is furlough,

---

* Sir Arthur T. Harris, called "Bomber" Harris by the press, was Air Officer Commanding-in-Chief, RAF Bomber Command during the height of the British-American strategic bombing campaign against Nazi Germany.

† From July 17 to August 2, 1945, Churchill, Stalin, and Truman met at Potsdam, Germany. On July 26, the newly elected Clement Attlee replaced Churchill as the new Prime Minister and attended the conference in Churchill's place. On the agenda: the unconditional surrender of Japan, the division of Germany into occupation zones, and plans for the future of post-war Europe.

‡ Josef Kramer, commandant of Auschwitz-Birkenau and of the Bergen-Belsen concentration camps, was called the Beast of Belsen by camp inmates. Convicted of crimes against humanity, he was hanged on December 13, 1945.

not demobilization, the men chosen will be those with longer terms of overseas service still ahead of them. But this, of course, means that men who haven't been out here very long will see their loved ones before those who have. So there is still much discontent. Part of it arises from the rule that unmarried men must serve four years overseas while the marrieds are limited to three.

"Since You Went Away"—a very pleasant film with Claudette Colbert, Joseph Cotton, and the ever irascible/loveable Monty Woolley. Also, a divertingly grown-up Shirley Temple. This show is at the Camp Cinema here. Down in Rabat the other night, the program included a preview of the Errol Flynn film "Gentlemen Jim." Well, we recognized it as such, but the French had a different title for it, which translates as, "For the Blue Eyes of Kitty."

Friday, August 10. If this were the simple routine diary and perhaps should be, today would read as follows:

> 0745 hours. Got up, washed, went to breakfast—porridge, dried egg, bacon, and concrete-hard fried bread.
> 0815. Went to work. Few aircraft came in.
> 1100. Malcolm Club for a cup of tea. Weather hot.
> 1230. Tiffin [light midday meal]. Meat and veg stew. Apples and white sauce.
> 1250. Changed my library book. Drew out "Great Expectations," which I should have read years ago. And so on.

But today was no ordinary day, or rather this is no ordinary week, for it is just sinking into us what this Atomic Bomb really signifies. It was last Monday, a few of us were watching the departure of some French notable on a French Marauder, Moroccan troops lined up in his honour. A sergeant friend of mine whispered in my ear, "Heard the news? We've dropped a bomb on the Japs, an atom bomb it's called, more powerful than...." My eyes widened to his statistics. Next day, I visited M. Cormier who is bearing up bravely from the shock of his wife's death. Cormier expressed doubts as to the wisdom of ever inventing such a weapon, but agrees that if we can harness and control atomic energy, it could be utilized for the good of all humanity.

The following day, we heard of another blow against the Japanese—Russia's declaration of war.

All of which signals that peace is on its way. About time, too. Nearly one quarter of my life has been in a war. Once the Japanese give in, it will all be ended—but over the peace will now hang the threat of that terrifying mushroom cloud.

Sunday, August 12. This waiting, the suspense… More than 30 hours have elapsed since the Allied reply was made to Japan's surrender offer. Probably the status of Emperor Hirohito is the stumbling block. Should he be placed in Allied hands as a prisoner of war? Japanese regard him as a divine Emperor. Personally, I think the Imperial Majesty should be treated as a common war criminal.

Today may be the last Sunday of the War. Things are calm, here the weather cooler, two or three Transport Command aircraft flew in. Tomorrow night, Lofty Manners and I will present a record recital, the (sadly limited) choices including orchestral works Haydn's "Clock Symphony," MacDowell's "To a Wild Rose," and Nelson Eddy singing, of all things, "Danse Macabre."

It is difficult to find the right word describing the atmosphere or mood hereabouts. "Tense" will have to do. The usual monotony persists, but it is shot through, I fancy, with a feeling that of the joys of home: warmth of a cozy fire, slippers on the carpet, purring cat, singing kettle for tea, friendly relatives, the Saturday night dance, the town cinema, the corner pub, the girl next door, the smell of eggs and bacon frying while you contemplate having it in bed are closer now than ever they were since the first shot was fired six years ago.

But can we ever know true peace again in the new age of the Atomic Bomb, especially with its threat of still more fearsome potential? For the second device, dropped on Nagasaki, made the first (dropped on Hiroshima) out of date immediately. Stories of its terrible impact, of victims six miles from the explosion's centre, blinded by the glare, of buildings pulverized and humans vaporized—and the lingering doubts as to the ethics of its use (or misuse) all make for countless sleepless nights in the months and years ahead.

Monday, August 13. Night. At the recital tonight, as the strains of MacDowell's "To a Wild Rose" faded away, and before we settled down to hear the "Clock" symphony, the news was switched on. It was still the same. No reply from Japan.

Each bulletin last night and throughout today told of the Russian offensives across the Manchurian plains, of the vast Anglo-American armada in Japanese waters, of the intensification of the air attacks on the mainland. But silence from the Japanese government.

Meanwhile, we are learning more of the Atom Bomb. I saw, for the first time, a British newspaper report of it. The Daily Express. The entire front page carries the story under big black headlines: THE BOMB THAT HAS CHANGED THE WORLD.

Wednesday, August 15. Afternoon. On the morning of September 3,

1939, when Neville Chamberlain announced that Britain was at war, I was fast asleep. On the night of August 14, 1945, when Clement Attlee announced that Britain was at peace, I was fast asleep.

Even now, I have difficulty sorting out my feelings following the news that, at last, it's all over.

Before turning in last night, I dropped by the Sale Times office and watched Terry Haile, at work on the Victory number. (Incidentally, earlier rumours of Emperor Hirohito's suicide were rampant and sometimes accompanied by the crack that Hara Kiri had been asked for a statement but refused to commit himself [Ouch!])

Some celebrating has evidently started early in Rabat for as I crawled from under my mosquito net at 0730 and peered out at the morning sunshine, I could hear the distant wail of sirens and a rumble of gunfire. And in the breakfast queue, as we lined up for porridge, substitute egg, and bacon, I was told that "the war ended last night. Attlee broadcast at midnight, "Today and tomorrow are V-J days."

Work started halfheartedly, dwindled to nothing, and the sections dispersed for two days' holiday. I was pleased to see, on "Orders" that I'm not detailed for any duty. Below DROs was a typed message from our Canadian CO, popular W/Cdr. Bryant, expressing his wish that we enjoy ourselves celebrating—but should take care not to overdo it.

Gunfire echoed most of the morning. Fellows prepared to go out, the sunlit air rang with happy obscenities. In the radio room, I heard a commentary on the King and Queen's ride to Parliament. Never was a new Parliamentary session opened in more joyous circumstances. Britain's first Labour government—the first with real power—is taking control of the nation after six cruel and bloody years.

The war's final hours had their tragedies—one of the worst, the sinking of the American carrier, Indianapolis.*

Hirohito's extraordinary speech and the general reluctance of the Japs to admit defeat should warn us to be on our guard, to watch them closely.

Somehow, I seem to have forgotten what peace feels like. As far back as memory can reach, even long before the war began, I have known apprehension and uncertainty. Well, no time for introspection. This moment is for celebrating.

---

* USS *Indianapolis* was a heavy cruiser torpedoed and sunk by a Japanese submarine on July 30, 1945, shortly after delivering the internal components of the atomic bombs that were later dropped on Hiroshima and Nagasaki. Of the 900 men who abandoned ship, only 316 survived and were rescued. The *Indianapolis* disaster remains one of the worst tragedies in U.S. Navy history.

"And He shall judge among many people, and rebuke strong nations afar off, and they shall beat their swords into ploughshares, and their spears into pruning-hooks: nation shall not lift up a sword against nation, neither shall they learn war anymore."*

Friday, August 17. The peace has been with us now for two days. In London last night drizzling rain dampened celebrations, pubs quickly ran out of beer. But Londoners, and no doubt the rest of the country, displayed an exuberance probably the equal of that seen in New York or San Francisco.

But here in Morocco? Well, on V-J night in Rabat, there were lantern processions of Senegalese troops whose black smiling faces were in odd contrast to a depressed mien that seemed characteristic of the local French—certainly those I saw. I witnessed no Anglo-French fraternization—instead, if anything, sort of a detached toleration of the RAF boys' drunken boisterousness. The Rabat citizens (non–Arab), who swarmed into the cafés and restaurants, appeared unable to spread joy even among themselves. Between dances, they sat with sour, dejected expressions, seldom talking to each other and never—as far as I could tell—with British personnel.

The few Americans in Rabat suffered the same patent ostracism. Down in the [Café] Comédie's basement, I talked with two very friendly and intelligent Yanks. And when Terry Haile and other colleagues found me, I was rather much the worse for wear. It was 3 am on V-J plus one when I got into bed.

Today in Rabat was much the same. The French girls hung on to their compatriots, and as there are no English girls around here, the whole celebration was, for us, decidedly stag. And I rather suspect that few airmen sought feminine company in the brothels—for one reason, money was sparse, the Japs having inconsiderately surrendered just before payday.

As on V-E-Day, a giant V was erected outside Rabat railway station, made up of flags. I may be reading in the positioning of the flags something not intended at all, but during the V-E celebrations last May, the Stars and Stripes was placed a few flags below those of Britain, Russia, and France. At that time, Franco-American relations were less than cordial. Now, with the French irritated by British action in Syria, the Union Jack on Rabat's big V is almost at the very bottom, below France, USA, USSR, and China. I don't think all this is coincidence. Ah, well. I expect to be out of the RAF in a few months, will postpone my "victory" celebrating until Christmas.

---

* Daughter Vivien J. Olsen's note: *King James Bible*, Micah 4:3.

To celebrate V-J Day, a giant V was erected outside the Rabat railway station decorated with flags of the victorious Allied nations.

Earlier yesterday, Terry Haile and I explored the sandy desolation near the mouth of the Bou Regreg, the original location of the harbor. And we allowed our imagination to project a scene of three hundred years ago, when corsairs [pirates] sailed in and out of these waters. One pirate captain was an Englishman named Mainwaring, whose band of cutthroats were called the Sale Rovers.* Mainwaring, I believe, was an exile from one of the stately homes of seventeenth century England. We—Terry and I—were making notes on this topic when an errant breeze snatched Terry's papers away. He chased after it into what looked like a dried-up ditch. It was nothing of the sort. Terry's feet and ankles vanished into black-green slime, and the rest of him would have quickly followed had I not, with my feet braced on firmer ground, hauled him out. His feet great masses of evil-smelling slime, his voice befouling the fresh sea air with curses, Terry enlisted the aid of an ancient Arab beachcomber who took us into his pokey little hut and washed the bottom of Terry's trousers, his shoes and socks. And it turned out that despite Arabic name and appearance, the beachcomber spoke good German, showed us war certificates testifying to involvement in old campaigns.

---

* Sir Henry Mainwaring (1587–1653) served in the House of Commons before his earlier "career" as a pirate. After Parliament, he became a naval officer in the Royal Navy. Mainwaring supported the Royalist cause in the English Civil War (1642–1651).

Terry and I recovered from the experience ("Scum Other Slime" we sang in parody of the Frank Sinatra hit "Some Other Time") by lounging on the Sale beach ogling the sparkling sea and sundry locals, including a shapely young woman wearing a totally transparent bathing suit. Behind us reared the cliffs, the Medina, and the Kasbah of the Oudaias* gleaming in the sun. We closed our eyes to the sun's glare and rested our heads back upon the soft sand and thought of home or nothing at all. This, then, was Peace.

Monday, August 20. A York came in bringing VIPs—and English newspapers. Amid the accounts of peace celebrations and ceasefire terms imposed upon the enemy, a discordant note struck by the Dean of St. Albans, who ordered that his church bells <u>not</u> be rung, in protest against the use of the Atom Bomb.

Tonight, saw Judy Garland in "Meet Me in St. Louis." Nicely musical and nostalgic, though too long. Also, startling film footage of Japanese kamikaze attacks on American warships.

Thursday, August 23. What the hell is going on? Late this afternoon we were cheered by the government's announcement that a million men will be released from the RAF by the end of the year. This after weeks of rumour and speculation about home leave and demobilization. But tonight, we hear that the demobilization rate will not be as rapid after all. Is lack of shipping space to blame? Then why is the Queen Mary† taking thousands of <u>Americans</u> home? And why not use more air transport, for instance, our bombers?

Sunday, August 26. Eve of my 27th birthday. I have tomorrow off. Will listen to records newly arrived from France which a colleague and I bought last week, include Goodman, Ellington, Fats Waller, and some nice Dixieland produced by Hubert Rostaing and other French musicians. In the afternoon, Derek and I will get down to Temara for a bathe. And in the evening, there's the Corporals' Victory Dinner at the Paradis in town.

America's sudden and (seems to me) unnecessarily abrupt termination of Lend-Lease is sure to worsen the already bleak economic outlook back home. Poor Britain. After her six-year effort to rid the world of fascism, she receives no reward but industrial poverty and near-bankruptcy. Granted, unified effort of several nations was needed to

---

* The Kasbah of the Oudaias is a kasbah (citadel) in Rabat located at the mouth of the Bou Regreg River, opposite Salé, and adjacent to the old Medina of Rabat.

† RMS *Queen Mary* (the "Grey Ghost") was transformed into a troopship during World War II. In late July 1943, she set the record for the number of troops and crew on board: 16,683. That record still stands.

finally crush the legions of Hitler, Mussolini, and the still arrogant Hirohito. But it was all made possible only because Britain fought on alone and refused to quit in the years 1940 and 1941.

Terry and I visited Port Lyautey the other day. It's a quieter, smaller town than Rabat. And on the way, we passed several groups of Moorish ruins, some still with the remains of cannon jutting from the ramparts.

Tuesday, August 28. Cloudy, rain threatening. Grim rumours of disorder, even mutiny, among British soldiers at Gibraltar, reflecting mounting discontent over the speed—or lack of it—of the government's demobilization program. I hear the governor's residency on the Rock [Gibraltar] was stoned. Here, there is no sign of trouble, other than outbursts of grumbling and ill-temper.

In Washington, President Truman denies that dislike of Britain's socialist government prompted his early decision to end lend-lease.

My folks have visited Reading, stayed with relatives. The old man writes that "Ma is tired, but got through the London traffic all right. On the back of a folder of eight letter-card photos of "views of Reading" are scrawled: "Love from cousin Dorothy"—"Longing to see you—Cousin Bob" and "Heard a lot about you—Cousin Evelyn." Dorothy? Bob? Evelyn? Oh, and another: "You'd better pay us a visit—all my love, Muriel." I have never met, or even heard of these "relatives." But their sentiments are more than welcome!

Sunday, September 2. Tomorrow is the ninth anniversary of my enlistment. I was eighteen. The skies were gloomy. Cardiff General Railway Station was noisy, smelly. My mother was fearful, the old man anxious and full of well-meaning, if unnecessary advice—and I was a little scared, a little excited, and dressed in a shabby sports coat, shabby flannel trousers, and even shabbier shoes. I had left school four years earlier. But in a sense, my real schooling began the day I took the train to the RAF recruiting station at West Drayton.

Peace treaties* are signed, occupying forces enter Japan. Truman promises economic aid to Britain in the approaching winter. But news in general makes little impact around here these days, as morale dips because of impatience with the slow demobilization—and an unexpected spate of heavy work as Halifaxes and Yorks pass through.

Tuesday, September 4. The night before last, Derek and I dined with a Russian family that left the homeland during the Russian Civil War

---

* The documents signed aboard USS *Missouri* in Tokyo Bay on September 2, were "instruments of surrender," not peace treaties. The peace treaty between 48 of the World War II Allies and Japan was signed in San Francisco on September 8, 1951. The Soviet Union was not a signatory.

[1917–1922]. The husband is excellent company, speaks English perfectly, has a wonderful sense of humor. He and his wife suspect Stalin of craftiness—one doesn't need to be a Russian to do that! And the wife, with a shudder of loathing, pleaded with us not to mention Lenin's name again, after one of us had done so. In explanation, she went on to describe some of the atrocities committed by the Russian revolutionaries in 1917.

Sunday, September 16. Yesterday morning, the whole camp grumblingly took part in a brief color-hoisting parade at which a very self-conscious British consul and his wife attended, this being our own peculiar way of commemorating the victory over the Luftwaffe five years ago.

But over London, a far more fitting ceremony was that of a grand fly-past by 300 fighters led by W/Cdr. [Wing/Cdr.] Bader whose experiences in this war would (and doubtless soon will) fill a book.*

Last week down at Sale, a well near the petrol pipeline running from the railway station across the fields to our airfield, was reported as contaminated by leakage from the pipeline. The owner of the well sent two Arabs down to its bottom to effect repair. They were found dead, overcome by petrol fumes. I spent this morning at Sale in the dust and heat supervising the drainage of over a thousand gallons of petrol out of the pipeline. Personally, I think this line should have been replaced months ago—it is leaking in several places.

Thursday, September 20. Our moody and rather colourless CTO called me into his office this morning, surprised me by offering a cigarette, and asked how many bowsers I would need to serve two dozen multi-engine aircraft a day. We've never had twenty-four planes with more than two engines arrive here within a twenty-four-hour period. But it seems to me he has been told to prepare for such. We spent the next half-hour trying to calculate what would be needed. To my question, "Where are the men coming from?" he shrugged and said, "That's someone else's problem, not mine."

The visit wasn't altogether wasted. I flirted, albeit fruitlessly, with 17-year-old Andrea, the CTO's pretty French clerk, one of half a dozen French girls whose presence on this airbase appears to be quite unnecessary.

The removal of Duty-Free concessions in cigarettes to the armed forces will certainly help stamp out the black market. Even out here some sort of black market goes on. I have myself occasionally indulged in a mild spot of "le march noir," but with paid-for NAAFI cigarettes.

---

* Note from LFG in 1993: "Douglas Bader was a legless flier, Battle of Britain ace, prisoner of war, and escapee." See Paul Brickhill's biography of Bader, *Reach for the Sky*.

Last week, in the Comedie's basement bar, I sold 100 for 200 francs and two bars of English chocolate for 15 francs each.

Two days ago, Terry Haile and I enjoyed an interesting afternoon exploring the Roman and Arabic ruins with which the walled Chellah* abounds. We sketched and photographed old baths and temples and forums, savoured the wild beauty of dazzling flowers that grew in profusion among these relics of the distant past.

Corporal Fred Wallace, in my billet since Jack Marsden left, has himself departed for home, flew off in a Stirling this morning. He was a strange bird. As Damon Runyon would say, "A story goes with it. But I won't relate it here."

Sunday, September 30. I suppose it reflects a rather sudden realization on the part of the Americans that they are, right now, the world's dominant industrial and economic power. Or perhaps pressure of domestic politics, Anyway, Truman has asked Britain, with some firmness, to open up Palestine to Europe's displaced Jews. So far, no answer from London.

Yesterday morning I wore myself out again down at Rabat's "Stadt Maroc" playing tennis with Terry Haile. Did I say playing? My tennis is on a par with my swimming.

Notwithstanding appeals by the government to be patient during this snail-pace release program, the men seem to be getting angrier. Last night's broadcast by the Ministry of Labour satisfied no one. Instances of shaky morale occur often. Today, when I told one of my fellows to replace hosepipes on the petrol tanker so they wouldn't be accidentally run over, he said, "Fuck the hosepipes. The RAF don't give a damn about me, why should I? etc. etc."

He was one of those who shouted loudest in support of the Labour Party during the election campaign. But something is certainly amiss. Yorks and Dakotas on BOAC training flights have passed through here lately homeward bound, with ballast consisting of sandbags. Needless to say, men—who feel they could serve as ballast for the flight home—are reluctant to work on these aircraft.

The latest pronouncements from London make clear that thousands of servicemen, who expected to be home by Christmas, will be disappointed.

Well, I have some idea when I will be en route home—about three months from now. But maybe sooner than that—for on DROs today, it says I must report tomorrow for my release-medical check-up. Also

---

* The Chellah or Shalla is a medieval fortified Muslim necropolis located near Rabat on the south (left) side of the Bou Regreg River estuary.

unexpected—I asked the CTO's pretty French clerk Andrea for a dinner date before my departure and she replied, "I'd be delighted."

The BBC broadcaster and self-styled philosopher C.E.M. Joad* was invited to a swing concert. His reply to the concert's sponsor: "I have very little acquaintance with either jazz or swing, but that little rendered me most reluctant to enlarge it... No doubt, if you made it worth my while to pay me for this painful experience you propose, I would come. I cannot conceive, however, what possible interest the opinions of musicians on a non-musical subject such as jazz or swing could have." Fair enough—but since when did the bombastic Joad consider himself a musician?

Sunday, October 7. Successfully passed my release-medical two days ago. I seem to have lost weight out here though—a mere 137 pounds. But the MO told me there is nothing wrong with that.

A horrible postwar boredom has set in. Tales of misery and starvation in bomb-battered Europe of strikes, wild parties, and crime waves in America, of revolutions in Latin-America, of newly reported concentration camp atrocities, all evoking little or no reaction. Futility appears the fate of attempts to create a new and better world. Even those very words sound trite and hackneyed.

Monday, October 15. Pierre Laval has been executed.† He spent his last night on earth writing letters to his wife and daughter. Half an hour before facing the firing squad, he took poison in a last attempt to cheat justice. Well, that's the way it is usually described—cheat justice. And we hear of justice being "satisfied." What do these words mean? But I've no time for philosophical musings. Laval was universally condemned as a traitor and, as such, has been shot. That's all there is to it—I suppose.

The newspaper called the "People" is going in for sensationalism, seems to me, with its stories of British soldiers in Germany allowing themselves to be attracted to and seduced by German girls. But it does rather irk one to read of British officers taking German girls to a dance while our own girls of the ATS [Auxiliary Territorial Service], not being of commissioned rank, are left on the outside looking in.

I was on guard last night. Whiled away the hours studying algebra and reading "Tess of the d'Urbervilles." Was rewarded with a splendid pre-dawn view of the constellation Orion. And at this [time of] year, the glare of Sirius is an even steelier blue than when it is only visible before midnight.

---

* Cyril Edwin Mitchinson Joad was an English philosopher and frequent guest on the BBC.

† Pierre Laval, who served in the Vichy government, had been found guilty of plotting against the security of the state and collaboration with the enemy.

This camp is becoming overcrowded. The great transportation of de-mobbed and ex–POWs from the Far East, through our region and across France for home, has been in progress some weeks now.

Saturday, October 20. As the days speed past, all my thoughts now are concentrated more and more upon my casting off of uniform—after nine years of wearing it. About six or seven weeks to go, I calculate. I am eager as anybody to get back into civvy street, but there are features of service life I'll certainly miss, not the least of which is the feeling of being "looked after," the conviction, for instance, that one's physical health in the service is the service's responsibility. Also, these days, I am virtually my own boss. I choose my own days off, am rarely interfered with by others so long as I can keep my section's head above water—or should it be petrol? This state of affairs has lasted for much of two years.

And there is that unique comradeship that I don't think can be fostered outside the military environment.

All that being said, however, the military remains plagued by its traditional bugaboos, most conspicuously that rank snobbishness (rank in its double sense), which can produce injustice, incompetence, even a form of tyranny. The trouble is not only that of a gulf existing between high-level officers, CO included, and OR (other ranks). The administration branch, officers and staff alike, seem unconcerned with and act superior to the Flights—those sections where aircraft land, are refueled, and serviced to fly again, the Flights with their "chiefies" [flight sergeants], oil-drums, overalls, and tool-chests, hangars and trestles, and Forms 700, crew-rooms and wheel-chocks, the immortal Flights on whose tarmacs and landing strips was won the Battle of Britain.

All too often, the begrimed and hard-working members of the Flights are disdained as social inferiors by the pen-pushing sedentary squad. It is as if, now the war is ended, the Flights no longer form the very hub of the Royal Air Force.

And there is the soul-crushing uniformity against which the independent spirit rebels from the day the body first dons uniform.

Oh, well, I'd better bear all this in mind and thus avoid any tendency to regret leaving the RAF. I have, after all, been a part of it during the most glorious period in its history. I've learned much, including the most important fact, namely, that there is so much more to learn. I have made many friends and learned how to win over enemies, some anyway. I have the service, and the war, to thank for showing me life at its ugliest and life when it is sublime. So, while I shan't regret leaving the RAF, neither will I regret having joined it.

Wednesday, October 24. News that a Liberator, bound for England with eighteen RAF personnel, crashed on take-off at Maison Blanche, killing all of them, hardly cheered me in view of the likelihood of my going home by air. To go home by sea would be more interesting, and I would be allowed to carry more baggage. I have over twenty gramophone records that make up quite a heavy load.

My scheduled departure date is November 26. Released with me will be Corporal Tommy Finnegan, whom I have known since the old Ras el Mar days. In London last night, the anniversary of the Battle of El Alamein* was celebrated. Field Marshal Montgomery presented Churchill with a volume of Eighth Army poems.† Said Churchill: "Before El Alamein we survived; after El Alamein we conquered."

Thursday, October 25. The panic is on. Last night, throughout the dark hours, Liberator after Liberator came in—eight in all, followed by a Stirling and a Halifax. For me, it proved one of the most grueling nights yet. And we are experiencing a scandalous shortage of batteries for our torches. Most of the refueling and other work was done in pitch darkness, accompanied by the mixed sounds of refueling tankers pumping away, engines running up, and plenty of yells, and curses. Fl/Lt. Baines, our CTO, was anxiously around and about, and I stressed the need for light, more light, and he told me that his efforts to secure batteries from Gibraltar had failed.

Except for one or two near-mutinous outbursts, the lads worked obediently enough, probably reminding themselves that these aircraft were taking comrades home. Each Lib carries about sixteen men, mainly RAF, from the Far Eastern front.

We were obliged to improvise light sources—including utilizing the fire-engine's bright beams. But all too often we had to depend upon the moon for illumination.

This morning, dog-tired, I fell into bed and slept so soundly I did not hear the Libs taking off. Nor their return half-an-hour later, recalled due to fierce gales sweeping western Europe and the British Isles.

More "troopers" came in today, men are feeding at the Malcolm Club, some sleeping tonight in hangars.

I'm not working tonight. One of the new corporals will have to cope alone. But I don't think so may aircraft will be in this time.

---

* El Alamein is a town on Egypt's Mediterranean coast. The battle, which was fought nearby from October 23 to November 11, 1942, was a decisive British victory over German-Italian forces. This defeat of Axis armies in North Africa was considered to be a major turning point for the Allies in World War II.

† Book of poetry published on January 1, 1944, entitled *Poems from the Desert: Verses by Members of the Eighth Army*. The Introduction was written by General Montgomery.

Saturday, October 27. Yesterday the CTO expressed his satisfaction with the "good show" we put up during the recent mass diversion of troop-carrying aircraft through our staging post. In 32 busy hours from 6 pm on the 24th until 2 am on the 26th, we pumped 32,165 gallons—well over half in hours of darkness. All the troopers have gone now, carrying up to 500 "time-expired" servicemen—some I noticed, wearing odd headgear, clutching Japanese souvenirs, thus bringing to this generally dull base a breath of the Far Eastern war.

Over the objections of colleagues Terry Haile, Dick Lewis, and Derek Roberts, I advised that we postpone our new-formed Rhythm Club's first recital, fearing competition from the band at the Sergeants' Mess dance. I was to read the notes at the recital, and finally, I rather churlishly told my friends to go ahead without me. Which they did—and the recital was a success, the echoes from the Sergeants' Mess not interfering one whit with the waxed works of Dorsey, Goodman, Shaw, Ellington, Basie et al. But relations are currently strained between Terry and Co. and myself.

Sunday, November 4. These are uneventful days now. I am called out for work only sporadically. My emotions are somewhat mixed, excitement sometimes stirs as I count the declining days before I bid my friends farewell and fly home to shed my uniform and nine years of military service.

First though, I will have a week's leave, with Derek as my companion.

Yesterday's "going home" list contained 73 names. These men will depart by train for Algiers tomorrow. All but one—a fellow who works for me and had applied some days ago for a 48-hour pass. His application reached the Station Warrant Officer yesterday and got no further. Defiantly the fellow left camp anyway last night, heading for Casablanca, unaware that his name was among the latest selected for home leave. In vain did we try to contact him via the Union Jack Club in Casablanca. The latest lucky home-bound batch goes off without him. His name, it so happens, is Fortune.

Derek and I called upon our Russian friends, the Ignatievs, in Casablanca. They gave us their version of the Rasputin* affair, having lived through those years, and seemed quite convinced that the holy (unholy?) monk did indeed exert a hypnotic influence on the Tsar's

---

* Grigori Rasputin (1869–1916) was a self-proclaimed Siberian holy man in Russia, who told Czar Nicholas II and Czarina Alexandra that he could heal their son's (Alexei) hemophilia. After gaining increased influence over the Czarina and the royal family, combined with his increasingly scandalous behavior, Rasputin, also known as the "mad monk," was assassinated on December 30, 1916.

family, especially the Tsarina. Ignatiev got out of Russia in 1920, crossed Poland and Latvia, finally reached France, and met his bride-to-be in Paris. She herself had fled the Red Terror, escaping via Turkey.

Wednesday, November 7. First day of my last leave—and I'll take it alone, for Derek's pass has been cancelled due to the large number of men gone on home leave. Sections are sorely depleted, the wireless section (where Derek works) no exception. I'll putter about Rabat, Port Lyautey, Fedala, and Casablanca for the next few days. Weather is blisteringly hot and windy.

Saw two good films, each the product of a master: "Blithe Spirit," Noel Coward's comedy featuring Rex Harrison and Margaret Rutherford (a delight!) and a Hollywood version of Oscar Wilde's "Picture of Dorian Gray" in which newcomer Hurd Hatfield looked too morose a hedonist, and George Sanders, fairly well cast as Lord Henry, spoiled things a bit by uttering the Wilde epigrams too fast. Angela Lansbury's brief contribution was nice. But the portrait stole the picture.

Sunday, November 11. Last night Derek and I returned from Casablanca by train. We had spent a pleasant two days there, mainly in the company of M. Cormier and his friends, the Paris family. During dinner, I again had reason to silently curse my meagre—well, all but non-existent—knowledge of French for my companions were most interesting people.

M. Paris, like the Cormiers, was a staunch member of Casablanca's Resistance Movement and had experienced quite a few dangerous thrills operating clandestine radio transmitters and so forth.

Very shortly, I shall be running around with my clearance chit [official notice], preparing to enter civilian life which, I have been gloomily assured by recent returnees from UK leave, is a cold, aloof, grumpy, ill-considerate environment. Well, I want no flags flying or bands playing. All I want is my home, a job, and prospects of joining Helen, the girl in America to whom I write.

[Prime Minister] Clement Attlee is in Washington engaged in what I am tempted to call "panic" talks. This blasted atomic bomb is panicking everybody. "We shall have atomic energy—and other energy also," said [Soviet Minister of Foreign Affairs Vyacheslav] Molotov the other day. That's just it. We are all going to get it, but through competition, not cooperation. Therein lies the tragedy—and danger of catastrophe.

Saturday November 17. A howling wind bending the trees, black clouds sweeping across the moon, periods of heavy rain—truly a stormy night. But I've little to worry about, tucked in cosily abed. Yesterday I collected my clearance chit and Release 1A Booklet—that amazing collection of forms and dotted lines and instructions and reminders—every possible detail of the complicated process of actual release is covered. A principal reminder is that one is not being actually discharged but "released," and liable to recall if necessary. Indeed, a money order valued five shillings is enclosed, to help pay the fare to the re-mobilization centre. And one must keep one's uniform clean, ready for use ... just in case. H'm.

According to schedule, I'll be leaving here Thursday with Corporal Finnegan and two lesser-known types. I'll be getting "cleared" until Monday, which leaves me little time for last minute purchases or farewells.

Felt so relieved handing in all the junk I've had to cart around for years. Much of it stuff we never needed to use, all the anti-gas impediments, for instance. KD (khaki drill), battledress, boots, the whole lot went over the counter, disappearing into the gloomy rack-walled recesses of the Main Store. All I have now is my personal cleaning stuff, underclothing for both seasons, blue uniform, diaries (which I intend parceling up and mailing), and my records, which form the bulk of my possessions.

40,000 Welshmen braved bad weather today at Ninian Park [football stadium] in Cardiff and saw an example of the Russian drive we heard so much about during the war. Despite an early good showing by Cardiff City, the Russians swarmed all over our team, defeating them by the astounding score of 10 to 1! And at the close of the game, the Moscow Dynamos seemed as fresh as ever. This must be the "other energy" Molotov spoke of the other day.

Now to settle down and read William Bolitho's "Murder for Profit." Gives some rare insight into the minds and motives of mass murderers.

Talking of mass murderers, over a dozen of the Belsen concentration camp bosses have been sentenced to death.

Tuesday November 20. Received my final pay before going home. And it looks as if I'll be getting away on time. I'll have no chance to buy any last-minute items or hunt up a few people I've lost track of in recent months—Josine and Renee, for instance, and Paulette. Can't be helped. I'd better regard them as characters in—not a chapter, but a book about to be closed.

I am somewhat apprehensive about stepping into "civvy street." Shouldn't be, I suppose. But perhaps there will indeed be moments of loneliness, times when I will scowl, "Damn this civilian life, I wish I were back with the lads... Terry... Derek," and so on.

But then, surely all I'll need to do is remind myself of the unpleasantries of service life—the lack of social contact, the physical labour needed to perform the most mundane of tasks e.g., walk (or run) to the washhouse, to the dining hall. The difficulty of hearing music when you want to and what you want to. The lack of intelligent conversation.

[On that rather lackluster note] I closed my service diary. That week with Corporal Finnegan and several others, I boarded a DC-3 that flew us to Gibraltar. Taking off from that notoriously short airstrip, I prayed that the extra load I'd brought on board against orders—78 rpm records and three or four V-discs*—wouldn't be just enough additional weight to send us into the sea. But our Dakota staggered aloft, flew us across the North African coast to Algiers. Here we became part of a mass of British servicemen and women, all from sundry stations in Algeria, the Middle East, the Far East, and God knows where else, forming a huge pool of military personnel awaiting flights home. Since that was where we were all bound—home—the general mood was lighthearted, and the crowded canteen rang nightly with songs and drunken laughter.

In due course, our turn came—we left Algiers in a Stirling bomber, which obviously had seen its share of wartime action, the fuselage floor had shrapnel holes, stuffed now with wadding. We crossed the Mediterranean in glorious weather. As we approached the coast of South France, our pilot sent word back to us that if we looked out the right window, we could see the Tyrolean Alps, if we looked left, we could see the Pyrenees in Spain. I was unable to confirm either as the heads of my fellow passengers blocked each view. So I returned to my book, "Murder for Profit."

We reached the English Channel, losing altitude and considerable visibility, rainclouds swallowing us. We burst out of the murk and there it was below us, the green sodden fields of dear old England. Not that much of their greenery was visible for evidence of the massive building-up was everywhere—aircraft and tanks and all kinds of military vehicles smothering every meadow. Clearly our side had become well prepared for a much longer war.

We landed on an RAF airfield at Hednesford, somewhere in the Midlands. A WAAF medical orderly greeted each one of us with a question to be answered before alighting. And the first words spoken to me upon returning to England after two and a half years' absence were, "Have you, at any time abroad, had cholera?"

---

* V-Disc ("V" for Victory) records involved the production of several series of recordings during the World War II era by special arrangement between the United States government and several U.S. record companies. The 12-inch, vinyl 78 rpm gramophone records were produced for the sole use of U.S. overseas military personnel. Many popular singers, big bands, and orchestras recorded special V-Disc records.

The Diary: 1945

Notes on the back of a diary page
Favorite pubs—1940–1942
Closest pub and most favorite to Honiley (285 Squadron AACU) was the Tom O'Bedlam on the main Birmingham-Stratford road (or Birmingham-Warwick); Kenilworth: Virgin and Castle: (where I was given a send-off party March 1943); Birmingham: Golden Eagle and Castle (especially its lounge); Manchester: George and Dragon [and] Britannia.

Afterthought

"From Cardiff to Kansas through sixty-two years. Greatest generation? For Americans arguably so. For the British, the most lovable, lonesome, loyal, lion-hearted, looniest, and lucky generation ever. I know. I was there."

In June 2009, Leonard F. Guttridge wrote these words during what would be the last week of his life.

Glossary of Aircraft Mentioned

Fighters/Interceptors (British)

Hurricane (Hawker)	single engine fighter
Spitfire (Supermarine)	single engine fighter
Defiant (Boulton Paul)	single engine interceptor/night fighter
Whirlwind (Westland)	twin engine heavy fighter

Light Bombers (British)

Hart (Hawker)	single engine, twin-seat biplane (light bomber)
Audax (Hawker)	single engine, twin-seat biplane (light bomber)
Battle (Fairey)	single engine light bomber
Blenheim (Bristol)	twin engine light bomber
Hudson (Lockheed)	twin engine light bomber (U.S. built for RAF)

Medium Bombers (British)

Whitley (Armstrong Whitworth)	twin engine medium bomber
Wellington (Vickers)	twin engine medium bomber
Manchester (Avro)	twin engine medium bomber
Hampden (Handley Page)	twin engine medium bomber

Heavy Bombers (British)

Halifax (Handley Page)	four engine heavy bomber
Lancaster (Avro)	four engine heavy bomber
Sterling (Short)	four engine heavy bomber

Torpedo Bombers (British)

| Beaufort (Bristol) | twin engine torpedo bomber |

Multi-purpose (British)

Beaufighter (Bristol)	twin engine multi-purpose nightfighter
Warwick (Vickers)	twin engine multi-purpose
Mosquito (de Havilland)	twin engine multi-purpose
Boston/Havoc DB-7/A-20 (Douglas)	twin engine multi-purpose (U.S. in Brit. Service)

Transports (British)

| York (Avro) | four engine transport |
| Scion (Short) | twin engine light transport |

Miscellaneous/Scout, Training, Liaison, Private, Commercial (British)

Tutor (Avro)	single engine biplane (training)
Lysander (Westland)	single engine scout and liaison
Oxford (Airspeed)	twin engine training
Puss Moth (de Havilland)	single engine high-wing monoplane (private and commercial aviation)
Dragon Moth (de Havilland)	twin engine biplane (commercial use)
Leopard Moth (de Havilland)	single engine monoplane (private aviation)
Monospar (General Aircraft)	twin engine utility aircraft
Percival	single engine low-wing monoplane (light training)

U.S. Aircraft

Marauder B-26 (Martin)	twin engine medium bomber
Flying Fortress B-17 (Boeing)	four engine heavy bomber
Liberator B-24 (Consolidated)	four engine heavy bomber

Glossary of Aircraft Mentioned

Catalina PBY (Consolidated)	twin engine flying boat/amphibian patrol bomber
Dakota DC-3 (Douglas)	twin engine transport

German Aircraft

Focke-Wulf Fw 190	single engine fighter
Messerschmitt Bf 109	single engine fighter
Dornier Do 217	twin engine medium bomber
Heinkel He 111	twin engine medium bomber
Junkers 88	twin engine fast/medium bomber

RAF Bases Where Posted (1937–1945)

Ringway	RAF station south of Manchester
Wittering	RAF station near Peterborough, Cambridgeshire
Henlow	RAF station, Bedfordshire
South Cerney	RAF station, Gloucestershire
Baginton	RAF station near the village of Baginton, Warwickshire, southeast of Coventry (now Coventry Airport)
Honiley	RAF station near the village of Honiley in Wroxall, Warwickshire, seven miles southwest of Coventry
Ras el Mari	Unknown
Rabat/Salé	Located in Salé, 5 miles east-northeast of Rabat, both the RAF and the United States Army Air Forces shared this airfield until June 1, 1943, when the USAAF left (now Rabat-Salé Airport).

Index

Aachen 155, 155*n*
Achilles, HMS 51, 51*n*, 57*n*
Afrika Korps 110*n*
Airborne Invasion (John Hetherington) 181
Aitken, William (Lord Beaverbrook) 121
Ajax, HMS 51*n*, 57*n*
Albania 38, 39, 97
Algeria 69, 158, 189, 214
Algiers, Algeria 132, 134, 137, 147, 158, 175, 193, 211, 214
Altmark (German Navy) 56, 56*n*
Andrews, Dana 190
Anschluss (annexation) 146
Anzacs in Battle 117
Anzio (landing) 135
Arden, Eve 173
Ardennes (Bulge) 164, 164*n*, 169
Arise, My Love 104
Ark Royal, HMS 110*n*
Arnhem (Market Garden) 155, 153*n*
Arsenic and Old Lace 192
The Assassin (Liam O'Flaherty) 88
Astaire, Fred 34, 108, 122, 152
Athenia, SS 46, 46*n*, 47
Atlantic 97, 97*n*
atomic bomb 200, 201, 212
Atrocity (concentration) camp 184, 192, 194, 198; *see also* Auschwitz-Birkenau; Belsen; Buchenwald, Dachau
Attlee, Clement 33, 39, 62, 198, 201, 212
Audax 27, 27, 7*n*
Aumont, Jean-Pierre 153
Auschwitz-Birkenau camp 198; *see also* Atrocity (concentration) camp; Belsen; Buchenwald; Dachau
Australia 85, 128
Austria 146, 185
The Awful Truth 26
Azores 129, 154, 156, 162

Babes on Broadway 116
Bachelor Mother 55
Bader, Douglas 194, 194*n*, 206
Baedeker Raids 118*n*
Balfour Declaration 34*n*
Ball, Lucille 175
Barrymore, Ethel 174
Basie, William "Count" 211
Battle 14, 41, 60, 65, 70, 95
Beaufighter 83, 92–94, 101, 103, 123, 127, 150
Beaufort 58
Belgium 59, 61, 62, 63, 64, 67, 95, 151, 154, 165, 172
Belsen (concentration) camp 184*n*; *see also* Atrocity (concentration) camp; Auschwitz-Birkenau; Buchenwald; Dachau
Beneš, Edvard 29–30
Benghazi 84
Benny, Jack 156
Bergman, Ingrid 160
Berlin 184, 184*n*
Berlin, Germany 36, 75, 95, 172, 177–178, 184–185, 195
Bevin, Ernest 191, 198
Birmingham, England 13, 79, 80, 97–99, 104, 106, 108, 110–117, 123–125, 127–128
Bismarck (German Navy) 104, 104*n*, 105
Blenheim 64, 78, 89, 92–93, 95*n*, 104, 107
Blithe Spirit 212
The Blitz 2, 71, 75, 80, 82, 91–92, 101, 111, 118, 179
Bogart, Humphrey 155
Boissevain, MS (Dutch) 128, 128*n*
Bonnet, Georges 29, 29*n*
Boyer, Charles 47, 80, 160
Brazil 175
Brighton Rock (Graham Greene) 129

Bristol, England 79, 84, 121
British Broadcasting Corporation (BBC) 19, 31, 40, 46–47, 62, 70, 81, 103, 108, 123, 153, 177, 197, 208
British Expeditionary Force (BEF) 49
British Historical and Political Orations from the 12th to the 20th Century (Ernest Rehs) 110
Broadway 116
Brooke, Alan 148
The Brothers Karamazov (Fyodor Dostoevsky) 195
Buchenwald camp 184; *see also* Atrocity (concentration) camp; Auschwitz-Birkenau; Belsen; Dachau
Budapest, Hungary 158
Bulgaria 85, 151
Burma 112, 147, 150, 184

Caen 139, 139*n*
Cagney, James 68
Cairo, Egypt 157, 158, 192
Canada 85, 97, 122, 126, 129, 162, 175
Cape Matapan 96*n*
Captains Courageous 20
Cardiff Blitz 91*n*
Cardiff Wales 3, 8, 13, 18, 20, 22, 24–25, 32–35, 39, 41–42, 47, 50, 55, 59, 66, 68–70, 72–76, 81, 88–92, 96, 99, 106, 108, 110, 116, 120–122, 134, 141, 172–173, 177, 194, 205, 213, 216
Carducci (Italian Navy) 96
Carson, Jack 173
Carter, Benny 172, 175
Casablanca, Morocco 129, 132–135, 142, 146, 153–155, 157, 160, 162, 164, 172–174, 180–181, 183, 187, 189, 192–193, 211–212
Casablanca Conference 161*n*
Cavalcade (magazine) 34, 34*n*
Chamberlain, Neville 27, 46, 78, 201
Chaney, Lon, Jr. 67
Chaplin, Charlie 170, 170*n*
Cherbourg, France 138, 141–142
China 28, 34, 36, 92, 202
Churchill, Winston 7, 8, 33, 51*n*, 54, 57, 61, 61*n*, 62, 74, 80, 84, 99, 107, 109*n*, 111, 115*n*, 116*n*, 118, 119, 126, 136, 138–139, 141, 146, 148–149, 157, 161*n*, 162, 167, 167*n*, 173, 175, 180, 185, 186–187, 188, 191, 194, 196, 198, 198*n*, 210
Citizen Kane 112
Colbert, Claudette 104, 199
Collier's (magazine) 129
Cologne, Germany 118, 118*n*, 175
Condon, Eddie 183

Cooper, Gary 111
Cossack, HMS 56
Cotton, Joseph 160, 199
Courageous, HMS 47, 47*n*
Coventry, England 13, 76, 78, 80, 97–99, 104–106, 109, 111–112, 114, 119, 126, 189
Coward, Noel 8, 71, 174, 181, 212
Crete 96, 104, 104*n*, 105
Crimea Declaration 173; *see also* Yalta Conference
Crosby, Bing 151, 152, 183
Crosby, Bob 40, 175
Cross of Lorraine 153
Cugat, Xavier 183
Czechoslovakia 27, 28, 29, 32, 38, 117, 118

D-Day 139; *see also* Normandy
Dachau camp 184; *see also* Atrocity (concentration) camp; Auschwitz-Birkenau; Belsen; Buchenwald
Daily Express (newspaper) 28, 35, 36, 64, 88, 111, 114, 121, 140, 158–159, 175, 190 194, 196
Daily Herald (newspaper) 138, 188, 196
Daily Mast (newspaper) 194
Daily Mirror (newspaper) 71, 71*n*, 118
Daily Worker (newspaper) 112, 118
Dakota 158, 182, 196, 207, 214
Daladier, Édouard 29, 29*n*, 31, 32, 63, 63*n*
Dark Victory 50
Darlan, Jean 147*n*
Davis, Bette 44, 50
Daylight on Saturday (J.B. Priestley) 130
Dead End 25
Defiant 71, 84, 92, 94, 97, 103, 114, 121, 124
De Gaulle, Charles 136
Denmark 60, 67, 104
Denmark Strait 104*n*
De Velera, Eamon 105*n*
Dewey, Thomas 157
Dieppe Raid 127, 127*n*, 138
Dodge City 57
Dollfuss, Engelbert 146, 146*n*
Dorsey, Tommy 149, 211
Double Indemnity 169
The Doughgirls 173
Dublin, Ireland 105
Dunkirk, France 64, 64*n*, 65, 95, 106, 135, 194
Dunn, Irene 47
Dusseldorf, Germany 124

Echo de Maroc 164
Eden, Anthony 62, 62*n*, 112, 119, 146
Edward VII (England) 44
Egalise (newspaper) 164
Egypt 81, 84, 110, 154
Eisenhower, Dwight 138, 158
El Alamein 210, 210*n*
Elizabeth, Princess (England) 135, 162
Ellington, Edward "Duke" 8, 23, 25, 26, 39, 204, 211
England 21, 23, 49, 52, 58–59, 64, 68, 70, 72, 85, 94, 101, 113, 117, 118, 130, 132, 134, 138, 139–140, 143, 144, 147–148, 150–151, 153, 169–170, 174–175, 180, 187, 194, 203, 209, 214
English Channel 63, 70, 81, 111, 139, 141, 168, 214
Ethiopia 84, 96
Exeter, HMS 51, 51*n*, 57*n*
Exmouth, HMS 54, 54*n*

Fairbanks, Douglas, Jr. 117
Fantasia 114
Finland 53, 55
Fiume (Italian Navy) 96*n*
Flying Fortress 162, 182, 196
Flynn, Errol 57, 65, 136, 199
Focke-Wulf 128
Follow the Fleet 108
Foreign Correspondent 85
The Fountain (Charles Morgan) 96
France 9, 14, 19, 25, 27, 29, 36, 39, 42–43, 48–49, 53, 54, 59, 63–64, 65–69, 83, 92, 95, 103, 119, 139–141, 148–150, 153–154, 158, 161, 172, 175, 194, 202, 204, 212, 214
Franco, Francisco 20, 160
Frankfurt, Germany 172
French Foreign Legion 129
French Without Tears 62

Gamelin, Maurice 63, 63*n*
Gandhi, Mahatma 125, 125*n*
Garland, Judy 116, 175, 180, 204
Gaslight 160
Gentleman Jim 199
George II (Greece) 133, 133*n*, 163
George V (England) 44
George VI (England) 28, 31, 45, 81, 94, 119, 146, 148
German-Soviet Non-Aggression Pact 43, 130*n*
Germany 9, 13, 27, 28–29, 31–32, 36–38, 42–43, 45–46, 49, 56, 69, 71, 97, 102, 107–108, 111, 116, 120, 130, 146–147,

155, 157, 170–172, 179, 180, 182, 184, 191, 198, 209
The Ghost Breakers 79
Gibraltar 109–110*n*, 174, 184, 193, 198, 205, 210, 214
Giosuè (Italian Navy) 96
Glorious, HMS 65, 65*n*
Gneisenau (German Navy) 111
Goebbels, Joseph 37, 37*n*, 71, 90, 123, 158, 170, 186, 186*n*
Goering, Hermann 31, 31*n*, 188, 189
Going My Way 145
The Good Earth 20
Goodman, Benny 8, 25, 26, 152, 183, 204, 211
Grable, Betty 113
Graf Spee (German Navy) 51, 51*n*, 56, 57, 57*n* 113
Grant, Cary 18, 26, 174, 192
Great Contemporaries (Winston Churchill) 109
Great Expectations (Charles Dickens) 199
The Great Man's Lady 110
Greece 76, 97, 99, 106, 133, 161, 162–164, 172
Greenmantle (John Buchan) 122
Grenville, HMS 54, 54*n*
Guadalcanal 125*n*

H. M. Pulham, Esq. 120
Hail the Conquering Hero 164
Halifax 126, 144, 138, 144, 148, 205, 210
Hampden 113
Hanover, Germany 85, 95
Hardy, Thomas 175, 183
Harris, Arthur 198, 198*n*
Harrison, Rex 212
Hart 23, 23*n*, 24, 26*n*, 37, 40, 46, 48, 51, 54, 57
Haver, June 175
Havoc 116, 118
Hawkins, Coleman 172
Hayworth, Rita 123
Heflin, Van 120
Heinkel 119, 126
Henlein, Konrad 28, 28*n*
Herriot, Édouard 147, 147*n*
Hess, Rudolph 102, 103
Heydrich, Reinhard 117, 117*n*, 118
Higher and Higher 141
Himara 81, 81*n*
Himmler, Heinrich 146, 146*n*, 189
Hirohito, Emperor 200, 201 205
Hiroshima, Japan 200, 201
Hitchcock, Alfred 85, 128, 148

Hitler, Adolf 26–33, 41–43, 45, 49, 51, 52, 64, 66–68, 71, 77–78, 85, 90, 92, 99, 103, 107, 109, 111, 116, 147, 151, 172, 175, 184, 191, 205
Holland 59–62, 67, 95, 172
Hollywood, California 8, 65, 80, 113, 117, 135, 149, 160, 171, 173, 212
Home in Indiana 175
Hood, HMS 104, 104*n*, 105
Hope, Bob 79
Hore-Belisha, Leslie 23, 23*n*
How Green Was My Valley 124
How Green Was My Valley (Richard Llewellyn) 122
Hudson 58
Hungary 29, 32, 151
Hurricane 7, 13, 63, 68, 83, 97, 98, 83, 97, 98, 101, 115, 115*n* 116, 118, 126
The Hurricane 25

Indianapolis, USS 201, 201*n*
International Share-out (Barbara Ward) 109
Introduction to Politics (Harold Laski) 176
Ireland 38, 40, 47, 68, 105, 141, 178
Irish Republican Army (IRA) 38, 38*n*, 43
Italy 15, 38, 65, 67, 69, 76, 97, 127, 134, 135, 141–142, 147, 150, 153, 170, 172, 184
Iwo Jima 191, 191*n*

James, Harry 149, 152
Jane Eyre 151
Japan 16, 67, 148, 157, 188, 198, 200, 205
Japanese surrender 200, 205
jazz music 2, 5, 8, 17, 26, 27, 35, 48, 51, 59, 68, 77, 86, 103, 113, 120, 123, 149, 150, 152, 165, 184, 208
Johnny Eager 120
Joyce, William 49*n*, 97, 99, 192
Juliana, Princess (Holland) 19
Junkers 126

Kain, Edgar "Cobber" 65, 65*n*
Kelly, Gene 153, 175
Keren 96
Kesselring, Albert 146, 146*n*, 188
King, Mackenzie 161
Kings Row (Henry Bellaman) 129
Kiser, Kay 175
Kristallnacht 36*n*
Krupa, Gene 41, 70, 120

Lady (Don't Turn Over) (James Hadley Chase) 118

Lamour, Dorothy 34, 196*n*
Lancaster 198
Laski, Harold 194, 194*n*
Latvia 212
Laughton, Charles 19
Laura 190
Laval, Pierre 208, 208*n*
Lawrence, Thomas 89, 89*n*
Lend-Lease 85, 92*n*, 204
Leopard Moth 77
Liberator 129–131, 135, 138, 148, 150, 154, 156, 158, 162, 164, 175, 178, 180, 184, 209–210
Libya 81, 84, 97, 110, 117, 120*n*, 158
Life (magazine) 169
Lifeboat 148
Life's Little Ironies (Thomas Hardy) 175
Lilliput 8, 61, 61*n*, 90
Liverpool, England 13, 52, 59, 60, 65, 73, 77, 79, 80, 96
Lloyd George, David 61, 61*n*, 119, 180
London School of Journalism 159
Look (magazine) 139
Lord Haw-Haw *see* Joyce, William
Love Affair 47
Luxembourg 61, 164
Lynn, Vera 158, 158*n*
Lysander 7, 14, 64–65, 68, 78, 83, 85–86, 88–89, 93–94, 99, 100–101, 104, 107–108, 112

MacArthur, Douglas 173
MacMurray, Fred 169
Malcolm Club 136, 136*n*, 139, 148, 152, 156, 159, 162–166, 169, 180, 184, 186, 197, 199, 210
Malta 65, 95, 117, 158
The Maltese Falcon 155
Manchester 60, 65–66
Manchester, England 33, 58–59, 60–61, 63, 65–67, 69–74, 76–77, 81–82, 89, 95, 104–105, 112, 126–127, 191
Manila, the Philippines 173
Marauder 199
Maroc Matin (newspaper) 139
Marrakesh, Morocco 158, 180–183
Marshall, George 115*n*
Mary, Queen (England) 31
Maugham, Somerset 183
Mayerling 80
McCrea, Joel 85, 110
Meet Me in St. Louis 204
Mein Kampf (Adolf Hitler) 35
Melody Maker (magazine) 5, 113, 149–150, 152
Meredith, Burgess 67

Index

Messerschmitt 68, 72, 102, 102*n*
Middle East Diary (Noel Coward) 174
Milland, Ray 104
Miller, Glenn 8, 143, 149, 168, 168*n*
Miracle of Morgan's Creek 141
Missouri, USS 205*n*
Mr. Smith Goes to Washington 65
Moll Flanders (Daniel Defoe) 110
Molotov, Vyacheslav 43*n*, 119*n*, 212, 213
Monospar 58–59
Montaigne's Essays (Michel de Montaigne) 8
Montevideo, Uruguay 51*n*, 57*n*
Montgomery, Bernard 141, 141*n*, 179, 210
Morocco 8, 129, 140, 142, 145, 151, 158–159, 160, 162–163, 169, 189, 202
The Mortal Storm 80
Moscow, Soviet Union 126, 213
Mosley, Oswald 63, 63*n*
Mosquito 150, 152, 158, 165–166, 175, 177–178
Muni, Paul 20
Munich, Germany 27, 28, 29, 33, 49, 174
Murder for Profit (William Bolitho) 213
Murmansk, Soviet Union 126
Mussolini, Benito 15, 31, 32, 36, 65, 184, 205
Mystery of Edwin Drood (Charles Dickens) 148

Nagasaki, Japan 200, 201
Narvik, Norway 60, 61
Nation (magazine) 169
Nehru, Jawaharlal 125, 125*n*
Neutrality Act of 1935 47*n*, 48
Neutrality Act of 1937 47*n*
Neutrality Acts (repealed) 48*n*
New Statesman (magazine) 169
New Zealand 65, 85, 128
News Chronicle (newspaper) 141
News of the World (newspaper) 16, 16*n*
Niven, David 55, 65
No Orchids for Miss Blandish (James Hadley Chase) 117
None But the Lonely Heart 174
Normandy, France 127, 137, 139, 141–142, 147; Invasion 137–141; *see also* D-Day
North Africa 128–129
North Sea 19, 29, 63, 65, 94, 118
Norway 49, 60–61, 63, 65, 67, 76, 103, 106, 138, 147, 185
Nuremburg, Germany 26, 90

Of Mice and Men 67
Only Yesterday: An Informal History of the 1920s (Frederick Lewis Allen) 89
The Ordeal of Richard Feverel (George Meredith) 169
Oxford 14, 23, 23*n*, 33–34, 46, 51, 51*n*, 53, 70, 95*n*, 114, 124
Oxley, HMS 49, 49*n*

Palestine 28, 34, 36, 158, 207
Panay, USS 16, 17
Paris, France 27, 42, 52, 65–66, 134, 140, 149, 150–151, 168, 172, 212
Passage to India (E.M. Forster) 154
Patton, George 177, 178
Percival 66
Pétain, Philippe 140, 140*n*, 150
Petite Marocain (newspaper) 181
Phantom of the Opera 157
Phenix (French Navy) 42, 42n
Phony War 59*n*
Picture of Dorian Gray 212
Picture Post (magazine) 154, 169
Pola (Italian Navy) 96*n*
Poland 13, 29, 38, 42, 43, 45, 46–47, 74, 86, 103, 151–152, 154, 174, 186, 212
Potsdam Conference 198, 198*n*
Powell, Eleanor 175
Power, Tyrone 113
Price, Vincent 190
Prinz Eugen (German Navy) 111
prisoners of war (POWs) 154, 177, 195, 209
Private Life of Henry VIII 25
Punch (magazine) 196
Puss Moth 14, 58

Queen Mary, RMS 204, 204*n*
Quisling, Vidkun 147*n*

Rabat, Morocco 8, 129–130, 136, 138, 140, 142, 144–145, 147, 149–151, 159, 162, 163–165 167–168, 170–171, 173–174, 177, 179–180, 183, 185–190, 191–193, 196–197, 199, 201–203, 204–205, 207, 212, 220
Radio Maroc 8, 180, 183, 186, 193
Rains, Claude 157
Rangoon, Burma 112, 184
The Razor's Edge (Somerset Maugham) 178
Rebecca (Daphne du Maurier) 80
Red Cross 70, 72, 76, 142, 181
Rembrandt 19
Reynaud, Paul 63
River Plate 57*n*, 113

226 Index

Road Floozie (Darcy Glinto) 118
The Roaring Twenties 68
Robinson, Edward G. 169
Rogers, Ginger 8, 55, 111
Rome, Italy 20, 135, 136, 138, 141, 146, 158, 174
Rommel, Erwin 110n, 120n, 147
Rooney, Mickey 175
Roosevelt, Franklin 16, 47, 66, 70, 77, 84, 92, 109, 119, 146, 157, 161, 172, 173
Royal Oak, HMS 48, 48n

Saboteur 128
Sailfish, USS 41, 41n
Sale Times (newspaper) 201
Sanders, George 85, 212
Saturday Evening Post (magazine) 129
Scapa Flow 48n
Scharnhorst (German Navy) 111
Scion 77
Scotland 15, 19, 46, 48–50, 54, 73, 80, 102, 128, 159, 194–195
Selected Letters of T.E. Lawrence (David Garnett, ed.) 88
Sergeant York 111
Shaw, Artie 211
Short Stories (Damon Runyon) 101
Sidi Barrani 81, 84
Sinatra, Frank 131, 139, 145, 157, 183, 204
Since You Went Away 199
Sinclair, Arthur 62, 112
Singapore, Malaya 109n, 111, 116
The Sisters 44
Snow White and the Seven Dwarfs 36
Solomon Islands 125
Sons and Lovers (D.H. Lawrence) 154
South Wales 32, 66, 70, 76; *see also* Wales
South Wales Echo 43, 68, 179
Soviet Union 29, 43, 47, 55, 92, 107–108, 117, 119–122, 126, 151, 164, 172, 186, 202, 205, 211–212
Spain 16–17, 20, 26, 28, 36, 153, 160, 214
Spanish Civil War 15, 34, 38
Spitfire 7, 13, 40, 69, 73, 74–76, 83, 92, 94, 98, 103, 115n, 117
Squalus, USS 41, 41n
Stalin, Joseph 107, 119, 119, 126, 157, 173, 189, 193, 198, 206
Stalingrad, Soviet Union 122, 128, 134
Stanwyck, Barbara 110, 169
Stars and Stripes (newspaper) 133, 139, 187
The Stars Look Down 59
Steinbeck, John 107

Sterling 144
The Struggle for Peace (Neville Chamberlain) 46
Submarine *U-81* 110n
submarine warfare 20, 41–42, 49, 56, 147, 201
Summa 55
Sun Valley Serenade 112
Sunday Graphic (newspaper) 161
Sunday Pictorial (newspaper) 62, 135, 142, 150
Suomussalmi 53n
Sweden 60
swing music 25, 33, 39, 41, 47, 48, 52, 76, 105, 208

Tatler (magazine) 83, 83n
Taylor, Robert 33, 120
Teagarden, Jack 70
Temple, Shirley 160, 199
Tess of the D'Urbervilles (Thomas Hardy) 208
Thetis, HMS 41, 41n, 42, 52
Thousands Cheer 175
Thunderbolt, HMS 41, 41n
Tierney, Gene 190
Time (magazine) 34, 129
Tito, Josip Broz 152
Tobruk 81, 84, 99, 120n
Tom Brown's School Days 80
Tom, Dick and Harry 111
Topper 18
Tracy, Spencer 20
A Tree Grows in Brooklyn (Betty Smith) 178
Tribune (magazine) 180
Triton, HMS 49
Truman, Harry 198, 205, 207
Tutor 38

Union Jack (newspaper) 139, 167
United States 9, 55, 77, 92, 170, 214
Uruguay 51n

V-discs 214, 214n
V-E Day 185–187, 191, 193, 202
V-J Day 203
V-1 (buzz bomb) cruise missile 141, 141n
V-2 ballistic missile 158, 158n
La Vigie Marocaine (newspaper) 150
Vittorio Alfieri (Italian Navy) 96
Von Bock, Fedor 117, 128, 189, 189n, 205
Von Ribbentrop, Joachim 43n
Von Rundstedt, Karl 146, 146n

Index

The Wagons Roll at Night 109
Wales 3, 8, 16, 18, 21–24, 32, 40–48, 65, 87, 89, 96, 177; *see also* South Wales
Waller, Thomas "Fats" 8, 26, 27, 55, 204
Warsaw, Poland 45, 152, 170
Warsaw Uprising 152*n*
Warwick 140, 148
Washington, D.C. 4, 5, 65, 119, 142, 164, 205, 212
Wasp, USS 117, 117*n*
Webb, Clifton 190
Welles, Orson 112, 151
Wellington 135, 138, 140–141, 148, 155, 181–182
Weygand, Maxime 63, 63*n*
Whirlwind 98
Whitley 54, 69–70, 76
Why Britain Is at War (Harold Nicholson) 57
Williams, Emlyn 32
Willkie, Wendell 77, 77*n*, 84, 154
Wilson, Arthur 1, 9, 95, 97, 100–101, 104–107, 109–112, 114, 116, 117, 119–122, 125, 126, 128, 144, 171–172, 175, 191
Winter War (Finland-Soviet Union) 55*n*
Women in Love (D.H. Lawrence) 152
Woolley, Monty 199
World Press Review (magazine) 169
Wuthering Heights 50
Wyman, Jane 173

Yalta Conference 173, 173*n*
A Yank in the RAF 113
Yanks 9, 89, 123, 139, 153, 173, 195–196, 202
York 136, 146, 152, 173, 178, 184, 204–205, 207
You Can't Take It with You 39
You'll Never Get Rich 123
Young, Robert 120
Yugoslavia 97

Zara (Italian Navy) 96*n*

www.ingramcontent.com/pod-product-compliance
Lightning Source LLC
Chambersburg PA
CBHW032040300426
44117CB00009B/1130